"Must reading for all who sincerely seek the clearest explanation yet for the Christian attitude toward homosexuality. I pray that this work will have the impact on all segments of our society that it deserves."

D. JAMES KENNEDY, PH.D.
Senior Minister,
Coral Ridge Presbyterian Church

"To be caught in the trap of homosexuality is difficult enough, but to be held captive in the snare of the 'strong delusion' of a false gospel requires the stronger arm of truth. Writing the truth in love, Joe Dallas reveals how to set the captive free."

JANET PARSHALL
Nationally syndicated
talk show host and author

"*The Gay Gospel?* is a magnificent word that shines the light of truth on a 'feel good' culture. We are living in a time when many no longer listen to sound doctrine but would rather have their ears tickled; they are seeking smooth-talking teachers and turning away from the truth to run towards myths. Thank you, Joe, for speaking absolute truth in such an understandable way. May this book bring sight to many who have been deceived."

ALAN CHAMBERS
President, Exodus International

"More than ever, Christians are challenged to articulate and defend the Bible's position on homosexuality. In *The Gay Gospel?* Joe Dallas—one of Christianity's most able and articulate spokesman on human sexuality—codifies the arguments and arms us with clear, concise and convincing answers. This resource is both compelling and compassionate."

HANK HANEGRAAFF
President of the Christian Research Institute
and host of the *Bible Answer Man* radio broadcast

W9-BJL-583

THE Gay Gospel?

Joe Dallas

HARVEST HOUSE PUBLISHERS

EUGENE, OREGON

Cover by Koechel Peterson & Associates, Inc., Minneapolis, Minnesota

Cover photo © Tom Henry/Koechel Peterson & Associates

THE GAY GOSPEL?
Updated and expanded edition of *A Strong Delusion*
Copyright © 1996/2007 by Joe Dallas
Published by Harvest House Publishers
Eugene, Oregon 97402
www.harvesthousepublishers.com

ISBN-13: 978-0-7369-1834-3 (pbk.)

Library of Congress Cataloging-in-Publication Data
    Dallas, Joe, 1954-
        [Strong delusion]
    The Gay Gospel? / Joe Dallas.
        p. cm.
    Originally published: Strong delusion. Eugene, Or. : Harvest House Publishers, © 1996.
    Includes bibliographical references.
    ISBN: 1-56507-431-9
    1. Homosexuality—Religious aspects—Christianity. 2. Homosexuality in the Bible. 3. Homosexuality—
Biblical teaching. 4. Dallas, Joe, 1954- I. Title.
    BR115.H6D36 2007
    261.8'35766—dc22   2006024683

Printed in the United States of America

12   13   14   15   /   VP-CF   /   10   9   8   7   6

To the Leadership of
Exodus International
KEEP STANDING

*If I profess with the loudest voice
and clearest exposition every portion of the
truth of God except precisely that little point
which the world and the devil are at the moment
attacking, then I am not confessing Christ,
however boldly I may be professing
Christ. Where the battle rages,
there the loyalty of the
soldier is tested.*

MARTIN LUTHER

Contents

Between Comfort
and Truth

*"Nothing is so easy as to deceive oneself;
for what we wish, we readily believe."*

Demosthenes (384–322 bc)

I remember clearly, and with inexpressible regret, the day I convinced myself it was acceptable to be both gay and Christian.

It was the fall of 1978, and the local Metropolitan Community Church was opening its morning service just as I slipped into a seat near the back. I had passed the plain white building hundreds of times before, having once been the associate pastor of a Foursquare church not three blocks away, and I'd heard plenty of stories about this gay-friendly denomination that had recently been founded by an openly homosexual minister named Troy Perry. I knew that most of its members were homosexual. I also knew it subscribed to the belief that homosexuality and Christianity were compatible, and that it was a visible and outspoken advocate for a number of gay causes. What I didn't know, those countless times I'd driven past the church shaking my head at the very thought of "gay Christians," was that I'd someday step inside and identify myself as one of them.

Who'd have guessed? I was, after all, a conservative, born-again believer who'd cut his teeth under the teachings of Pastor Chuck Smith, founder of the Calvary Chapel movement, during the heady days of what's often called the Jesus movement. I'd been an ordained minister and lived a sheltered, sanctified lifestyle since my teens, so how could I—or anyone, for that matter—predict my next stop would be the gay church? Back then, the idea was unthinkable.

Not that homosexuality was foreign to me. Unbeknownst to my friends and associates, I'd privately wrestled with it since childhood. In fact, by the time I converted to Christianity at age 16 I'd had numerous sexual experiences with both men and women. But I'd assumed that, having come to Christ, my sexual desires would either vanish or somehow conform to biblical standards and behave themselves until I was married. Sex wasn't discussed much in church back then, so I wasn't quite sure how this little miracle of transformation would come about. But I was certain that, with adequate prayer, fellowship, and Bible study, I'd eventually achieve a lust-free existence where no sexual fantasies or desires, homosexual or heterosexual, would intrude.

But they did, again and again. Even as I grew spiritually and my ministry expanded, my mind would often wander back to past sexual encounters or pornographic magazines I'd viewed years earlier. Without realizing it, I'd spent the early part of my life amassing a library full of erotic images, lodged in my brain like old books ready to be taken out and browsed through. Becoming a Christian hadn't erased them, and at times I have to admit they held a certain appeal. So when the rigors of ministry or personal stress made themselves felt, I'd retreat to my sexual fantasies for entertainment and comfort. I didn't feel good about that, but I consoled myself with the fact that I wasn't "doing" anything—viewing porn, for example, or committing fornication. So my sexual fantasies, while sinful, didn't seem *that* sinful. I was, in other words, indulging in a mental compromise that was setting me up for a bigger fall than I thought I was capable of.

One step into an adult bookstore seven years after my conversion was all it took to end my ministry and plunge me into a series of sexual excesses, culminating in a yearlong relationship with the owner of a gay bar. He was "committed" to another man, but no matter. We'd meet every night after hours, and I'd drive home drunk at four in the morning, then rise for work, exhausted and confused.

After finally breaking off my relationship with him, I took a hard look at myself and what I'd come to. I was only 23 years old, yet already I'd been ordained, then defrocked. I'd disgraced the ministry when my escapades had come to light and then committed adultery with the wife of a close friend, losing a child to abortion as a result. I had hired prostitutes, developed a drinking habit, joined the gay community, and endured a nightmarish relationship. Now that the relationship was over I was alone again, and life looked incredibly bleak.

So did my options. Repenting and returning to my old church seemed out of the question, much as I longed to. I missed the fellowship of Christian friends, but I thought they'd never take me back. And why should they, after the way I'd betrayed them? Yet the promiscuous, hard-driving lifestyle I'd adopted was a dead-end street as well. I wanted to indulge my sexual tastes, but not so wildly. I also wanted Christianity, but not without my sexuality. In short, I wanted it all, a common malady of the times.

So now it was desperation, rather than the amused curiosity I'd felt earlier, urging me to visit the Metropolitan Community Church that October morning in 1978. I wanted to see if it was possible to be actively homosexual, Christian, and confident of a right standing before God.

I knew better, of course. I knew the scriptural condemnations of homosexuality in both the Old and New Testaments were clear and final, and any attempt to get around them was purely self-serving. But it *was* self, after all, that I was serving in those days. Every major decision I'd made that year—entering the pornographic bookstore, the adultery, the homosexuality—had been based on what *I* wanted, not on what I knew to be right. In that darkened frame of mind, I was ready to believe what

I *wanted* to believe instead of what I *truly* believed. And what I wanted to believe, more than anything, was that my self-centered sexuality and faith could live together peacefully. In visiting the gay church, I was looking for something to confirm that.

The first confirmation came through music. The choir opened the service with, of all things, an anthem by popular evangelical songwriters Bill and Gloria Gaither! I was caught short, then comforted, as the familiar melody washed over me. I relaxed a bit, then spotted a worship book in the pew. Opening it, I was delighted to find many of the solidly evangelical hymns and choruses I'd sung years ago. *With songs like these,* I reasoned, *this* must *be a Christ-centered church.*

People were singing along with the choir now, some even lifting their hands. If not for the name on the building and the fact that some same-sex couples were linking arms, the service was looking like that of any conservative, mildly charismatic church. I glanced sideways at the women and men around me. Until then my exposure to the gay community had been limited to what I'd seen in the bars—tight Levi's, muscle shirts, and sexually suggestive behavior. Now I was confronted with a congregation full of moderate-looking gays and lesbians of all ages, none of whom conformed to the stereotype so many people have of homosexuals. The men, by and large, dressed, spoke, and carried themselves normally; the women's manners were generally feminine. And so a second confirmation dawned on me: *Gay* did not have to mean *sleazy* or *outlandish.* These were normal-looking people, leading respectable lives. My hopes grew—maybe I could be one of them!

Minutes later we were on our feet, singing and clapping through a string of upbeat choruses, when the most incredible feeling swept over me. My chest seemed to cave in, my eyes filled, and my legs buckled. It was the music. I was singing praises to God, something I thought I would never do again.

I had to sit down and weep. After a year of chaotic, utterly godless living, it felt so good to sing again—so blessed and familiar, like returning home from a war.

Something warm surged through me—something powerful,

consoling, reassuring. *Just rest,* it seemed to say as I relaxed and let the tears flow. *Everything's going to be fine.*

By the time I pulled myself together, the sermon had begun. The pastor's style was folksy, well-suited to his hefty build and jolly appearance. I liked him instantly, though within minutes I could see we were worlds apart theologically. His sermon included questionable ideas ("God gave us only two commandments: to love Him and to love each other. Everything else is fluff.") and ludicrous statements ("I don't like the term 'born again.' I prefer to say we're recycled!"). But when he got on the subject of homosexuality and the church, my thoughts ventured in directions they'd never gone before.

"Gays have solidarity," he explained, "not so much because of who we are but because of how we're treated. There's no group in the country so reviled as us. And so slandered! Listen to almost any television preacher talk about us and you'll hear lies upon lies."

A bit of an exaggeration, I felt, but only a bit. The Anita Bryant campaign in Florida had recently triggered a national debate on homosexuality, and some high-profile preachers had jumped into it ill-prepared, throwing out harsh rhetoric about gays over the airwaves. I shared the pastor's anger over that.

And yes, there *was* solidarity at this church; I recognized it as soon as I stepped into the sanctuary. Years earlier, I'd experienced it in the Jesus movement. We too had been maligned at times, ridiculed by a world that couldn't understand us. So I was familiar with the power of solidarity in a tight-knit group, and I missed it. I also missed having a cause, or a mission. Might I find it with these people?

"They condemn us," the pastor continued, "and call our love a sin. If that's what they truly believe, why don't they do anything to help us get over it?"

Nods and murmurs of agreement rippled through the congregation.

"Ask yourselves this," he challenged, pointing at all of us: "Could any of you, in the churches you grew up in, raise your hand during a prayer meeting and say, 'I'm a homosexual and need help; please pray for me'?"

The very idea provoked an eruption of laughter. I joined in, knowing all too well the improbability of such a thing.

But why?

The thought stopped my laughter cold.

Why indeed? I had seen people request prayer in church for any number of problems—sin problems, mind you, like selfishness, lust, and bitterness—without raising eyebrows. Yet I'd known people in those same churches who would never have admitted a problem with homosexuality. The repercussions would have been unthinkable.

For that matter, I had heard testimonies, received by the church with enthusiasm, of people overcoming drug addiction, alcoholism, and immorality of all sorts. Except *this* sort.

Which meant one of two things: Either God delivered very few people from homosexuality or, more likely, those who were homosexual were too ashamed or intimidated to admit it.

But again, *why?* Why was homosexuality so unfairly, and so unbiblically, set apart as the "Unspeakable Sin"?

The question persisted. I felt a peculiar anger rising—the self-righteous ire of a victim. The pastor had touched a nerve.

"Perhaps," he mused, "it's a good thing your church didn't offer you help. If they had, it would only have fed the notion that you needed their so-called help for your so-called problem when, in fact, you didn't!"

Applause broke out.

"Because it *isn't* a problem!"

Whistles and shouts of "amen" sounded.

I hesitated to join in. It was one thing to indulge, rebelliously, in something you knew to be wrong, but saying the thing itself was *not* wrong was another matter. That required a radically changed mind-set.

But wasn't that what I had come for? I teetered over the thought as he repeated himself: "It isn't a problem!"

Maybe it isn't, I thought, closing my eyes. *Please, let it not be a problem. Please let this be true.*

"But because so many of us think it's a problem," he continued, "because so many of us have been told it's a problem, we've grown up hating ourselves."

He paused to let it sink in.

"*Hating* ourselves!" he stressed. "Hating the very core of our being, the thing that defines us. Do you all know what homophobia is?"

The verbal response indicated they certainly did.

"Do you think homophobia is something only the bigots feel?"

The question was rhetorical; no one answered this time.

"It's right here!" he snapped, thumping his chest. "Right in our hearts! We swallow their lies, we believe we're perverts, so we *act* like perverts! No wonder so many of us have been promiscuous! No wonder so many of us have lived half our lives getting drunk in bars, or high on drugs, or prowling in bathhouses. When you've been oppressed, and when you've been told all your life you're the rottenest kind of sinner, you believe it! *That's* why there's so much self-destructive behavior in our community!"

I was startled to hear an "amen!" leap out of me, but that didn't stop me from repeating it, louder and stronger, even as the lightbulbs went on in my head.

It wasn't my fault, I marveled.

"Amen!"

The sleeping around, the abortion, the craziness—I was only acting out the role society had cast me in.

"Amen!"

THEY were wrong, not me. They LIED to me. They—what was the word he used?—they OPPRESSED me!

"Amen!"

The confirmation I wanted lay in that single word. I was oppressed—all gays were oppressed. *Oppression* was responsible for my misconduct.

I could forgive myself now. The thought drew fresh tears.

I could forgive myself and move in another direction with a new identity: *gay Christian.* And it was oddly liberating to put the two words together.

Gay Christian. Homosexual, but sexually responsible, not promiscuous. A God-fearing, churchgoing gay man with a cause: to combat homophobia and the oppression of all gay people.

The idea thrilled me. To have a cause again—something to live for, to fight for.

The pastor's next words seemed to be directed to me personally: "But Jesus said the truth would set us free. And hasn't it? Hasn't learning the truth—that God loves you just as you are, that He doesn't condemn you, that Jesus died not just for the heterosexual but for the homosexual as well—hasn't that truth liberated you?"

When the applause died down, he added, "And doesn't that compel you to take that liberation everywhere? To tell our people they can be gay and Christian? And to stand up to the fundamentalists and say, *'No more! God is our God, too!'*"

Yes, I agreed, swept up in his passion along with the others. His words struck a defiant chord in me. I laughed and clapped and repeated "Yes, it does" over and over. It was exhilarating.

When the mood finally settled again, I looked around me and smiled, mentally forming a decision: *This is what I've been looking for. These people—gay and Christian—could be my people. I could belong here.*

Even as I considered it, I was flooded with peace.

The pastor ended his sermon. Now staff members joined him to prepare the altar for communion, and I couldn't wait. Taking the Lord's Supper, I felt, would initiate me into this group, and I was more than ready.

"Behold the Lamb of God," he announced shortly, holding the host and chalice in the air as the staff lined up to serve the elements. "The table is prepared. Come."

Randomly, people began leaving their seats, and I was starting to leave mine when a wave of doubt slammed into me.

Joe, what on earth are you about to do? I froze halfway out of my seat.

It was my early training, my years of Bible study and sound teaching, posing the question, trying to dissuade me from a fatal decision. Because I knew, somehow, that if I stepped into that aisle and took communion—in *that* church, with *those* beliefs—I would seal a commitment that could take years, perhaps a lifetime, to reverse. Was this what I really wanted?

I settled back into the pew, shaken, as another question presented itself: *What about the Bible?*

I touched my forehead and noticed I'd broken into a sweat.

This gay pastor had indicted the church for misunderstanding homosexuals. But did that justify homosexuality itself? Suppose he was right: Suppose gays had a legitimate beef against society. Suppose Christians did need to be more loving toward homosexuals. Suppose some preachers were too harsh when referring to the subject. Did that make all the biblical injunctions against homosexuality null and void?

My discomfort was growing by the minute.

All my Christian life I had known the importance of judging everything by Scripture, not feelings. Not once, I noted, did this man back his assertion that homosexuality is okay in God's sight with any biblical support—because, of course, there was none.

And if there was none, the argument was settled. No matter how peaceful, exhilarated, or relieved I had felt earlier, exuberant feelings would not and could not make something wrong into something right.

I slumped forward, deflated.

That last point was inarguable, but I wasn't willing to accept it, not having just found some relief from the inner turmoil I had suffered for 12 endless months. My mind raced for a rebuttal, something to bring back the peace I'd known minutes earlier, when an entirely new line of thought occurred to me: Even if it wasn't right, was it so terribly wrong?

I clutched the idea, toying with it.

Compared to drinking and carousing, wasn't the life I was considering at least an improvement? I would be in church again, after all, singing and praying with people whose standards were much higher than those of the bar crowd I'd been running with. Surely God approved of what could only be called a step in the right direction.

Just then a couple of handsome, well-dressed young men passed my seat, arms entwined, moving toward the communion table.

Look at them! I chided myself, watching them kneel and hold hands, sharing the bread and wine. They were so serene, beaming health and security. *They're not worrying about a few little Bible verses; why should you? Besides, look at the songs we're singing and the way everyone is worshiping. All these gay and lesbian Christians are obviously devoted to God and are comfortable with themselves, so what's your problem?*

Some peace trickled back—and that kind of thinking definitely felt better. I scanned the congregation, most of them making their way to the altar, singing or humming quietly along with the organist. They all looked so content, so free of turmoil over their sexual behavior. If I would only give up my letter-bound obsession with the Bible, I could be content too. And I would be comfortable with myself, like them. Didn't that count for something?

I closed my eyes and sighed, knowing I had just hit the bottom-line issue: a contest between comfort and truth. I could either believe what made me comfortable, or I could believe what I knew to be true. Never had the choice been clearer; and to this day, I am amazed at how easily I made it.

I would do it. I would go to the altar, receive communion, and take my place with my gay brothers and sisters. I would join this church, this ideology, and make it my own. My life would again serve a purpose. I could already envision myself as an activist. It was the logical thing to do, I assured myself, and it was right. And even if it wasn't right, I would learn to live with it.

So with that in mind, I opened my eyes, stood tall, and stepped into the aisle...

1

WHERE WE
ARE NOW

*"The attempt to determine spiritual and
moral truth by personal preference will lead to certain
disaster, as it did in ancient Israel when
'Everyone did what he considered right' (Judges 17:6)."*

JOSH MCDOWELL
The Last Christian Generation

Writing about homosexuality is like reporting on the weather. Things change so quickly, and sometimes so drastically, that what you write today seems irrelevant within weeks.

I wrote the first edition of this book in the spring of 1996 under the title *A Strong Delusion,* completing the last sentence three hours before my son Jeremy was born. Bill Clinton was our president at the time, and the hot topics relative to homosexuality were gays in the military, public funding for HIV education, and a few scattered school districts adopting pro-gay curriculum. The gay-rights movement had certainly gained momentum and public support, but in light of all that's happened since then, 1996 seems almost quaint.

Back then we thought Rosie O'Donnell, Richard Chamberlain, and Ellen DeGeneres were straight. The Matthew Shepherd tragedy was still two years off, hate-crime legislation was somewhat novel, and gay/straight alliances in high schools were unheard of. Antisodomy laws were still on the books in some states, there was no *Will and Grace, Queer as Folk,* or Fab Five. The thought of an openly gay Episcopal bishop seemed laughable, and no county, state, or nation anywhere on earth had sanctioned same-sex marriage. In short, when *A Strong Delusion* was first released, we were living in very different times.

Some things relative to homosexuality remain the same, though, and one of them is the struggle experienced by women and men who wrestle with a conflict between their beliefs and sexual desires. In the years since I left both the gay church and community in 1984, I've seen my story repeated too many times, in too many lives. It's time we recognized those lives, and the seductive effect the gay religious movement is having on them.

Webster refers to a movement as a "tendency, a trend, or a series of organized activities working toward an objective." The gay Christian movement meets all three qualifications. It represents a tendency among Christians who are homosexually tempted to yield to that temptation and then try to justify it. It represents an ongoing trend within parts of the Christian church to legitimize homosexual behavior. And it's brimming with organized activities working toward an objective of widespread acceptance of homosexuality in both the church and society.

In that sense, it's much like the broader gay-rights movement in that it seeks legitimization (not just tolerance) of homosexuality. Gay spokesmen have made no secret of the fact that this is their goal. Activist Jeff Levi put it plainly to the National Press Club during the 1987 Gay Rights March on Washington:

> We are no longer seeking just a right to privacy and a protection from wrong. We also have a right—as heterosexual

Americans already have—to see government and society affirm our lives. Until our relationships are recognized in the law—in tax laws and government programs to affirm our relationships, then we will not have achieved equality in American society.[1]

But pro-gay theology takes it a step further by redefining homosexuality as being God-ordained and morally permissible:[2]

> I have learned to accept and even celebrate my sexual orientation as another of God's good gifts.
> —Gay author Mel White

> How could we go on being ashamed of something that God created? Yes, God created homosexuals and homosexuality.
> —Reverend Troy Perry, founder, Metropolitan Community Church

> I offered thanks to God for the gift of being gay.
> —Gay priest Malcom Boyd

When God is alleged to sanction the abominable, a religious travesty is being played out, and boldly. The travesty is twofold. Not only are believers falling into homosexual sin and legitimizing it but uninformed heterosexual Christians are applauding them as they do! Prominent religious figures and Christian organizations are giving a friendly nod to gay ideology, making Isaiah's famous warning more relevant than ever: "Woe unto them that call evil good, and good evil; that put darkness for light, and light for darkness" (Isaiah 5:20 KJV).

A Growing Movement

To get a sense of the prevalence of darkness being called light, even among professing Christians, consider just a few of the gains the pro-gay religious movement within the Christian church had made as of mid-2006:

- Four of America's most visible mainline Protestant denominations—the United Methodist Church, the Evangelical Lutheran

Church of America, the Presbyterian Church USA, and the Episcopal Church—contain thriving pro-homosexual groups that tirelessly lobby their denomination to officially condone homosexual practices and ordain openly homosexual pastors.

- The Episcopal Church's House of Bishops voted in 2003 to confirm the Rev. Gene Robinson as the first openly homosexual Episcopalian bishop. Regardless of the distress and division the confirmation generated within the denomination, official Episcopal Church spokesman Daniel England hailed the confirmation as "an important step for the church."[3]

- The son of radio teacher and pastor Chuck Smith, who is regarded as one of today's foremost Bible teachers and is founder of the widely respected Calvary Chapel church fellowship, has publicly declared he is no longer certain the Bible condemns homosexuality. "I need to investigate more thoroughly," said Chuck Smith Jr., pastor of Calvary Chapel Capistrano Beach in Southern California, when asked about biblical references to homosexuality. Departing radically from his father's orthodox views, Smith Jr. also condones gay adoption and affirms that "gay" and "Christian" aren't contradictory. "I know two young men who've been monogamous partners for seven years," he states. "They've adopted a son who's thriving, they're good people, they've asked Jesus into their hearts and seek to live Christian lives."[4]

- An October 2000 episode of the popular television series *The West Wing* featured the President of the United States (a fictitious character named Bartlet) reciting a lengthy pro-gay interpretation of the Old Testament Levitical codes prohibiting homosexuality. The character is portrayed in a positive light as he humiliates a woman who still believes the Old Testament prohibits this behavior.[5]

- Grammy Award–winning gospel singer Cynthia Clawson, a prominent figure in Christian music for decades, has become a regularly featured guest singer at gay churches and pro-gay events. When criticized for publicly aligning herself with churches that condone homosexuality, Clawson dismisses the subject as a nonissue, stating,

"Jesus never said anything about gay people. How important could it have been to Him if He did not mention it?"[6]

- Ken Medema, another popular gospel artist who frequently performs at conservative Christian events and churches, is also a defender of the pro-gay religious movement. Though heterosexual, he endorses the notion that homosexuality is legitimate in God's sight and, like Clawson, lends his talents to meetings of "gay Christian" groups.[7]

- Former president Jimmy Carter, when addressing a meeting of the Cooperative Baptist Fellowship, compared homosexuality to other secondary issues that "in God's eyes, fade into relative insignificance, as did circumcision in the first days of the early church."[8]

- Brian McLaren, widely known as an author and leader within the emergent church movement, seems to share President Carter's ambiguity on the subject. In an interview with *Christianity Today*'s online *Leadership Journal*, he recounts his refusal to give a straight answer when asked where he stood on homosexuality. "Many of us don't know what we should think about homosexuality. We've heard all sides but no position has yet won our confidence." In light of his (and supposedly many others') inability to decide what's right or wrong on the matter, he recommends a "five year moratorium on making pronouncements," during which he suggests we "keep our ears attuned to scholars in biblical studies, theology, ethics, psychology, genetics, sociology and related fields."[9]

McLaren's words echo a common sentiment growing among people who claim the Bible is either vague when it comes to sexual ethics, or perhaps just needs a little help from the social sciences. While stopping short of saying "Homosexuality is okay," he and others suggest that Scripture is unclear on the matter and, to gain clarity, we need to consider not only what Paul and Moses had to say, but also what today's psychologists, sociologists, and philosophers think.

Adding to the problem are the denominations that, despite their official positions on homosexuality, are reconsidering the matter or allowing their members to ignore their stated policies on sexual conduct. A confused believer does not have to visit a "gay church," as I did, for affirmation of his homosexuality. Several Protestant bodies contain both leaders and parishioners who fully embrace the pro-gay position, even while their denominations technically reject it.

What Do We Find in Churches Today?

So a curious mixture is brewing in Christendom. Major denominations may be filled with women and men committed to biblical integrity, yet a pro-gay contingent has been allowed to flourish alongside them. So when a homosexual person seeking truth enters a mainline church, what might he find today?

In Mainline Denominations

In the Episcopal church, he might encounter some "progressive" bishops who have been ordaining openly homosexual priests for "decades—more than 100 since 1977, by some estimates." In 1994, he'd learn, a number of Episcopal bishops signed a statement agreeing that homosexuality and heterosexuality are "morally neutral," that both "can be lived out with beauty, honor, holiness, and integrity," and those "who choose to live out their (homosexual) orientation in a partnership that is marked by faithfulness and lifegiving holiness" should not be excluded from the ministry.[10] The congregation he visits might well agree. Indeed, a 1993 survey in the *National and International Religion Report* indicated that 75 percent of U.S. Episcopalians think sexually active gays can still be faithful Christians.[11]

Among Presbyterians he would find an ongoing debate dating back to at least 1970, when a church panel declared that "sexual expression cannot be confined to the married or about to be married." The panel's recommendation was narrowly voted down. The discussion continues, though the Presbyterian General Assembly in 1991 rejected a similar report that claimed a "moral right" to sexual expression for "all persons, whether heterosexual or homosexual, single or partnered."[12]

Among the United Methodist congregations, the visitor might stop by the Foundry Methodist Church in Washington, DC, that has been home to, among others, former President and Mrs. Bill Clinton. There he might hear a visiting speaker describe the apostle Paul as a "self-hating gay man," or he might listen as Foundry's pastor considers whether or not Jesus was a cross-dressing "drag queen."[13] *

Also, when looking into the Methodist church, the visitor could choose between two diametrically opposing programs that coexist in the same denomination. Should he wish to embrace his homosexuality, he might join the Reconciling Congregations group, which advocates pro-gay theology. Should he decide to abandon homosexuality, the Transforming Congregations group will, thankfully, be available to him as well.

The visitor could listen in on dialogues already underway in the Reformed Church of America to determine the appropriate view of homosexuality. He could ponder the Christian Church's (Disciples of Christ) election of a man who favors ordination of active homosexuals to head their denomination. And he'd be interested to note that two Lutheran Churches (ELCA—Evangelical Lutheran Church of America) in San Francisco hired homosexual ministers who refused to remain celibate, even though ELCA church policy dictates otherwise.[14]

Surely he'd scratch his head when hearing the Reverend Karen Bloomquist, director of a sexuality study within the ELCA, cite "all kinds of culture wars going on around issues of sexuality in wider society" as the cause for her denomination's debate.[15]

Our curious visitor may well wonder: *Should culture wars in society dictate to the church what the church should believe?*

That's a frightening thought, considering cult authority Dr. Ron Rhodes's assessment of who should be influencing whom:

> The culture-forming energies of Christianity depend upon the church's ability to resist the temptation to become completely identified with, or absorbed into, the culture.[17]

---

* Although the official Methodist position on homosexuality is far more conservative than Foundry's, unorthodox ideas about the apostle Paul and homosexuality are hardly new to Methodism. Victor Paul Furnish of Southern Methodist University, in a 1979 book, questioned whether Paul really condemned homosexuality in the New Testament.[16]

Indeed, the fact we're arguing over homosexuality is evidence of, as radio teacher Chuck Smith says, "a sign of weakness within the church. It should not even be a question, because the Bible is very clear on the subject." It's also a sign of accommodation. The world's shifting morality is affecting our own, spelling bad news for Christianity. "When the church begins to look and sound like the world," warned the late Dr. Greg Bahnsen of the Southern California Center for Christian Studies, "there is no compelling rationale for its continued existence."[18]

And large parts of the church are indeed looking and sounding more like the world, promoting ideas that sound increasingly secular and decreasingly biblical. In that sense there really is a "gay gospel," though it's a false one. It features a new and improved Jesus who's been stripped of His less-appealing qualities. Forget repentance, cross-bearing, and sanctified living. The sins that matter to Him mostly concern social justice, ecology, and the evils of fundamentalism (especially among the Religious Right). Other matters—sexual morality, personal holiness, and clear, uncompromised evangelism—are of secondary (if any) importance. This improved Jesus doesn't care if you're gay or straight, so long as you love whoever you're with. And He'll not only accept you as you are, but He'll also not impose restrictions on your life that you deem unreasonable.

Considering this new Jesus' growing popularity, evidenced by the weakness and moral uncertainty evident in many church bodies, it's small wonder pro-gay theology has made such strides.

In Conservative Denominations

By contrast, most evangelical, fundamentalist, and charismatic churches remain relatively untouched by the debates raging in their more liberal counterparts. Yet since 1987, my work counseling Christians with sexual problems leads me to believe there is something amiss in many conservative churches as well.

By and large, these churches are taking a clear stand against homosexuality while, however, showing indifference to or ignorance of the many believers in their own ranks who struggle with same-sex attractions. When homosexuality is mentioned from the pulpit, it's usually framed as a problem "out there in society." When denouncing it, though, few pastors add, "Perhaps someone here is wrestling with this sin, as well. Resist it—God will be with you as you do. And so will we."

As one who has known countless women and men who have renounced homosexual practices and who resist, sometimes daily, temptations to return to them, I can attest to the world of difference one encouraging remark like that from a pastor can make.

This neglect of a significant problem among believers can be found in Christian outreach or support programs as well. Special ministries exist in many churches for people dealing with chemical dependency, alcoholism, marital problems, postabortion trauma, emotional dependency, and eating disorders. Yet the question I heard the gay minister pose in 1978—"Why don't they do anything to help us get over our sin?"—remains largely unanswered.

One possible reason is ignorance. Conservative Christians may simply be unable to believe that such a problem could be plaguing one of their own. "I've never run across that in *my* church," a local minister assured me when I tried to acquaint him with my ministry to repentant homosexuals. Ethics and common sense kept me from informing him that his own choir director came to me twice a week for counseling.

Reluctance to tackle the messy issues homosexuality raises might be another reason to avoid the topic, though there's a certain inconsistency in that. I remember a friend of mine once suggesting to a pastor that his church might develop a support group for men wanting to overcome homosexuality. "That's unnecessary," the minister retorted. "We believe in the power of the Word to transform lives. We teach people the Bible and send them home; we're not professional counselors."

No, they are not, and no one was asking them to hire any. But this same church had, weeks earlier, started a support group for people who were "codependent." Moreover, a group for the chemically addicted had been meeting there for years. And sadly, one of this man's former associate ministers had fallen into homosexuality and died of AIDS.

So why the double standard? Why weren't the codependent, the drug-addicted, and the alcoholics also just "taught the Bible and sent home"? Why the willingness, in this church and so many others, to let pastors or group leaders address complex problems like addiction and dependency while relegating the homosexual issue to "professional counselors"?

Of course, many fine churches have no support groups of any sort, and who's to say they should? But among the thousands of churches that *do* offer special care for a myriad of other problems, doesn't it seem odd that so little support is offered to the repentant homosexual?

Where Is the Real Help?

So the homosexual is caught between two voices: the liberal and the conservative Christian, both of whom are repeating part—but only part—of Christ's words to another sexual sinner, the adulterous woman:

"Neither do I condemn you; go and sin no more" (John 8:11).

"Neither do I condemn you," the liberal theologian comforts today's homosexual. "Go and sin."

"I *do* condemn you," the conservative Christian too often seems to retort, "so go and sin no more!" Or else he just says, "Go!" The sinner is then left alone to figure out just how to "sin no more."

No wonder the gay Christian movement looks so appealing to the woman or man struggling with homosexuality. It offers them acceptance and understanding that they may never have found in the church. That doesn't absolve them of responsibility if, like me, they decide to embrace pro-gay theology. But if we have offered them little help on their way toward making that decision, don't we bear some responsibility too?

Ron Rhodes makes a good observation on this point:

> A person does not usually join a cult because he has done
> an exhaustive analysis of world religions and has decided that
> a particular cult presents the best theology available. Instead,
> a person generally joins a cult because he has problems that

he is having trouble solving, and the cult promises to solve these problems.[19]

Sadly, we seem to forget that we evangelical Christians can promise solutions too. We can address the expanding gay Christian movement, refute its claims, and equip ourselves to answer its revisions of the Bible. We can learn to intelligently debate pro-gay advocates in our denominations by knowing their arguments and the reasoning behind them. And we can promise to develop a more effective response to the repentant homosexuals in our churches who crave—and deserve—our support. Having done that, we can address the broader gay-rights movement by faithfully serving in both truth and love, refusing to compromise one for the sake of the other.

Answering Pro-Gay Theology

Promises such as these are long overdue, but many believers today seem eager to both make and keep them. That's why *A Strong Delusion* has been revised and rereleased under the title *The Gay Gospel?* It's written to equip Christians to answer the claims of pro-gay theologians, who insist homosexuality and Christianity are compatible. A Christlike, biblically based response to these claims is more urgent than any of us could have imagined in 1996, so when Harvest House Publishers asked me to update this book, I eagerly accepted.

The Gay Gospel? is based on a series of talks I began presenting to churches and conferences in 1991, titled "Answering Pro-Gay Theology." Several people mentioned how helpful the series would be if put into written form. Members of denominations debating the issue, for example, said such a book could be a valuable tool to them as they took a stand in their churches. Family members with gay loved ones said it could help them better understand their sons, daughters, or siblings who were part of the gay Christian movement, and concerned believers said this information could help them dialogue more effectively at their schools, workplaces, and social gatherings. That's when I determined to make a book out of the seminar.

Three things seem necessary to effectively answer pro-gay theology:

1. An understanding of its origin and evolution over the years.

2. A point-by-point knowledge of its claims.

3. A point-by-point response to each claim.

With that in mind, the next two chapters of this book will overview the importance of the subject and provide some background on the gay religious movement and the influences in modern Christianity that have contributed to it.

Chapters 5 through 8 will detail common pro-gay arguments such as "Gays are born that way"; "Homosexuals can't change"; and "Homophobia, not homosexuality, is the problem." Then, in answer to the often asked question "What do gay churches do with the Bible verses on homosexuality?" chapters 9 through 13 will outline what I call the "revisionist" interpretations of the scriptures that mention homosexuality. An answer to each argument and revision will be provided, as well as a sample dialogue/debate as a model for person-to-person discussions. In chapter 14, I've offered some thoughts on what does and does not work well when arguing these points, and in chapter 15, I've included more of my own life story, as well as my hopes for the church as it deals with pro-gay theology in the coming years.

Not all pro-gay theological arguments are included here; no book could adequately address them all. Some change regularly or are refined with time—and some, having been presented for a season, disappear entirely.

But some have stayed pretty much intact for years, even decades, and these are the ones I've included. They're the ones I believe are most likely to be encountered and, therefore, need a response. Some of what I'd consider the more far-fetched arguments—attempts to sexualize David and Jonathan's friendship, for example, or morph Ruth and Naomi into lesbian lovers—are rarely, in my experience, taken seriously and don't merit the space needed to explain and contradict them. And the occasional attempts to paint a romance between Jesus and John the

Beloved are so repugnant and ineffective I'd rather not dignify them with any mention, though perhaps someday they too will be more commonly accepted and will require a response.

Despite this book's title, I don't find *gay* and *gospel* compatible. The gospel is the good news of God's love expressed in the person of Jesus Christ and His atonement. The gospel is not homosexual or heterosexual, though its invitation is extended to both groups, and this title isn't meant to imply otherwise. But God's good news to all people is being revised and presented as God's *approval* of all people, and this is what I consider the "gay gospel" to be about. It's a revision of the basics on human sexuality, with broader implications for the way we interpret the Scripture and approach Christian living. For that reason we'll use the term *revisionists* for those fighting for a pro-homosexual revision of the church's position on homosexuality, and the term *traditionalists* for those holding to the traditional and, I'm convinced, the doctrinally correct view that homosexuality is condemned in Scripture in unassailable terms.

"Sanctify the Lord God in your hearts," the apostle Peter admonished. "And always be ready to give a defense to everyone who asks you a reason

The Word Gay

I'm aware of, and respect, the objections many people have to the use of the word *gay* when referring to homosexuals. *Gay* originally had a different meaning, after all, and it has been co-opted to put a more positive spin on homosexuality. But for better or worse, *gay* has become a commonly understood term meaning not only homosexual, but *homosexual-affirming* as well. So when a person says, "I'm gay," he's normally not just admitting his homosexuality. He's also saying, in effect, "I celebrate my homosexuality and accept it as normal and good."

This, to my thinking, is what *gay* means in modern culture, and it is in that context I use it. So when referring to a person, institution, or mind-set that affirms homosexuality, I may at times use *gay* as a descriptive term. In so doing I am not affirming homosexuality as being literally gay, happy, and so on. Instead, I'm using a term identified with the approval of homosexuality.

for the hope that is in you, with meekness and fear" (1 Peter 3:15). This book was written toward that end, and with the hope that it will equip the servant of the Lord, as Paul so aptly said, to

> not strive; but be gentle unto all men, apt to teach, patient, in meekness instructing those that oppose themselves; if God peradventure will give them repentance to the acknowledging of the truth; and that they may recover themselves out of the snare of the devil, who are taken captive by him at his will (2 Timothy 2:24-26 KJV).

As one who was graciously given repentance to the acknowledging of the truth, I hope that *The Gay Gospel?* will be profitable to those who can instruct, and to those needing instruction.

Because both groups are everywhere.

PART ONE

A Basis for Understanding

2

WHY BOTHER ARGUING?

---

*"Controversy for its own sake is a sin.
But controversy for the sake of the
truth is a divine mandate."*

DR. WALTER MARTIN

Imagine a movement whose goal was to legitimize gluttony.

Suppose it was spearheaded by grass-roots activists, most of whom were overeaters themselves and who felt mistreated and ostracized by society. They'd struggled with their appetite since early childhood, and initially they'd hated themselves for it. But after trying every diet available, only to find themselves regaining whatever body fat they lost, they finally decided to stop trying to change and decided to try to accept themselves as they were. "We couldn't change, so God must have made us this way," they reasoned, "and there's nothing wrong with it. From now on, we won't tolerate *anyone* telling us that gluttony is bad!"

Soon the movement was joined and championed by medical doctors who argued that gluttony was genetic, psychologists who said overeaters were as emotionally sound as anyone else, sociologists who lamented that civilizations routinely discriminate against such citizens, and clergy who declared God loves the glutton as much as He loves the temperate.

Members of this movement gradually gained visibility and support. They wrote books and appeared on TV talk shows telling heartbreaking stories about the mistreatment they'd endured. They founded Web sites and started discussions. Their horrifying accounts of name-calling and abusive behavior outraged their sympathetic listeners; and so the public, exposed routinely to the gluttony movement's message, came to agree it was cruel and senseless to denigrate people just because of their eating habits. Soon it was unfashionable to even imply that gluttony was unhealthy, and those who did were regarded as bigots.

That didn't stop some, though, from opposing the movement. A few thoughtful doctors spoke out, saying that although it was wrong to call gluttonous people names or to reject them as people, a high percentage of body fat was still unhealthy and could lead to serious problems. Some psychologists also suggested gluttony might be symptomatic of deep-rooted emotional problems; and many pastors, alarmed at the growing acceptance of this behavior, declared that although God indeed loved overeaters, He did not make them that way nor did He approve of their gluttony.

At that point a strange trend developed. When those who opposed the pro-gluttony movement were pressured to change their views, they got bolder instead. Ironically, before the movement began, they hadn't thought much about obesity. But now that the country—indeed, much of the world—seemed to be saying, "Overeating is good; anti-gluttony people are hateful!" they had no choice but to defend their views. "There is such a thing as an objective standard of health," they insisted, "and anything falling short of that standard isn't good."

Yet no matter how calmly they presented their case, they were labeled divisive, discriminatory, hate-filled. "Why are you people so obsessed with gluttony?" they'd be asked by journalists, academics, and members of the gluttony movement. "Aren't there other serious health issues, like cancer and leukemia, that you should be more concerned about?"

Exasperated, the anti-overeaters (as they came to be called) replied, "We didn't start this! We're not obsessed with overeating—and of course there are other serious health issues. But there's no widespread movement pressuring people to view cancer or leukemia as being healthy, as there is for gluttony. Obsessed? No. We're just responding to your demand that we approve of something we believe is wrong. *That's* why we keep arguing about this!"

This morning before starting work on this chapter, I picked up a copy of our local Southern California paper, the *Orange County Register.* There in bold type at the top of the editorial page was the question, "What is it with conservative Christians and homosexuality?"

The columnist, Paul Campos of the University of Colorado, went on to opine that conservative Christians were obsessed with homosexuality, that our obsession had no basis in ethics or theology, and that we were hypocritical and self-righteous because we so vigorously denounced this sin, but were largely indifferent to other, more serious ones.[1]

I've heard all that before, but I still had to laugh when reading it. Because when it comes to the conservative Christian response to homosexuality, the facts tell a very different story.

In the late 1960s, a movement began whose goal was to legitimize homosexuality.

It was spearheaded by grassroots activists, most of whom were gay themselves and who felt mistreated and ostracized by society. They'd struggled against homosexual feelings since early childhood, and initially many of them hated themselves for having such feelings.

But after attempting to go straight, only to find themselves still attracted to the same sex, they finally decided to stop trying to change, and decided to try to accept themselves as they were. "We couldn't change, so God must have made us this way," they reasoned, "and there's nothing wrong with it. From now on, we won't tolerate *anyone* telling us that homosexuality is bad!"

Soon the movement was joined and championed by medical doctors who argued that sexual orientation was genetic, psychologists who said gays and lesbians were as emotionally sound as anyone else, sociologists who lamented that civilizations routinely discriminate against homosexuals, and clergy who declared God loves gays as much as He loves straights.

Members of this movement gradually gained visibility and support. They wrote books and appeared on TV talk shows telling heartbreaking stories about the mistreatment they'd endured. They founded Web sites and started discussions. Their horrifying accounts of name-calling and abusive behavior outraged their sympathetic listeners; and so the public, exposed routinely to the gay-rights movement's message, came to agree it was cruel and senseless to denigrate people just because of their sexual orientation. Soon it was unfashionable to even imply that homosexuality was unhealthy, and those who did were regarded as bigots.

That didn't stop some, though, from opposing the movement. A few thoughtful doctors spoke out, saying that although it was wrong to call gay people names or to reject them as people, homosexual sex was still unhealthy and could lead to serious problems. Some psychologists also suggested it might be symptomatic of deep-rooted emotional problems; and many pastors, alarmed at the growing acceptance of homosexuality, declared that although God indeed loved gay people, He did not make them that way nor did He approve of sexual behavior between people of the same sex.

At that point a strange trend developed. When those who opposed the gay-rights movement were pressured to change their views, they got bolder instead. Ironically, before the movement began, they hadn't thought much about homosexuality. But now that the country—indeed, much of the world—seemed to be saying, "Gay is good; anti-gay people are hateful!" they had no choice but to defend their views. "There is such a thing as an objective standard of morality," they insisted, "and anything falling short of that standard isn't good."

Yet no matter how calmly they presented their case, they were labeled divisive, discriminatory, hate-filled. "Why are you people so obsessed with homosexuality?" they'd be asked by journalists, academics, and members of the gay-rights movement. "Aren't there other serious moral issues, like violence and adultery, that you should be more concerned about?"

Exasperated, the anti-gays (as they came to be called) replied, "We didn't start this! We're not obsessed with homosexuality—and of course there are other serious moral issues. But there's no widespread movement pressuring people to view violence or adultery as being healthy, as there is for homosexuality. Obsessed? No. We're just responding to your demand that we approve of something we believe is wrong. *That's* why we keep arguing about this!"

There May Be Consequences to Face

In the face of ongoing pressure to change her views, the church has no choice but to argue. If we fail—if we find it too difficult or too intimidating—then I believe there are at least three general and drastic consequences we'll face:

1. The denigration of biblical authority.

2. The sexual exploitation of children.

3. The loss of a coherent definition of *family.*

Whether or not we have to face these consequences will largely be determined by the success of the pro-gay movement within the church, a movement that, if not confronted, *will* succeed. A quick glance at the determination that pro-gay groups have shown when pursuing their goals in the Presbyterian, United Methodist, Episcopal, and Disciples of Christ churches—not to mention the Metropolitan Community Church's decades-long effort to be recognized by the World Council of Churches—proves that these groups are nothing if not tenacious.[2]

If the church is unable to resist this movement, it will result in a massive change of standards in most mainline Protestant denominations—and quite possibly many independent, fundamentalist, evangelical, and charismatic churches. Thus America may one day receive, from her own churches, a definition of normality that includes (and approves of) gay marriage, pro-gay education (beginning with the primary grades) on the normality of homosexuality, and the general portrayal of same-sex unions as healthy and legitimate.

Not all churches will go along with this, certainly, but no matter. If the majority, or even a significant percentage of them, cave in to gay ideology, it will amount to a religious sanctioning of the gay movement's demands. No one knows this better than gay leadership. Gay columnist Paul Varnell states,

> The chief opposition to gay equality is religious. We may conduct much of our liberation efforts in the political sphere or even the "cultural" sphere, but always undergirding those and slowing our progress is the moral/religious sphere. If we could hasten the pace of change there, our overall progress would accelerate—in fact, it would be assured.[3]

With that assurance, normality and morality will have been successfully redefined, and both church and society will begin to reap the spiritual and cultural consequences.

The Denigration of Biblical Authority

The body of Christ will suffer immeasurably because sound doctrine—and even the Bible itself—will have to be taken less seriously if pro-gay theology is widely accepted. You simply cannot tamper with one part of Scripture (in this case, a very significant part) without dismantling its authority in general. And when the authority of the Bible is denigrated, the church of Jesus Christ, the light of the world, will be without any clear guidance of her own.

"The Bible," states Hank Hanegraaff of the Christian Research Institute, "not only forms the foundation of an effective prayer life, but it is fundamental to every other aspect of Christian living—[it] is God's primary way of communicating with us."[4] When God's primary way of communicating with us is compromised, an ancient sin is revived in which compromised obedience to God in one area cripples respect for His Word in other—perhaps all—areas of life and conduct.

"Fairness" and "Rightness"

It began when Eve allowed herself to mull over the serpent's question, "Hath God said?" (Genesis 3:1). Notice that Eve did not reject God's instructions entirely; she simply listened as the serpent explained their "unfairness." The satanic argument, as always, was couched in the most reasonable of terms—"Is it really *fair* for God to not want you to be like Him?" (see Genesis 3:4-5).

Eve bought the "unfairness" argument, and it's an argument people are still buying.

"It is inconceivable to me that God would create someone like me who is unable to change," a lesbian minister asserts, and "then condemn that person to hell."[6]

A familiar theme: God's standards seem unfair, therefore they must not really be God's standards. No matter how sincerely gay Christians claim to believe in biblical authority, their compromise in this one area weakens their position in others as well.

The Dilemma

When I belonged to the Metropolitan Community Church (MCC), there was an ongoing debate between their conservative and liberal congregations. Many leaders and members of the MCC were from fundamentalist/evangelical backgrounds and continued to refer to themselves as theologically conservative. (The MCC's "Statement of Faith," in fact, contains the basics most Christians agree on.) But others held radical, sometimes blasphemous, views.

One lesbian minister wrote in the church's official publication that it was idolatry to worship Jesus as God. Another stated in print her discomfort with the cross, implying a link between references to the blood of Christ and sadomasochism. And on at least one occasion I spoke with a pastor who said he wasn't sure what being born again meant, so he had no intention of encouraging people to do it.[5]

When conservatives in the MCC argued for a return to biblical authority, their liberal opponents reminded them that the position they all shared on homosexuality was at odds with Christian tradition and conservatism, so how could they (the conservatives) now push for biblical literalism? That was an argument I never heard a convincing rebuttal to.

Accepting the pro-gay theological view will weaken the church's position on issues of life and conduct too. We might consider the diminished respect for biblical authority and lowering of standards in other areas that are evident in the gay Christian movement.

For example, gay author and minister Mel White (formerly of Fuller Theological Seminary), describes his first homosexual encounter—which he engaged in while still married—as "inevitable." He describes his partner in adultery/homosexuality as "one of God's gifts."[7]

Troy Perry, a former pastor with the Church of God and the founder of the Metropolitan Community Church, takes a similar view of a similar experience. Recounting a tryst he had with another man (while his own wife was in the next room), he recalls, "Eventually, I came to realize that what we were doing seemed right for me. It stopped short of being love, but was a marvelous education."[8]

Adultery described as "right" and "a marvelous education"? Does acceptance of homosexuality lead to an altered view of marital commitment in general? It certainly did for Perry, who stated in a 1989 interview that how you define adultery is up to you, and that sex outside of marriage may not be wrong:

> If you have an open [inclusive of other sexual partners] relationship, that's fine and dandy.[9]

Years later, Reverend Perry's views on sexuality would show themselves to be more radical than ever. During a lengthy interview on the Web site of *Gay Guide Toronto,* in which Perry was introduced as a "proud leatherman," he described his taste for sadomasochistic sex:

> I tell people that S/M (sado-masochism, which combines the giving and receiving of pain with sex) means "sensuality and maturity"…I discovered that leathermen have a deep spirituality, and that includes pagans, Hindus…There is a mutually agreed-upon exchange of power, the top/the bottom, the slave/the master, the daddy/the boy…Some of the sensuality involved in the leather community is so intense it takes you into your spiritual self. Some of the things I've

witnessed at leather gatherings are akin to reading about the saints filled with rapture at being so involved with God and God's love.[10]

At the risk of overemphasizing the obvious, let me ask you to please reread Reverend Perry's statements, keeping in mind that he is the founder of the largest, most visible pro-gay denomination in existence, as well as one of the most influential spearhead figures for the "gay and Christian" movement.

This former Pentecostal pastor now believes, as a self-professed gay Christian, that ritualized sex between men, involving bondage and role-playing in sexual scenes depicting a father and son or a slave and master, is a form of "deep spirituality"—and such rituals between men are, according to Perry, similar to the holy experiences of "saints filled with rapture at being so involved with God."

It's unlikely Reverend Perry taught such loose views of marriage and sexual expression when he served as a pastor with the Church of God. Mel White, likewise, could hardly have written of an adulterous encounter as "inevitable" nor of a companion in either homosexual or heterosexual adultery as "God's gift" when he was a professor of preaching and communications at Fuller Theological Seminary. Something changed in their understanding of fidelity. This change cannot be unrelated to their acceptance of pro-gay theology.

Discarding Inconvenient Concepts

The first openly gay Episcopal priest to be ordained, Robert Williams, goes further than Perry and White by declaring in *Newsweek* magazine, on the subject of monogamy, "If people want to try, OK. But the fact is, people are not monogamous. It is crazy to hold up this ideal and pretend it's what we're doing, and we're not." Williams ends his remarks with an unusually tasteless flourish when he suggests, in the most vulgar terms, that Mother Teresa ought to have a sexual experience.[11]

The late Reverend Sylvia Pennington, a heterosexual advocate for the gay Christian movement, included an alleged revelation about marriage and divorce in her book-length argument against the possibility of anyone overcoming homosexuality:

> When any human relationship begins to infringe on the most important and eternal relationship—which is our union with Christ—the Lord Himself will end that human relationship. When the pain of an unsuccessful marriage begins to separate either party from God, then it is God, and not the people, who ends the marriage.[12]

Contrary to Jesus' specific reference to fornication being the only grounds for divorce (Matthew 19:9), Reverend Pennington gave the go-ahead for divorce proceedings to anyone feeling his or her marriage has begun to "infringe" on his or her relationship with God.

The Presbyterian Task Force, in their gay-affirming 1991 report titled *Keeping Body and Soul Together*, didn't even bother with inconvenient concepts such as marriage and monogamy. Instead they opted for the clever notion of "justice love," declaring that appropriate sexual conduct should be judged by "whether the relationship is responsible, the dynamics genuinely mutual, and the loving full of joyful caring."[13] One need not dwell too long on the carnal varieties and combinations one could call "responsible, mutual, and full of joyful caring."

What They End Up Saying

Can such low moral standards among people naming the name of Christ reflect anything but a diminished view of Scripture? While most in the gay Christian movement insist they consider the Bible to be authoritative, a look at some of their remarks about Scripture betrays another view:

- "What influences lead us to new ways of understanding Scripture?" writes Troy Perry. *"New scientific information, social change, and personal experience* are perhaps the greatest forces for change in the way we interpret the Bible and develop our beliefs."[14]

- In reference to the apostle Paul's views on homosexuality, gay Episcopalian minister Robert Williams comments, "So what? Paul was wrong about any number of other things, too. Why should you take him any more seriously than you take Jerry Falwell, Anita Bryant, or Cardinal O'Connor?"[15]

- Writes lesbian author Virginia Mollenkott, "I can no longer worship in a theological context that depicts God as an abusive parent and Jesus as the obedient, trusting child. This violent theology encourages the violence in our streets and nations."[16]

- Jane Spahr, cofounder of CLOUT (Christian Lesbians Out Together) and lesbian evangelist for the Downtown Presbyterian Church of Rochester, claimed her theology was first of all informed by "making love with Coni," her lesbian partner.[17]

- Melanie Morrison, cofounder of CLOUT, says, "I know in my heart that the canon is not closed—I know this because the Bible does not reconcile me with the earth and the Bible does not reconcile me with my sexual self."[18]

Again, it should be understood that many in the gay Christian movement would disagree with some of the above remarks. Some would even find them outrageous. But compromise begets compromise. The disrespect for biblical standards among the radical elements of the gay Christian movement is the unquestioned result of the biblical revisions the movement itself is based on.

Can we expect any less to happen in our own sanctuaries if we, as the gay Christian movement did, allow a similar compromise of biblical integrity? No, according to Kristi Hamrick, press secretary to the Family Research Council:

> This is why lines must be drawn, standards discussed, and battles fought. Because when people push the envelope of morality and get away with it, they don't sit back to enjoy the sensation. They reach further—touching the lives of the

people around them—touching the lives of your children, and someday, mine.[19]

The Sexual Exploitation of Children

At the outset, let me clarify that I do not view homosexuality and pedophilia (sex between adults and children) as the same. While both are clearly immoral and unnatural, they also involve different behaviors, cross different moral boundaries, and have different consequences.

Likewise, I don't assume that homosexual men are likely—simply because they're homosexual—to molest children. What I have observed firsthand (which is limited, certainly) leads me to believe most homosexuals are not interested in sexual relations with children.

I have counseled more than 100 homosexual men and a handful (five or fewer) of pedophiles. None of the men who identified themselves as homosexuals reported any sexual feelings whatsoever for children. Of the pedophiles I counseled, none reported being aroused by adult men of the same sex, furthering my belief that homosexuality and pedophilia ought to be viewed as separate conditions.

My experiences in the gay community also confirmed this. As a staff member, delegate, and pianist of the Metropolitan Community Church, I knew hundreds of gay men. Not one of them, to my knowledge, had any sexual interest in children.

Still, I'm convinced that the acceptance of homosexuality will pave the way for the acceptance of pedophilia. This is so, not because homosexuals desire sex with children, but because the approval of one previously taboo practice makes room for approval of the next, more serious taboo.

Progressive Loss of Taboos

In the early 1960s, before the "sexual revolution" hit, the two major taboos were adultery and fornication. Both were generally frowned on, and those who practiced them usually kept quiet about it. Then, during the upheaval characterizing the later '60s, people began to take a kinder and gentler view of these practices. Films such as *The Graduate,*

Love Story, and *Bob and Carol and Ted and Alice* began portraying these practices in first a sympathetic, then downright positive light. Popular songs like "Let's Spend the Night Together" glamorized them; theater productions such as *Hair* and *Oh! Calcutta!* portrayed them on stage; comedians joked about them. Soon what was taboo became commonplace. And homosexuality began peeking out from behind the next curtain.

By and large, those who broke the taboos in the '60s didn't openly support homosexuality. It was seldom mentioned, much less promoted, and when it was discussed, this was done in less than sympathetic terms. Yet the swingers of the '60s were the unwilling doormen for the budding gay-rights movement. If sex between consenting men and women apart from marriage was now permissible after all, then why not between consenting adults of the same sex?

The marriage boundary around sexual behavior had been removed. The next boundary's removal was less than five years away.

Films toward the end of the '60s and the early to mid '70s—*Boys in the Band; Fortune in Men's Eyes; Norman, Is That You?*—portrayed homosexuality in first a sympathetic and then positive light. Popular songs such as "Lola" glamorized it. Theater productions like *The Ritz* and, again, *Fortune in Men's Eyes* portrayed it on stage. And comedians joked about it.

No Longer a Disorder?

But homosexuality's biggest boost toward acceptance came when the American Psychiatric Association removed homosexuality from its list of disorders. Supporters of this decision argued a number of key points. I've listed them below with quotes from medical or psychiatric experts who supported these points—in order to compare the points experts made about homosexuality 30 years ago to the points they're making about pedophilia today.

1. *Homosexuality represents a problem only to those homosexuals who are distressed by it.* "If a homosexual is distressed about his orientation," said Dr. Judd Marmor, an influential psychiatrist, "the appropriate

diagnosis should be the underlying psychological disorder, e.g. anxiety reaction—depressive reaction."[20]

2. *Society's anti-homosexual prejudice creates more problems for homosexuals than their sexuality does.* A memo from a gay organization in New York City to the American Psychiatric Association made this point clearly: "We are told, from the time we first recognize our homosexual feelings, that our love is sick, that we are emotional cripples...The result of this in many cases is to contribute to a self-image that often lowers the sights we set for ourselves in life."[21]

3. *Homosexuals are no less emotionally stable than heterosexuals.* The Chair of the APA Task Force "concluded that homosexuals showed no significant signs of pathology."[22]

4. *Homosexual relationships can be healthy and affirming.* The Chair of the APA Task Force also "concluded that a significant portion of homosexuals...could function well interpersonally."[23]

The push to normalize homosexuality, based on these points, was successful. The board of the American Psychiatric Association voted to change the diagnostic status of homosexuality. (See chapter 6 for a full account of the events leading up to the APA vote.)

This landmark decision began with a group of homosexuals who gathered data, networked, and rallied support from a culture that was reluctant (at first) to accept them. They also effectively utilized their allies within the leadership of the American Psychiatric Association.[24]

And pedophilia watched from behind the next curtain, waiting.

Comparing the Arguments

Today, we are hearing the same arguments from "experts" defending pedophilia as we heard 30 years ago from those defending homosexuality. Compare these points, and the quotes from psychiatrists and doctors to support them, with the points listed above.

1. *Pedophilia represents a problem only to those pedophiles who are distressed by it.* "According to the new DSMIV (Diagnostic and

Statistical Manual of the American Psychiatric Association) a pedophile [has a diagnosable condition] ONLY if he feels bad or anxious about what he's doing."[25]

2. *Society's anti-pedophile prejudice creates more problems for pedophiles than their sexuality does.* William Pomeroy, formerly of the Alfred Kinsey Research Team, "told *Citizen* magazine that adult/child sex can be 'wonderful and beautiful,' adding that the only downside is that the 'consequences' society applies against such behavior 'can be absolutely horrendous.'"[26]

3. *Pedophiles are no less emotionally stable than non-pedophiles.* "Pedophilia, according to [Dr. John] Money, should be viewed as a sexual orientation, not a disease or a disorder."[27]

4. *Child/adult sexual relationships can be healthy and affirming.* "People seem to think that any contact between children and adults…has a bad effect on the child. I say this can be a loving and thoughtful, responsible sexual activity."[28]

Culture has been lagging behind the "experts" on this subject. No songs or plays have yet, to my knowledge, lauded pedophilia, and I've heard no stand-up comedy routines on the subject.

Approval from Experts

Meanwhile, as gay activists before them did, advocates of pedophilia are gathering data, networking, and rallying support from a culture reluctant to accept them. And they are utilizing their allies within the leadership of the American Psychiatric Association. Those allies already include:

• The previously quoted Dr. John Money of Johns Hopkins University. In an interview with *The Journal of Pedophilia* in the Netherlands, Money said, "If I were to see a case of a boy aged 10 or 11 who's intensely erotically attracted toward a man in his twenties or thirties, if the relationship is mutual—then I would not call it pathological in any way."[29]

- Dr. Deryck Calderwood, chairman of the SIECUS (Sex Information and Education Council of the US) board of directors, says, "When no one gives the child a bad conscience…intercourse between adults and children causes no mental harm."[30]

- Dr. John DeCecco, openly gay professor and head of the Human Sexuality Department at San Francisco State University, believes that "the decision [to have child/adult sex] should largely rest in the hands of the people who are entering into the relationship. If I'm 12 and I decide to have sex with a 19-year-old or a 20-year-old or a 50-year-old, that is really a choice I have."[31]

- Dr. Wayne Dynes, professor at Hunter College, who shares DeCecco's views: "[I'm] not sure that a 7-year-old can give informed consent. That doesn't mean that one should necessarily exclude sexual relations with them."[32]

- Lester Kirkendall, PhD, SIECUS founding board member, anticipates that future sex-education programs "will probe sexual expression…across generational lines. These patterns will become legitimate."[33]

- Harvard Health Services psychologist Douglas Powell, commented, "I have not seen anyone harmed by this [child/adult sex] so long as it occurs in a relationship with somebody who really cares about the child."[34]

But even with blessings from the academic elite, could the advocates of pedophilia really win the public's sympathy, much less its approval? Unthinkable.

But then, public approval of homosexuality was once unthinkable too. We should know by now that a campaign's success depends not on its rightness but on how well it's packaged and how aggressively it's promoted. In this respect, Dr. Money advises pedophiles to take their cue from gay activists:

> When the gay rights activists became politically active, there wasn't a sufficient body of scientific information for

them to base their gay activism on. So, you don't have to have a basic body of scientific information in order to decide to work actively for a particular ideology. As long as you're prepared to be put in jail. Isn't that how social change has always taken place, really?[35]

Opening the Door

In an interview on the *700 Club* television show several years ago, I cited many of these quotes as evidence that the gay-rights movement was serving as a doorman to the pedophile movement. Is this really what gays want?

I doubt it. Leadership in the gay community is divided over what support, if any, it should lend the pedophile movement. NAMBLA (the North American Man-Boy Love Association—founded in 1977, the most visible pedophile organization) petitioned to march in the Stonewall 25 Gay Pride Parade. They had the support of some gay leaders, yet the organizers of the parade banned them from participating.[36]

Most gays forcefully denounce both NAMBLA and any form of adult/child sex, though a scant few see NAMBLA as a logical extension of the gay community.[37] One thing is certain: The pedophile movement could not have made significant gains if the gay-rights movement hadn't paved the way by challenging existing norms and restrictions on sexual behavior.

Which brings us back to the church. If she—unable or unwilling to confront the gay Christian movement—yields to it, the gay Christian movement will, with religious authority, open the door for the gay-rights movement to overhaul America's values. And, whether deliberately or not, the gay-rights movement will then hold open the door for the pedophile movement and its own pernicious agenda.

History will hopefully run its course before we see what's biding its time behind the *next* curtain.*

---

* Review the sins listed in Leviticus 20 and you might find a clue. Along those lines, a remark made by gay activist Sarah Cohen at the Yale Annual ball is noteworthy: "What's wrong with a little bestiality?"[38]

The Loss of a Coherent Definition of Family

Of all the cultural consequences I believe we will suffer, the loss of family definition will be both the reason for, and the result of, the first two.

If the church allows marriage and family to be redefined, then a circular deterioration will start: There will be an increase in the sexual confusion and exploitation of children as a result of the redefinition of family, and there will be an even further redefinition of family as a result of the sexual confusion and exploitation of children. Given enough time, the original concept of "family" could be driven right out of our consciousness.

Not that the family isn't already hurting; it is presently in danger, and it's not homosexuals who put it there. Spousal assaults, abandonment, divorce, adultery, child abuse, and incest have battered the family for years. I was once asked by a Christian radio host what I felt the greatest threat to the nuclear family was. Since the show was on homosexuality, I knew the answer she was looking for, but I couldn't give it: "The greatest threat to the nuclear family," I said sadly, "is the nuclear family."

But the family remains (as of this writing) with its definition intact, which is crucial. So long as the family is recognized for what it is and remains sanctioned as such, it can survive; its problems can be corrected. Redefine it, though, and through redefinition it loses its very worth.

Is Love Enough?

I have heard gay couples argue they can do a fine job of raising children. Some say they are better at it than some heterosexual couples they've known. Likewise, in the 1993 Gay Rights March on Washington, a number of participants were asked how they defined a family. A young lesbian couple pointed to their adopted sons as evidence of their family status. One group of marchers said "family" could be man and woman, man and man, or woman and woman. Another group included various combinations—for example, two men and a woman—saying that what is right for *them* (the alleged family) was all that mattered.

"Where there is love," they said confidently, "there is a family."[39]

So if love, for whatever reason, dies, does the family relationship die as well? If parents stop loving their children, can they, under this new definition, throw their kids out?

The real question is not whether there is love. The question is whether love *by itself* should qualify people to undo centuries of traditional and theological understanding of the term *family* to make it accommodate them and their desires.

To illustrate the importance of definition, let's look at the concept of the church of Jesus Christ. It is defined in Ephesians 1 as women and men who, having been born again by the Spirit of God through faith in Christ, are now the visible members of His body on earth. The church, then, is the body of Christ.

The church also has problems. Let's assume (and it shouldn't be hard) that the body of Christ is not functioning the way it was meant to. Suppose a panel of experts was convened to discuss solutions to the church's problems, and suppose one of the experts offered the following:

> You know, there are plenty of nice people who are not Christians, but who do have some sort of faith and who'd love to be part of the church. They could do the work of the church; why, some of them could do it better than some Christians do! Besides, the church obviously isn't functioning well in its present state. Why not redefine it to include not only born-again Christians, but also people of other faiths or nonbelievers who have faith in themselves and who want to be recognized as part of the church? As I see it, wherever there's any kind of faith, there's the church!

A poetic idea, but a wrong one. Faith alone saves nobody—the One we have faith in, Jesus Christ, defines us as Christians, not just faith itself. And if a person's faith is not specifically in Christ, then he is not a part of Christ's body. That does not mean he's not a wonderful person with much to offer; it does not mean he's not deeply loved and valued by God. It simply means that, by his status as a non-Christian, he cannot truly be part of the body of Christ.

If the experts decided to redefine the church to include the non-Christian, that still would not make him a part of the church in God's sight. It would, though, weaken the witness and effectiveness of the church in general. Reconceptualized to include virtually anyone, the church could hardly preach the gospel; why bother with messy concepts like atonement and judgment if anyone with any kind of faith can now be called "the church"? And so the church, now watered down by redefinition, would no longer have the impact it was meant to have.

This is true of the family too. Redefining it to accommodate same-sex couples will never make such combinations a family in God's sight. It will, though, weaken the effectiveness of the family in general. Standards such as monogamy and fidelity will have to change when the qualifications for "family" change, to make room for a whole new concept.

That's because the redefinition of "family" won't stop with same-sex couples. Just as the gay-rights movement is now a platform for sadomas-ochists, transsexuals, and bisexuals (and in some cases, pedophiles), so these same groups can be expected to jump on the marriage bandwagon once the pro-gay movement has opened the door.

With "love" as the standard for the "new family," any one of these groups, and other groups as well, can claim to love their partners. Logically, then, bisexual trios, a man and a transsexual, an adult and a child, and a "master" with his "sex slave" should be able to claim family status. Is this what gays want when they clamor for same-sex marriages? I doubt it. But this is the inevitable result of tampering with a God-given model.

What Is the Ideal?

When studies confirm that boys raised without fathers have higher rates of impulsivity and antisocial behavior; when children have a better chance of success when both mother and father are present in their homes; when a 1987 study of violent rapists shows that 60 percent of them came from single-parent homes; when 75 percent of teenage suicides come from broken homes; and when girls raised without fathers are shown to be sexually active sooner in life and at higher risks of having children out of wedlock;[40] can we seriously deny the need children have for both a mother and a father?

At this point, lesbian or gay male couples might argue that they too can provide a safe family environment, and that as responsible, hardworking citizens, they will instill good values in their children. For the sake of argument, let's assume they're right. Suppose they remain monogamous and stay together for a lifetime, adopting and raising children in a safe, loving environment. Many heterosexual couples are unable to do the same. Doesn't that prove that we should, as the gay Christian movement asks us to, redefine "family" to include them?

No—because the question assumes that if something works, it must be right; or that if something does not match the ideal yet still produces good results, then the ideal should be modified.

Certainly a moderate, responsible gay couple could provide a better home life than, say, an abusive heterosexual couple who beat their children or abuse drugs. But that's pitting the best-case gay scenario against the worst-case heterosexual scenario. We might just as well say that, because a responsible, loving single mother is better equipped to raise children than an irresponsible, unloving couple, then single motherhood is, in general, just as good as a two-parent home.

But it isn't. The ideal situation is still a healthy two-parent home. Just because some two-parent homes are unhealthy does not mean the two-parent ideal should be changed.

The answer to family problems is to *correct* the problems, not redefine the family. No matter how benign a homosexual couple may be, if you compare what the average same-sex couple has to offer with the average opposite-sex couple, the opposite-sex couple will win out because they include a mother *and* a father.

Some people feel that homosexual couples are less than ideal as parents because of their homosexuality. I would argue it's not necessarily their homosexuality that makes them less than ideal; it's their sameness. Two men or two women together—whether as a homosexual couple or as roommates or friends—cannot give a child what a heterosexual couple can. Children need the influence of both a man and a woman; anything less may be good to a point, but never ideal. And to be of any real use, a standard must represent what is ideal, not what is good to a point.

Protecting a Standard

Dr. Dennis Praeger, founder and president of the Micah Center for Ethical Monotheism, gives us some insight into the development of this standard in his excellent essay "Why Judaism Rejected Homosexuality":

> When Judaism demanded that all sexual activity be channeled into marriage, it changed the world. The subsequent dominance of the Western world can be attributed to the sexual revolution initiated by Judaism and later carried forward by Christianity. This revolution consisted of forcing the sexual genie into the *marital bottle*.[41]

Dr. Praeger refers to the "utterly wild" nature of human sexuality, which, when unbridled, expresses itself in every conceivable coupling and combination. The Torah called for a civilizing influence, creating and protecting the notion of a family by rigid definitions and roles. In so doing, God decreed that sexuality conform to a specific standard—a standard that cannot yield to accommodate deviant sexuality.

This is why, when gays claim their sexuality is "natural" to them, I am inclined to say, "So what?" *Natural* (in the subjective sense, as in "natural to me") does not mean *right;* the created intent for sexual expression must dictate what forms of sexual expression are acceptable. So if people choose to pursue their "natural" sexual inclinations, we may grant their right to do so. But we cannot grant their demand that the standard for marriage and family be revised to suit what is natural to them, yet unnatural in fact.

So why bother arguing? Because if the church is to be, as Jesus said, the salt of the earth (a preserver of right standards and truth) and the light of the world (a guide to righteousness and life), then her responsibility to the world is to love it as Christ did—by speaking truth to it, not by accommodating its demands. Nor can the church join its assaults on standards of marriage clearly spelled out in the Bible. Dr. Praeger writes that he understands the reasons some groups have for making these assaults. "What I have not understood," he adds, "is why Jews or Christians would join the assaults. I do now. They do not know what is at stake. At stake is our civilization."[42]

3

HOW THE
"GAY CHRISTIAN" MOVEMENT
BEGAN

*"So there you have it: This ecclesiastical Phoenix
rising from the ashes of Sodom. It cannot,
will not be ignored. The heterosexual Christian is now
forced to declare himself and reaffirm or
disregard his beliefs about what the scriptures teach."*

DR. PAUL MORRISON

Major denominations ordaining homosexuals, priests and clergy presiding over same-sex weddings, sanctuaries invaded by boisterous gay activists, debates over homosexuality ripping congregations apart—who would have guessed we'd ever reach such a point in church history?

A vigorous debate between Christians and homosexuals should not be surprising in and of itself. If Dennis Praeger is right when he says the Judeo-Christian ethic is responsible for the Western world's disapproval of homosexuality,[1] then conflicts between the church and the gay-rights movement are not only understandable, they're inevitable.*

So the tension we see today between conservative Christians and gay-rights advocates is no surprise. It is a clash between two opposing philosophies: one confining sexual behavior to a specific standard, the other fighting for something much broader. They can hardly be expected to coexist peacefully. Our culture's acceptance of homosexuality should not surprise us either, since the Judeo-Christian ethic has been spurned in many ways for the past three decades.

The Phrase "Gay Christian"

Most conservative Christians—myself included—believe homosexuality in any form is a violation of biblical standards. And for that reason we don't feel that "gay" and "Christian" are compatible. "Gay Christian" movement, then, may seem a contradiction in terms or a tacit approval of the movement itself. In this book, neither is the case. I use the phrase only to describe the broad movement that claims to be both gay and Christian, and it seems redundant and sarcastic to keep putting the words *gay* and *Christian* in quotation marks.

What *is* surprising, though, is that we have reached a point where these ethics are being not only challenged, but rewritten as well. To better understand how they are being rewritten, and why, we first need to review the evolution of the gay-rights movement in America, the subsequent development of the gay Christian movement, and the church's response to both.

The more you know about a group—what they've experienced, where they've been, what events have shaped their beliefs—the more effectively you can respond to them. And while learning about their background, you just might develop a more insightful, sympathetic attitude toward them.

---

* While acceptance of homosexuality in ancient cultures is well documented,[2] the past 2000 years of Western thought have, by and large, rejected it,[3] and the influence of both the Old and New Testaments can be credited for that.[4]

My favorite author, Charles Dickens, was a master of sympathetic insight. His stories feature characters guilty of horrible deeds, but when he explains their backgrounds, we can't help but feel some pity for them even as we despise their actions.

The miserly old Scrooge in *A Christmas Carol* can't be excused for his cruelty to the poor. But his own bleak childhood helps us to understand what hardened his heart. Miss Havisham, the demented spinster of *Great Expectations,* appalls us when she uses her adopted daughter to hurt men of all ages. But when we learn how she was jilted in her own youth, we feel some compassion for her. When the peasant masses in *A Tale of Two Cities* rise up with unreasonable fury against all aristocrats, Dickens reminds us of the abuse they endured, and so we understand them better. We hate what they did, but we see why they did it.

The better we understand the events that lead a group of people to behave in a certain way, the better we are able to deal with them. For that reason, before confronting the gay Christian movement, it is important to know the elements that gave rise to it.

Movements are not monolithic, by the way. Members of any movement have some common, general beliefs, and some different ideas as well. Ask a feminist, for example, what the priorities of the women's movement are, and she may tell you they are equal pay and affirmative action; ask another feminist the same question and she might say "reproductive freedom." Two different feminists, two separate priorities. Yet both will tell you their general commitment is to women's rights.

The gay-rights and the gay Christian movements are similar. As each has grown, its members have become more diverse in their beliefs and approaches while retaining some common, general goals. Compare the gay-rights movement of 1969, with its emphasis on demonstrations and "coming out of the closet," to that of today, and you will see a more diversified, sophisticated, sometimes even fragmented group. The same can be said of the gay Christian movement.

So it's not wise to assume that all members of a group or movement believe exactly the same thing. But you can, in most cases, gain a general idea of what they stand for. To do that, it's best to examine the statements and actions of their leaders, the body of writing they have produced, and the common themes running through each. Those three elements can provide an accurate picture of a group's general views while allowing for some differences among its members. With that in mind, let's take a look at the development of both the gay-rights and the gay Christian movements, and the church's response to each over the past four decades.

The Early Years

Although there were some challenges during the first half of the twentieth century to the common belief that homosexuality was unnatural,[5] there was no visible homosexual movement in America until the 1950s. This is not to say there was no homosexual *subculture* before then; there was, and it thrived. But the origin of the gay-rights movement can be traced to 1950, with the founding of the Mattachine Society (for homosexuals of both sexes) and the Daughters of Bilitis (a lesbian organization).[6]

Both groups were conservative in their approach. "Evolution, not revolution" was the means Mattachine sought to use in achieving its goals; the Daughters of Bilitis showed similar restraint. The movement's goals were to reform the public image of the homosexual (from "pervert" to respectable citizen), to see homosexual acts decriminalized, and to see homosexuals gain "full participation" in American life.[7] By gaining the support of psychiatrists, scientists, and clergy, they hoped to achieve these goals through reason and public discussion.

In 1955 (five years after the founding of Mattachine), the first serious challenge to the Bible's condemnation of homosexuality was published. Dr. Derrick S. Bailey, an Anglican theologian who argued for the acceptance of homosexuality,[8] published *Homosexuality and the Western Christian Tradition.* In his book Bailey claimed that the destruction of Sodom in Genesis 19 came about not because of homosexual acts, but because of inhospitality. This uncommon interpretation of Genesis 19 would be repeated for decades within the gay Christian movement.

The quiet approach the early gay-rights movement was taking met with little opposition from churches. This was not an indication of approval (though some liberal theologians were already sympathizing with Mattachine's goals). Rather, since most Christians were unaware of these low-profile groups, there was little mention of homosexuality from America's pulpits. That was yet to come.

One exception was a group of 11 Quakers who were at least aware of homosexuality, if not the homosexual movement, and who took a friendly view of it. The Literary Committee of the Friends Home Service in England published, in 1963, a pamphlet on sexuality that reads like a 30-year forerunner to the controversial Presbyterian report of the 1990s. It allowed for premarital sex, approved of adultery in some cases, and viewed homosexuality as acceptable.[9] While not reflecting the official Quaker view at the time, and certainly not influencing Christian or secular thought on homosexuality in the early 1960s, the pamphlet stands out as an early milestone in the gay Christian movement.

The philosophy of the Mattachines and Daughters of Bilitis, meanwhile, was gradually evolving. Initially, some leaders in both groups considered their own homosexuality to be an illness, or at least a serious handicap. While supporting fair treatment for homosexuals, these leaders (themselves homosexual, or "homophile," as they were often called then) still believed their sexual state was less than ideal.[10] Early debates within the movement, in fact, centered on whether or not homosexuals should support psychiatry, since its general view was anti-homosexual. Some thought mental health specialists could be valuable allies in their fight against unfair treatment. Others, who felt perfectly comfortable with their homosexuality, viewed those same psychiatrists as enemies needing to be challenged.

The homosexual movement from 1950 to 1965, then, was marked by a struggle for self-definition and understanding.

From "Please Treat Gays Fairly" to "Gay Is Good"

By 1965 psychiatry was seen by gay leaders much the same way that the church is viewed by them today—as the primary institution frustrating the goals of the homosexual movement.

That same year, the movement produced a statement of gay pride that rejected the opinions of psychiatry and society. In essence, it said that homosexuality is not an illness, that solidarity among homosexuals is an important tool in reaching their goal of equality with heterosexuals, and that tactics more aggressive than public discussion and education were needed if they were ever to achieve their goals.[11]

A third published argument for the pro-gay theology came out two years later. Wainwright Churchill's *Homosexual Behavior Among Males* called for a "new morality in the sexual sphere," repeated Bailey's explanation of Sodom's destruction, and praised Bailey and the 1963 Friends' report for their groundbreaking conclusions.[12] Like its predecessors, Churchill's book was not written by a self-identified gay Christian. But also like its predecessors, it laid additional groundwork for the gay Christian movement.

The call for more aggressive tactics was answered twice in 1968, when homosexual activists demonstrated at the convention of the American Medical Association (AMA) in San Francisco, and at Columbia University's College of Physicians and Surgeons, where a panel on homosexuality was convening.[13] Inspired in no small part by the civil rights movement, they used leaflets, protests, and appeals to the public's sense of fairness to make their points.

At both the AMA convention and Columbia University, activists demanded participation in future professional conventions and discussions on homosexuality, arguing that it was time that the professionals "stopped talking *about* us and started being with us."[14] Even if not entirely successful, it was the beginning of empowerment and, as Ronald Bayer terms it, healing:

> Though not necessarily couched in terms of violence, action and rebellion were seen as antidotes to the shame, self-doubt, and self-hatred that had been imposed upon homosexuals by society.[15]

Apparently, then, public demonstrations not only made a statement—they felt good! That good, empowered feeling would be reported by gay activists again and again. But the true 1968 milestone for the gay

Christian movement occurred much more quietly than the demonstrations at Columbia and San Francisco.

The First Pro-Gay Denomination

On October 6, 1968, 12 people responded to an ad placed in *The Advocate* (a gay-oriented newspaper) inviting them to worship in a newly formed church for homosexuals. The ad was placed by a 28-year-old former Pentecostal minister named Troy Perry.

Nearly 40 years later, Reverend Perry is still one of the gay Christian movement's most influential leaders. As such, he is of interest to anyone hoping to understand pro-gay Christians.

The denomination Perry founded that October—the Universal Fellowship of Metropolitan Community Churches (UFMCC)—is, by his own claim, "the largest organization touching the lives of gays and lesbians in the world."[16] Nearly 300 UFMCC congregations now exist worldwide, and with social and political action encouraged among its members, Perry's claim about UFMCC's influence is probably true.

In his books *The Lord Is My Shepherd and He Knows I'm Gay* and *Don't Be Afraid Anymore,* Perry recounts the early experiences, both sexual and spiritual, that shaped his thinking. The oldest of five boys, he was raised by his doting mother, Edith, in a religious environment. After his father's death in a car accident, he survived abuse from a violent stepfather who battered Edith and evidently arranged for one of his friends to rape 13-year-old Troy as punishment for coming to his mother's defense.[17]

He found refuge in church and was especially attracted to Pentecostalism. His ministerial gifts showed up early. By age 15 he was a licensed Baptist preacher; by his late teens he was a paid evangelist with the charismatic Church of God. Shortly thereafter he married and took a pastorate in the latter denomination. Having been aware of homosexual attractions the better part of his life, Perry involved himself with other young men, both before and after his marriage, and was eventually excommunicated from the Church of God and divorced from his wife.

Years later, after joining the gay subculture, he was moved by the distress of one of his friends who had been jailed for simply being in a gay bar (a common occurrence at the time). Perry recalls the conversation with this friend, which led to his sense of calling to start a gay church:

> "We're just a bunch of dirty queers and nobody cares about dirty queers!"
> "Somebody cares," I said.
> "Who?"
> "God cares."
> Tony uttered a terrible laugh. "No, Troy. What do you mean, 'God cares'? Be serious!"[18]

That night he conceived the idea of a church for gay people to show them that God did indeed care. A year later he founded the Metropolitan Community Church. Today, the denomination springing from Perry's living room is represented in at least eight foreign countries and throughout most of the United States.

These early stirrings of the gay-rights movement, and the gay Christian movement, were quiet and subtle. From the 1950s to the late 1960s, the gay-rights movement grew and defined itself by saying, "We are not sick, we want validation, and we are prepared to fight for it."

The gay Christian movement, even more than the gay-rights movement, was in its infancy. With scattered support from a handful of liberal churches, it adopted a self-definition similar to that of the gay-rights movement, with an addendum: "God loves and accepts us just as we are; *and* homosexuality is okay with Him."

As they entered 1969, both movements were unaware of a coming earthquake that would begin to propel them into the nation's consciousness.

The Stonewall Riots and the Beginning of the Gay-Rights Movement

It happened without forethought, warning, or plan. No identifiable leaders were involved in it; no call to arms got it going. But it inflamed and, to an extent, redefined the homosexual movement. Revered by gays as the turning point from which they must never retreat, it is celebrated annually in gay-pride rallies and parades. It was called a riot by the local press when it happened. Today, it's known as Stonewall.

Reviewing the headlines from 1969, a reader could miss Stonewall altogether. It gets more press today than it did when it occurred, possibly because gay-related issues received little coverage back then. Or maybe the other newsworthy items of 1969—Woodstock, the Manson family murders, the first man on the moon—drowned it out. At any rate, it's impossible to review the gay-rights movement without giving space to the Stonewall riots.

In the early morning hours of June 28, nine plainclothes detectives entered a gay bar in New York's Greenwich Village called the Stonewall Inn. Intending to close the bar for selling liquor without a license, they ejected the nearly 200 patrons who were inside, then arrested the bartender, three transvestite customers, and a doorman. But when they escorted their charges outside, they found that an angry crowd had gathered on the sidewalk. Someone—exactly who and why are matters of discussion to this day—threw something at the detectives, and within minutes the crowd, which eventually swelled to nearly 400, also began hurling rocks and bottles at the police. The officers retreated and barricaded themselves in the bar until backup enforcements arrived, and within 45 minutes the rioting stopped.[19]

The scene repeated itself the next night when another crowd gathered outside the Stonewall Inn, chanting "Legalize gay bars!" and "Gay is good!" Fires were started, and bottles were again thrown at police, who battled with the demonstrators for two hours before they finally dispersed. Four nights later, yet another gay mob—this one nearly 500 strong—took to the streets in Greenwich Village, marching and shouting slogans.

Exactly what prompted Stonewall is uncertain. Some rather silly ideas have been proposed, one of which is that the recent death of gay icon Judy Garland had put homosexuals in a foul mood.[20] A better explanation would consider some of the social forces at work in the late '60s.

The Vietnam conflict, campus unrest, and the relatively young civil-rights movement had fueled scores of public demonstrations so that by 1969, a group of angry protestors was a common-enough sight. The times were almost wildly anti-authority; government was the dreaded "Establishment," adults over 30 were not to be trusted, campus administrators were openly defied, and police were written off as "pigs." (The Stonewall mob, in fact, chanted "Pigs," among other things, while they pelted the police with rocks and bottles.) Everything traditional was subject to question; it was honorable to challenge the norm. In this context both Stonewall and the aggressive new tone it gave to the gay-rights movement make perfect sense.

By then, many homosexuals saw themselves as a mistreated minority. Too often, they were right. Assaulted for no other reason than the sickness of people who hated them,[21] ignored at times in the legal process, and sometimes unreasonably harassed by police, they were, collectively, angry. The Stonewall riots gave public expression to their pent-up anger; the public expression, in turn, inspired a new defiance among gays.[22]

Immediately after the rioting, homosexual activist groups began forming, first in New York, then nationwide. Plans for future demonstrations, political action, and cultural reform began to take shape. Within months, Gay Power (a term birthed shortly after Stonewall) took its place alongside its cousins of the '60s: Flower Power, Power to the People, and Black Power.[23]

The homosexual population entered the 1970s with a fresh sense of unity and definition. *U.S. News and World Report* writer Erica Goode spells out the post-Stonewall elements that, at the time, gave both the gay-rights and the gay Christian movements their core of strength:

> The idea that sexual orientation was an important characteristic, that it set a group of people apart, defining them as different in some essential way, and a realization, among those attracted towards members of their own gender, that there were others like them, facing the same difficulties and concerns.[24]

The construction of a "gay identity" was crucial to this, so gay activists began educating the public as to how they should view homosexuality. No longer was homosexuality to be seen as a condition or a behavior; it was now to be considered a fundamental part of one's makeup, no less permanent than skin color or gender. By that reasoning, any objection to homosexuality now placed the objector in the same category as a racial bigot or a "sexist." By shifting the focus of homosexuality from *behavior* to *identity*, the gay-rights and gay Christian movements gained new ground by "gradually turning," as Goode explains, "what had been a series of sexual sins into an identity, a way of being."[25]

Stonewall was a declaration of war. Demonstrations would continue to play a key role, but war involves more than hand-to-hand combat; there are troops to mobilize, alliances to forge, and strategies to be laid. The written accounts of gay-rights meetings in 1969 and the early 1970s reflect that the strategy gay leaders seemed to agree on was threefold:[26]

1. Encourage all homosexuals to "come out of the closet" and declare their sexuality as a key part of their identity.

2. Form and strengthen alliances with groups and individuals sympathetic to the gay cause.

3. Confront people or institutions who resisted the gay cause.

Each strategy was a mandate for action. And as the gay-rights movement acted on each mandate, the gay Christian movement was never far behind.

Mandate One: "Come Out!"

The first mandate—encouraging gays to "come out" and identify themselves by their sexual desires—was furthered when the first anniversary of the Stonewall riots was celebrated in New York City in June 1970.

Nearly 10,000 lesbians and gay men—easily the largest public gathering of homosexuals in American history—marched down Sixth Avenue and gathered in Central Park. "Out of the closets! Into the streets!" they chanted, beginning a yearly tradition of celebrating Stonewall that continues today.

As the gay-rights movement got more press, men and women who kept their homosexual longings a secret (either for moral reasons or fear of retaliation) heard the invitation to "come out" and "accept who you truly are." It was an attractive invitation, especially to Christians who battled homosexual temptations. In their conservative churches they were hearing little to help them overcome their struggles; homosexuality was not, by and large, discussed. They were in a silent battle with themselves, and it was hellishly lonely. So when the gay-rights movement offered them support through a community of people who understood what it meant to be homosexual, they were interested. The only obstacle was their faith—how could they choose between being gay or being Christian?

The gay Christian movement removed that hurdle by telling them there was no choice to be made—gay *and* Christian was now an option! They responded in droves, some by leaving their more conservative churches to join the Metropolitan Community Church, others by seeking out "gay-friendly" denominations. And as they did, the gay Christian movement, emulating the gay-rights movement of 1969, stepped into the sunlight.

Gay Christian material began showing up in secular and Christian bookstores.[27] In 1972 Troy Perry published his autobiographical *The Lord Is My Shepherd and He Knows I'm Gay.* Four years later Malcolm Boyd, a renowned Episcopalian priest and bestselling author, openly declared his homosexuality, documented in *Take Off the Mask.* Tom Horner, another Episcopalian priest, submitted his revision of every biblical text on homosexuality in his book *Jonathan Loved David.*

Most notable of all the gay Christian literature in this period was Letha Scanzoni and Virginia Ramey Mollenkott's *Is the Homosexual My Neighbor?* Prior to the 1978 publication of this book, pro-gay writing (even that which found its way into religious bookstores) went largely unnoticed by conservative Christians. But now, for the first time in its history, the gay Christian movement had produced an explanation of its view that caught the attention of evangelicals and fundamentalists. Combining new interpretations of Scripture with earnest (if unconvincing) arguments, the book was praised by secular and Christian sources, including *Christianity Today, The Christian Century, The Journal of the Evangelical Theological Society,* and *The Christian Ministry.* Endorsements from such respected Christian publications was proof that the gay Christian movement was gaining momentum and credibility.

Further proof was seen in the growing visibility and influence of the Universal Fellowship of Metropolitan Community Churches (UFMCC). Troy Perry, the Fellowship's moderator, became internationally recognized within years of founding the organization. In 1972 he addressed a London convention on homosexuality; author and theologian Norman Pittenger attended and gave Perry's speech his approval. Two years later Perry assisted the Australian "Campaign Against Moral Pressure." The next year he was one of 80 leaders invited to meet Governor Jimmy Carter during his bid for the Democratic nomination, after which he led a "gays for Carter" campaign. In 1977 he was invited to Carter's White House to present, along with other gay leaders, his concerns on homosexuality in America.[28]

UFMCC ministers, meanwhile, gained increased exposure through talk shows and news conferences, and Metropolitan Community churches sprang up around the country. The gay Christian movement was successfully following the first mandate of the gay-rights movement. It was out of the closet, proclaiming homosexuality as a God-given gift and encouraging all homosexuals to do likewise.

Mandate Two: Form Alliances

The gay Christian movement also followed the second mandate of the gay-rights movement by forming alliances with its sympathizers. Troy Perry was (and is) especially good at this. When the Los Angeles Metropolitan Community Church was destroyed by arson in 1973, he took out an ad in *Variety* magazine soliciting donations to rebuild the sanctuary; a generous response followed. When he openly fasted for 16 days in front of the Federal Building in Los Angeles in protest of a ballot initiative restricting gay schoolteachers, he raised $100,000 from supporters across the country. And when he spoke at a fund-raiser targeting the same initiative, he was hailed by the likes of John Travolta, Burt Lancaster, and Cher.[29]

Alliances the mainstream church might envy—but will probably never attain—have come easily to the gay Christian movement. The news and entertainment industry, both highly supportive of the gay-rights movement, have forged a tidy bond with the gay Christian movement as well. I remember seeing signed portraits of Phyllis Diller and Mae West hanging at the Los Angeles Metropolitan Community Church. Troy Perry, the church's founder, counts Phil Donahue as one of his friends. When Mel White announced his homosexuality in 1993, media giants such as Barbara Walters and Larry King gave him generous coverage. At an AIDS fund-raiser, Shirley MacLaine offered her blessing to a gay minister while Stevie Wonder stood by.[30] Support from Hollywood is, in fact, a given among the gay churches.

Alliances with churches were also formed after Stonewall. On July 16, 1969, just weeks after the riots, the second "Gay Power" strategy meeting was held in a local Episcopal church. Two years later the United Church of Christ ordained the first openly gay minister in a major denomination.[31] And in January 1977, the Episcopal Church of New York ordained an openly lesbian woman.[32]

Gay networks soon developed within major denominations, where they operated with or without official church sanction. In 1974, Lutherans Concerned was founded for gay Lutherans and their supporters. Two years later, Affirmation was born among the United Methodists as an organization for "lesbian and gay concerns." Integrity (an Episcopalian gay group), Dignity (for Catholic homosexuals), and Kinship (the pro-gay Seventh Day Adventist group) established themselves in their respective denominations. Conference for Catholic Lesbians, Friends (Quakers) for Lesbian and Gay Concerns, and the United Church of Christ Coalition for Gay and Lesbian Concerns did likewise.[33]

With its visibility growing, alliances with prominent individuals secured, and groups and churches in place, the gay Christian movement was equipped to follow the gay-rights movement's next, and most dramatic, mandate.

Mandate Three: Confrontation

Before 1977, there were few clashes between the gay-rights movement and the conservative church. Aside from minor skirmishes—the Daughters of Bilitis staged a demonstration at St. Patrick's Cathedral in 1971, for instance[34]—public conflicts between the two groups were rare.

Gay leaders knew the conservative church disapproved of homosexuality, but in the early years of their movement, they had other concerns. If society was unsympathetic to their cause, they felt, it was largely because homosexuality was considered an illness. To change society's view, it was necessary to first change the view of the institution responsible for labeling them "sick." Thus the American Psychiatric Association (APA) became the target of relentless, well-organized gay protests beginning in 1968 and lasting five years. In 1973, the efforts of gay leadership paid off: The APA deleted homosexuality from its list of disorders (see chapter 6 for more about this).

After the APA changed its position, gays were armed with fresh ideological boldness. They could now confront politicians, educators, and even the federal government with a new approach. If American psychiatry no longer said homosexuality was abnormal, they reasoned, then antisodomy laws and restrictions on military service for homosexuals should be abolished. They further demanded, based on the APA's decision, that civil-rights protection be afforded to gays, and that schools teach students to regard homosexuality as normal.[35]

They demanded more than they got, but they got a great deal. By 1976, some 15 states had removed antisodomy laws from their books, and 33 cities had enacted civil-rights codes protecting homosexuals. The American Bar Association, the American Medical Association, and the American Psychological Association officially supported decriminalizing homosexual behavior, and the United States Civil Service Commission stopped excluding gays from federal employment.[36]

These advances were not entirely ignored by the conservative church. In 1974, the New York Catholic Archdiocese openly opposed civil-rights codes for gays. Two years later, a national coalition of conservative ministries formed to help those who wanted to overcome their homosexuality.[37] But, just as the gays felt that confronting the church was not yet a priority, so the church saw no pressing need to confront the gay-rights movement. Most likely, despite its progress, conservative Christians did not yet feel that the movement had encroached on their own rights.

One exception was a Christian entertainer whose name, whether justly or not, would come to symbolize confrontation between gays and Christians.

The Anita Bryant Campaign

In January 1977, the Board of Commissioners of Dade County, Florida, approved an ordinance prohibiting discrimination based on sexual orientation. Local Christian leaders opposed the ordinance, seeing it as an official endorsement of homosexuality. One of them was Anita Bryant, a 37-year-old singer, author, and runner-up in the 1958 Miss America pageant. When asked to spearhead a campaign to repeal the Dade County ordinance, she accepted.[38] She announced her intentions and began mobilizing support, and the press stepped up its coverage of her efforts—with good reason. While Dade County's gay-rights ordinance was not unique (similar laws were already on the books in other states), it was the first one officially opposed by a celebrity figure—a *female* celebrity, at that—who was also a Christian, a recording artist, and a former beauty queen to boot! The story was irresistible.

Anita Bryant's campaign propelled the Christian viewpoint of homosexuality into the national spotlight, where it could be examined and hotly debated. Miss Bryant was interviewed and editorialized by newspapers, magazines, and network television. On national talk shows she quoted Scripture and explained her moral opposition to gay rights. Gay spokesmen responded, at times furiously, and soon the gloves were off. Accusations and wild exaggerations were thrown out by gays and, sadly, by a few Christians as well.

Gays publicly compared Anita Bryant to Hitler. She was accused of inciting violence against them, causing them to lose their jobs, and threatening human rights in general.[39] Her name became a rallying cry among gays, a common enemy who united them.

Unfortunately, as Christian leaders jumped into the discussion, they too made some irresponsible remarks. On religious television and radio programs, gays were often referred to as potential child molesters, with no studies or facts to back such claims. They were said to "recruit" others into homosexuality, to be worthy of imprisonment, and to be insatiable in their lust. It was not enough for a Christian to simply object to homosexuality; it seemed necessary (in many cases) to paint lurid pictures of homosexuals as well. And so the wall between gays and the conservative church shot up, stacked with hostility and mutual distrust.

The Involvement of the Gay Christian Movement

None of this was lost on the gay Christian movement, which, perhaps even more than the general gay population, saw the Bryant campaign as an affront to their very identity. Not only was Miss Bryant condemning homosexuality, but she was using the Bible—the same Bible they claimed to believe in—as the moral authority behind her crusade. She emphasized, perhaps more than any public figure ever had, the chasm between "homosexual" and "Christian." Those who claimed to be both were compelled to defend their position. And so, in the spring of 1977, the gay Christian movement followed the third mandate of the gay-rights movement: confrontation.

As it turned out, gay Christian leaders were in a better position to confront Bryant than nonreligious gays, because they spoke her language. When she quoted Bible verses, they could respond with Scripture as well; when she claimed divine guidance, they could do the same.

To Christians who were biblically literate, the pro-gay religious arguments were easy to see through. But to the general public, many of whom would be voting on gay-rights bills in Florida and elsewhere, the gay Christian approach confused the issue. After all, if both sides claimed to be Bible-believing Christians doing God's will, how was the average citizen to know who was right? Troy Perry, explaining why he needed to debate Bryant's supporters on television, put it well:

> Our enemies are taking the language of Scripture and running wild with it. Nobody's talking classroom civics in Miami—this is a religious issue! And I speak the language![40]

Despite considerable pro-gay efforts, in June 1977, the voters in Dade County repealed the gay-rights ordinance by a 69-percent-to-30-percent margin. Anita Bryant claimed victory, and rightfully so. Not only had she fought in the public arena and won, but she had broken new ground while doing so. She had taken an unpopular stand without wavering. In retrospect, we might ask why more Christian men were not willing to oppose the gay movement as bravely as she did. She faced a media that was often hostile, endured innumerable insults, and set a new standard for Christian activism.

The battle, though, was far from over. It simply transferred itself to cities across the nation where similar gay-rights ordinances were being considered, debated, and voted on. In a sense, the Anita Bryant campaign was a turning point for Christians and gays.

New Awareness, New Resistance

The campaign marked a new awareness among Christians of homosexuality and the demands of the gay-rights movement. Just as Bryant had, in her words, a "live and let live" attitude until the Dade County ordinance forced her to take a stand, so the church, in the aftermath of Dade County's battle, realized that a "great transformation" had taken place in the homosexual movement:

> No longer content with mere tolerance, gay activist groups sought social acceptance, and the legitimization of homosexuality as an alternative sexual orientation.[41]

"Social acceptance" included laws prohibiting discrimination against homosexuals in housing and employment, as well as pro-gay education programs in public schools. Goals such as these could hardly be ignored by Christian businessmen, who now realized they might face lawsuits by not hiring openly homosexual employees. Christian landlords, forced to rent to gay couples despite their religious objections, were equally concerned. And parents of all faiths, envisioning their children being taught the "normalcy" of homosexuality, were understandably alarmed. Just as Dade County had put the Christian view of homosexuality in the public spotlight, so it had also displayed the gay agenda in the same glare. It too was scrutinized, debated, and reacted to.

As a result, Christian resistance to the gay-rights movement increased, at local and national levels, from 1977 onward. Whatever the outcome, each new battle found conservative Christians confronting, or being confronted by, the gay Christian movement.

Increasing Confrontations

In 1978, California State Senator John Briggs sponsored an unsuccessful ballot initiative to restrict public-school teachers from endorsing homosexuality. His primary and most visible opponent was Troy Perry. Dr. Beverly LaHaye founded Concerned Women of America (CWA), a formidable women's organization frequently at odds with gay causes. She would later be castigated by Mel White as one of his favorite "homophobic radio or television personalities," who "uses her own genteel brand of homophobia" to mobilize CWA. Dr. Jerry Falwell organized the Moral Majority in 1979 to combat, among other things, gay rights and abortion. His subsequent clashes with both the gay-rights and gay Christian movements are legendary.[42]

4

THE "GAY CHRISTIAN" MOVEMENT COMES OF AGE

"Our themes are: 'Gay, proud, and healthy,'
and 'Gay is good.' With or without you,
we will work vigorously toward their acceptance
and will fight those who would oppose us."

RONALD BAYER
Homosexuality and American Psychiatry:
the Politics of Diagnosis

As gay-rights battles were fought across the country, gay Christian spokespersons jousted with conservatives in television and radio debates. Each appearance gave new exposure to the gay Christian viewpoint, and exposure was a plus for the movement. When the pro-gay interpretation of the Bible was argued in public, sympathetic journalists and talk-show hosts picked it up and repeated it before national audiences. "That's just *your* interpretation of those Bible verses" became a common response from the likes of Phil Donahue when conservative studio guests explained their Bible-based objections to homosexuality. "There is a new way of looking at them, you know!"

Thus gay Christians spread their philosophy, both through their own materials and through their media allies. If success is measured by expansion and visibility, the gay Christian movement's achievements from 1970 to 1979 are inarguable. From a fledgling population, it had grown to become an eloquent and aggressive wing of the gay-rights movement. Brimming with media savvy and finding itself well-connected politically, it ended a decade of culture wars as a force to be reckoned with.

By 1980, there was an identifiable body of work, from a variety of sources, promoting the pro-gay theology. At least eight books, most of them published through major houses, were on the market,[1] while journals and articles debated the pro-gay position relentlessly. The gay Christian population was easy to spot as well, inside and outside mainline denominations. Gay caucuses flourished in traditional churches, while newer groups such as the Metropolitan Community Church, Evangelicals Concerned,[2] and independent gay churches continued their expansion.

With expansion came clout and, more importantly, the power of persuasion. So far, the gay-rights and gay Christian movements had influenced policies in local and federal government, education, the media,[3] and, of course, the American Psychiatric Association. Churches of a more liberal bent were also influenced toward a pro-gay position. Troy Perry, when explaining how easily liberal churches accepted his beliefs, made an interesting admission:

> I knew I would have few if any problems with the
> so-called liberal churches. Liberal churches do not usually
> deeply involve themselves with Scripture.[4]

But the final conquest—the conservative church—remained, and remains, immune to gay persuasion for the opposite reason: Conservative churches *do* involve themselves deeply with Scripture! To convince conservative Christians that God condones homosexuality, the gay Christian movement needed a rebuttal, in conservative terms, to the traditional biblical view. Ignoring the Bible would hardly be acceptable; attacking its authority would be even worse. For the gay Christian movement to convince its toughest critics, it needed to affirm the Bible as the ultimate authority and prove that the ultimate authority did not condemn homosexual behavior.

As of 1980, the movement hadn't yet succeeded in that formidable task. Troy Perry's writing, though full of interesting stories that were emotionally compelling, was doctrinally weak.[5] Scanzoni and Mollenkott spent nine chapters of *Is the Homosexual My Neighbor?* examining psychology, sociology, medical science, and personal testimonies of homosexuals who tried to change but "couldn't," yet they devoted only one chapter to a scriptural "defense" of homosexuality. Tom Horner's *Jonathan Loved David* concentrated on culture and history, then gave brief space to biblical concerns and admitted that the apostle Paul would most likely "not have looked kindly" on homosexual behavior.[6]

That may have been enough for liberal believers and gay sympathizers, but conservative Christians would never buy it. So the gay Christian movement could alternately ignore conservatives or fight them (both of which they certainly did) or, better yet, meet them on their own turf with Bible-based arguments.

Such arguments would serve three purposes. First, they would provide ammunition in the escalating war that gays were fighting with groups such as Jerry Falwell's Moral Majority. Conservative religious organizations were influencing public policy; they encouraged their constituents to fight "gay rights" on biblical grounds. If the gay Christian movement could show their grounds were just as biblical as their opponents', conservative Christians might lose credibility in the public's mind.

Second, persuasive biblical arguments could settle whatever self-doubts some gay Christians might be having and encourage other Christians struggling with homosexuality to accept it as a gift and join the gay Christian ranks.

Finally, it might win some heterosexual conservative Christians over to the gay Christian camp, making valuable allies out of them. Attorney and professor F. LaGard Smith recognizes the importance of this:

> Gays realize that they must deal with the whole of
> Scripture if they are to have any chance of convincing us—or
> themselves—that homosexual conduct is pleasing to God.
> It's a daunting task, but they set forth in confidence.[7]

That confidence was radically bolstered in September 1981, when the gay Christian movement's most impressive defense was released in bookstores around the country.

A New Foundation for Pro-Gay Theology

Christianity, Social Tolerance, and Homosexuality by John Boswell is to the gay Christian movement what *Uncle Tom's Cabin* was to the abolitionist movement—a reference point and an inspiration. Pick up any pro-gay religious book written since 1981, or listen to a debate on homosexuality and the Bible, and quotes from Boswell are likely to abound. His is unquestionably the most comprehensive defense for a revised view of Bible verses, in both testaments, referring to homo-sexuality.

While a professor of history at Yale University, Boswell spent ten years researching his 434-page defense for the pro-gay revision. *Christianity, Social Tolerance, and Homosexuality* argued that the Christian church has not always disapproved of homosexuality, and that the Bible verses assumed to condemn homosexual sex do not refer to homosexuality at all but to various other forms of immorality.

To back the first claim, Boswell explored and produced abundant material on the Middle Ages, arguing that the intolerance of that period toward unpopular minorities (including homosexuals) is what really began the Christian "tradition" of condemning homosexuality. To prove his second claim, he turned to the original language of the specific verses in Genesis, Leviticus, Romans, 1 Corinthians, and 1 Timothy that have been traditionally understood to condemn homosexuality. Here he attempts to prove that each verse has been mistranslated or misunderstood in modern times.

Boswell's tactics were brilliant. Early in his book he dismantles the reader's confidence in his own ability to understand the Bible—an important first step, since anyone reading the Bible cover to cover, without bias, would conclude that it prohibits homosexuality. He then moves on with a tour of ancient writings on sexuality, civil law, poetry, and religion, all in an attempt to assure us that early Christian writers were not as concerned about homosexuality as we are today.

Finally he examines the verses mentioned previously, breaking them down in their original language and putting them in historical context. Here Boswell is at his dazzling best. Claiming to understand Moses' and Paul's language—thus understanding what they *really* meant to say—he stands traditional beliefs on their heads by turning simple references to homosexuality into descriptions of rape, inhospitality, ritual impurity, or male prostitution. The reader, almost certainly unfamiliar with Greek or Hebrew, is left questioning the traditional teaching that the Bible condemns all homosexuality.

When an author's credentials are impressive and lengthy and his stature among academics is high, his conclusions may be swallowed whole by the public and the media. This is especially true of "experts" contributing to the homosexual debate. Alfred Kinsey's "ten percent of the population is homosexual" myth was accepted and repeated for decades before it was seriously challenged and disproven. Dr. Simon LeVay's 1991 study on the hypothalamus, allegedly proving that homosexuality is genetic, was snapped up by the media and continues to be cited as "proof" that gays are born gay, though LeVay himself denies he ever proved such a thing. And, of course, if the American Psychiatric Association decided that homosexuality is normal, who are we as mere laypeople to disagree?*

So it is with Boswell. His credentials were impressive, and no one reading his book could deny its scholarly tone. (Indeed, I have been in debates where my gay opponents whipped out their copy of Boswell and confidently pointed to his credentials as proof that we should unquestioningly accept his conclusions.[8]) But credentials and a scholarly tone do not necessarily yield truth. Before anyone accepts Boswell's

---

* See chapter 6 for refutations of Kinsey, LeVay, and the APA.

conclusions about homosexuality and the Bible, some points about him and his work need to be raised.

Concerns About Boswell

First, Boswell was gay.[9] (He died of AIDS in 1994.) That in itself does not disqualify him from writing on the subject, but his own stake in the issue cannot be ignored. He admits as much, perhaps inadvertently, when he opens his book by stating,

> No matter how much historians and their readers may wish to avoid contaminating their understanding of the past with the values of the present, they cannot ignore the fact that both writer and reader are inevitably affected by [their] assumptions and beliefs.[10]

Boswell was also "neither a linguist nor a classicist, but an historian,"[11] as Professor Elodie Ballantine Emig points out in her excellent series on Boswell and the pro-gay theology. Historians may write about language, of course, but when they do, it should be remembered that they write as historians, not as experts on language.

Also, though Boswell wrote with genuine respect for the Bible as a document, he had unusual ideas about its purpose. Of the New Testament, for example, he wrote,

> In general, only the most pressing moral questions are addressed by its authors. Details of life appear only to illustrate larger points. No effort is made to elaborate a comprehensive sexual ethic: Jesus and His followers simply responded to situations and questions requiring immediate attention.[12]

Boswell's view makes the Bible look almost accidental—a good but incomplete book, inadequate to answer the important questions of life. Compare this to the apostle Paul's assessment:

> All Scripture is given by inspiration of God, and is profitable for doctrine, for reproof, for correction, for instruction in righteousness, that the man of God may

be complete, thoroughly equipped for every good work
(2 Timothy 3:16-17).

Boswell's lack of confidence in the Bible's ability, on its own, to provide a "comprehensive sexual ethic" or to address far-reaching (not just "pressing") concerns, leaves readers with a convenient loophole: If the Bible doesn't sufficiently address sexuality, then guidance in that area must be sought elsewhere. And "elsewhere" will no doubt include the mental health and sociological disciplines, both of which take a much friendlier view of homosexuality than the Bible does.

Validation?

None of previously mentioned concerns kept Boswell's book from being widely celebrated upon its release. It was hailed by literary critics as "groundbreaking," "revolutionary," "astonishing," and it went on to win the 1981 American Book Award for History. More significantly, it became an anchor for the gay Christian movement. Finally, their view had been validated in what many felt were conservative biblical terms. Each verse referring to homosexuality had been explained in its original language and context, and no fundamentalist Christian could deny that this was the best way to interpret Scripture. Moreover, these verses were explained in what seemed to be airtight arguments. No one has improved on them, though they laid the foundation for future pro-gay authors like Robin Scroggs, Bruce Bowrer, Peter Gnomes, and journalist Andrew Sullivan.

But if Boswell was lauded by gays and journalists, he was largely ignored by the conservative church. Gay Christian materials were not likely to find their way into the libraries of conservative pastors, after all, and they were seldom if ever reviewed in magazines such as *Christianity Today* and *Moody Monthly.* Indeed, Boswell and the pro-gay theology remained almost unknown to conservatives for nearly a decade.

Eventually, his arguments began cropping up in debates within mainline denominations, though, forcing conservatives in those circles to analyze and respond to his claims. Only later, as the pro-gay theology emerged in fundamentalist and evangelical discussions, was it taken seriously by those groups. Yet as of this writing, *Christianity, Social Tolerance, and Homosexuality* is still a primary resource for pro-gay theologians.

Increasing Aggression

As the gay Christian movement continued finding allies in churches and secular circles, it also continued to follow the trends of the larger gay-rights movement. And the gay-rights movement's most noticeable trend, from the mid-1980s into the 1990s, was aggression.

The AIDS epidemic, in full bloom by the mid '80s, fueled a strident form of gay activism. Groups such as the AIDS Coalition to Unleash Power (ACT UP), Queer Nation, and the Lesbian Avengers caught the public's eye as they staged boisterous demonstrations and invaded churches and corporations they considered to be "enemies."

The gay Christian movement did not take long to develop its own style of aggression. Fundamental to its identity were two beliefs: Homosexuality is not unbiblical; and homosexuals can't change, even if they want to.

The reason for the first belief is obvious: The movement could not claim legitimacy if it didn't insist it was biblically legitimate. The necessity for the second belief was less obvious, but crucial.

An unwavering belief among conservative Christians is that homosexuals, like all sinners, need to repent. Having repented of their sin, Christ will enable them by His grace to lead godly lives without indulging in homosexual practices. It was—and is—vital to the gay Christian movement's success that it convince everyone, especially its critics, that homosexuality simply cannot be repented of, any more than skin color or gender can be abandoned.

If the testimonies of the gay Christian movement's members were the only ones the conservative church heard, they would make more progress—perhaps—in convincing the church that their sexual orientation was immutable. To their dismay, however, other testimonies were also being heard—from former homosexuals.

Exodus International, a coalition of ministries dedicated to helping people overcome homosexuality, had for almost two decades been proclaiming a message in direct opposition to the gay Christian movement: that homosexuality was a sin, and that Christ could free the homosexual. No message could be more intolerable to the gay Christian movement, and in the mid-1980s they determined it had to be silenced.

In 1989, Reverend Sylvia Pennington, whose career was devoted to assuring gay Christians that their behavior was acceptable to God, released her scorching analysis of the "ex-gay movement" titled *Ex-Gays? There Are None!* By compiling stories of women and men who had tried to change from homosexuals to heterosexuals (through Exodus and similar ministries), Pennington argued that anyone attempting to "go straight" was doomed to failure. Her book, the first published broadside against Exodus ministries, threw down the gauntlet from the gay Christian movement to any Christians who claimed to have overcome homosexuality. Debates between "Christian gays" and "ex-gays" were soon commonplace on talk shows and in print.

National Exposure

The gay Christian movement's aggression found an even wider platform when, in 1993, filmmakers Teodoro Maniaci and Francine Rzeznik produced a 90-minute documentary on Exodus International titled *One Nation Under God*. First shown at the 1993 Gay and Lesbian Film Festival, *One Nation* featured interviews with gay Christians who, having tried "ex-gay" ministries, now saw themselves in a position to "expose" them. Most of the film devotes itself to their criticisms, attempting to prove by sheer weight of testimony and emotion that no homosexual can ever be anything else. In 1994, PBS deemed the film worthy of national exposure on its Point of View series. For the first time, all of America was exposed to the arguments from gay Christians as they scoffed at the idea of anyone changing, even through Christ, their sexual orientation.

Then, in 1994, Rev. Mel White shocked both Christian and secular communities with the revelation that he was both gay and Christian. White, already a widely recognized Christian author and filmmaker, released *Stranger at the Gate,* an autobiographical account of his attempts to overcome homosexuality while employed as a ghostwriter by such men as Jerry Falwell, Billy Graham, and Oliver North.

White's two primary messages were made clear, both in his book and his public appearances: The Religious Right is homophobic and must be stopped, and anyone promoting the idea that homosexuality can be overcome must be silenced. This twofold message, not specific to White and, in fact, coming from many other sources as well, would become an anthem that played quite well in the coming decade, both to gays and pro-gay sympathizers. And nothing elevated it more effectively into the nation's consciousness than the brutal murder of a young Wyoming man that would shock a nation and galvanize the movement.

Matthew Shepherd and the Hate Crimes Debate

On October 7, 1998, two motorcyclists in Laramie, Wyoming, passed what they thought was a scarecrow, oddly positioned on a fence in a field. On closer inspection they realized they'd stumbled onto an unconscious male who'd been savagely beaten, lashed to the fence in near-freezing weather, and left to die. He was flown to the nearest hospital, where he remained in critical condition until he succumbed five days later, felled by this unusual cruelty.

He was a 22-year-old political science student named Matthew Shepherd, and his killers' subsequent apprehension and trial would shed light on one of the most notorious cruelties against a homosexual in American history. The night before he was found, he'd left a local bar with Aaron McKinney and Russell Henderson, two young men who drove him to the remote field where he was robbed, beaten, and then tied to the fence.[13] Their motives are still being debated. Shepherd's wallet was taken, suggesting robbery as a possibility, and McKinney and Henderson later claimed their use of amphetamines played into their violent behavior that night, leading to a drug-related mugging.

But there was no avoiding the general belief that hatred for homosexuals inspired the killing. McKinney's defense attorney, in fact, initially laid out a "gay panic" strategy, claiming that Shepherd had sexually propositioned the defendant and McKinney's anti-homosexual reaction was uncontrollable.[14] So the scenario most people have of the Shepherd murder is that two heterosexuals lured a young man they knew to be gay into their car, possibly with the suggestion of a sexual encounter, but definitely with an intent to overpower and assault him out of their hatred for homosexuals.

Reactions

Public outcry was immediate and widespread. National gay-rights organizations like the Gay and Lesbian Alliance Against Defamation, the Human Rights Campaign, and the National Gay Task Force sponsored demonstrations nationwide featuring high-profile figures like Helen Hunt, Elton John, and Ellen DeGeneres. Even then-president Bill Clinton made a public appeal for "hate-crimes" legislation he was hoping Congress would pass.[15]

The national conscience was rightfully shocked over the tragedy, but soon attention became focused not on the violence performed by the actual self-identified killers but on a broader, perhaps more politically convenient group: conservative Christians.

Shortly before Shepherd's death, a coalition of Christian groups such as Focus on the Family and the Family Research Council, had sponsored a national ad campaign featuring testimonials of women and men who'd been involved in homosexuality but had now rejected that behavior and, as Christians, encouraged others to do the same. The ads were understandably controversial, sparking loud opposition from gay-rights organizations, who claimed the ads legitimized homophobia and were misleading, ill-informed, and destructive.

Accusations

But Shepherd's murder escalated the objections to fever pitch, as both gay spokespersons and media allies indicted, directly or indirectly, the ads, the Christian groups who sponsored them, and by extension, *all* churches and believers who openly stated that homosexuality was wrong.

Matthew Shepherd's blood was not only on McKinney and Henderson's hands, they said—it stained the Christian church's as well.

On *The Today Show,* host Katie Couric interviewed Wyoming's then-governor Jim Geringer about the Matthew Shepherd case. Toward the end of the interview she dropped a bomb:

> And finally, Governor, some gay-rights activists have said that some conservative political organizations like the Christian Coalition, the Family Research Council, and Focus on the Family are contributing to this anti-homosexual atmosphere by having an ad campaign saying, "If you're a homosexual, you can change your orientation." That prompts people to say, "If I meet someone who is homosexual, I'm going to take action and try to convince them or try to harm them." Do you believe that such groups are contributing to this climate?[16]

Couric wasn't alone in making thinly veiled accusations. NBC reporter David Gregory offered similar ones:

> The ads were controversial for portraying gays and lesbians as sinners who had made poor choices, despite the growing belief that homosexuality may be genetic. Have the ads fostered a climate of anti-gay hate that leads to incidents like the killing of Matthew Shepherd?[17]

It was reminiscent of the accusations heard during the early days of the AIDS epidemic. In the horror of seeing scores of young gay men dying, a desire for someone to blame became irresistible. (This is a common dynamic throughout human history.) Many to this day level an accusing finger at then-president Ronald Reagan for not doing enough in the early days of the epidemic. Others blame religious teaching against homosexuality for influencing the general belief that this behavior is wrong, thus inducing in gay men a self-hatred that made them more likely to engage in the promiscuity that so often accompanied an AIDS diagnosis in the early 1980s.

So it was the church's fault. If only Christians hadn't taught that homosexuality was wrong, the public wouldn't be influenced by their moral teachings (which, not incidentally, were teachings promoted openly by President Reagan). Thus there'd be little public disapproval of homosexuality; gay men in turn would not hate themselves, and, as a result, they'd be less likely to be careless with their health and safety.

Connect the dots enough times and you get the picture: Christian teaching inspired homophobia; homophobia inspired self-hatred among gays and indifference among the public; Christian teaching, therefore, contributed to the AIDS epidemic.

Nearly two decades later, a similar portrait of guilt was being painted in the public's mind regarding Shepherd. Christian ads inspired homophobia; homophobia inspired Matthew's killers; Christian teaching, therefore, contributed to Matthew Shepherd's death.

Christian Teaching to Blame?

Unpack this reasoning, however, and it loses much of its force. First, the ads in question by no means suggested anyone should, as Couric rather wildly implied, "Take action and try to convince" a homosexual or "harm" him. They were testimonials, not instructions in violence. To assume people will read or hear a testimonial and then go out and try to force others to do what the "testifier" did, is a truly ludicrous jump in thinking. When weight-loss ads feature testimonials of people who've shed 30 pounds, do people read them and then get the idea to take action and try to convince an overweight person to diet or harm them if they don't? When Kirstie Alley ran ads featuring her own significant weight loss, did that foster a climate of anti-overweight hatred that endangered anyone struggling with obesity? Clearly, it takes much more than an ad to inspire a murder.

Secondly, McKinney and Henderson didn't go straight from church to the bar where they met and targeted Shepherd. Nor had they just left a Focus on the Family meeting, nor had they just viewed one of the "notorious" ads. Nothing in their trial, in fact, indicated they'd been aware of, much less influenced by, any Christian material.

Finally, in a later twist to the story, after being sentenced and having begun their life terms in prison, the killers themselves have denied anti-gay hatred had anything to do with their actions that night.[18] Whether those are the honest reflections of prisoners doing time or the disingenuous attempts of a couple of guys hoping to get their sentences appealed, we'll never know. But the evidence against Christian teaching is nonexistent in the Matthew Shepherd case, though the accusations against it continue.

The gay-rights movement had now turned a significant corner. Shifting from the rallying cry of "Treat homosexuals fairly" in the '60s to "Homosexuality is normal" in the '70s and '80s, a new theme was added in the late '90s, in the shadow of a horrendous crime: "Opposition to homosexuality must be stopped." That theme would be amplified, and continues to this day, as a focal point of gay rights.

Mainlining the Movement

In a lighter vein, in the late 1990s and early 2000s the open homosexuality of celebrities was becoming common, lending a tremendous boost of respectability to gay rights. Ellen DeGeneres's coming out, both personally and as a television character, was headline news. Rosie O'Donnell would soon follow, and pop stars like Boy George, Elton John, and George Michael were all now openly gay and proud. Add to the mix handsome movie stars like Richard Chamberlain and Tab Hunter, and you had an impressive display of women and men the public had grown to love and admire, now saying, "We were gay all along."

The likability factor was clearly in their court. When people we've viewed on TV or watched in films, whose music we've listened and danced to, are now declaring they're gay, we tend to still like them and, to a point, sympathize with their goals. Their happiness matters to us; they're like old friends we want the best for. In this symbiotic relationship between likeable celeb and doting public, we feel protective toward them. If I've watched Rosie, laughed with Ellen, or loved Elton John's music for years, I feel a deep affection for them. And in the course of our "relationship," their enemies become mine. So if I believe the conservative church is making their lives harder, my knee-jerk reaction is, of course, against the church.

Gay activists have seized on this, none more successfully than those promoting the "gay Christian" ideology. Claiming that conservative Christian teaching on homosexuality inspired hatred against gays and self-hatred among them, gay religious activist Mel White's newly formed "Soulforce" group began regularly protesting, and at times disrupting, Christian gatherings, churches, and universities, all in an attempt to persuade them to adopt new positions on homosexuality.

In his book *Stranger at the Gate,* White had openly challenged his former friends and colleagues such as Rev. Jerry Falwell and Dr. D. James Kennedy, along with Dr. James Dobson, Billy Graham, and others, to meet with him and discuss their views on homosexuality. By and large he was rebuffed, so he began a crusade to more publicly challenge conservative groups to change their positions and policies on the matter.

Organized protests at Pat Robertson's Christian Broadcasting Network facilities and Jerry Falwell's Liberty University were formed; public "fastings" (in the tradition of Gandhi's historical tactics) were staged at James Dobson's Focus on the Family headquarters; and disruptions of annual church denominational conventions became staples of Soulforce's approach. Their efforts soon extended to "Freedom Rides," in which gay activists and their allies boarded buses and headed out to Christian universities around the country—with the goal of changing the students' minds about homosexuality and convincing the Christian universities and Bible colleges to adopt more "gay-friendly" policies.[19]

The New Intolerance

Soulforce is hardly alone in these goals, which are shared by many groups engaged in similar efforts. But these efforts speak to the new trend in gay rights. No longer content to see homosexuality normalized in the culture, gay leadership shows an increasing intolerance for groups or individuals holding the traditional viewpoint, even in their own churches or Christian institutions—an intolerance that has gained impressive support in the years following the Shepherd tragedy.

A quote from one of the "freedom riders" provides a nice example. Citing the group's goal to confront schools teaching the traditional view, Soulforce spokesman Jacob Reitan states,

> We must cut off the suffering at its source. The source is religious-based oppression.[20]

The fact that this "religious-based oppression" is founded on the sinister belief that homosexuality is not God's will—a belief foundational to the Judeo-Christian definition of a family and taught regularly in private churches—makes those very churches the source at which Mr. Reitan states the suffering must be "cut off."

Legal Developments

This clash between conservatives and pro-gay advocates inevitably began making its way to the Supreme Court. In 2000, the Court heard arguments over whether the Boy Scouts of America had the right to maintain their official position that homosexuality and scouting were incompatible. In a closely watched decision, the Court narrowly ruled for the Scouts. Later, the rights of states to keep antisodomy laws on the books was challenged, and it was overturned by the High Court in *Lawrence v. Texas*.[21] Once the Supreme Court decided antisodomy laws were unconstitutional, few doubted that same-sex marriage would become the next battleground.

So it was no surprise when in 2003, the same year of the Supreme Court decision on antisodomy laws, Massachusetts became the first American state to legalize marriage between two members of the same sex. This set off state-by-state waves of protest, efforts to amend state constitutions to preserve the definition of marriage, cavalier judicial rulings in favor of gay marriage (which frequently flew in the face of public opinion), and a heated, ongoing national debate over what does and does not constitute a family.[22]

The impact of all this on the church has been immeasurable, felt most significantly when the Episcopal Church elected Gene Robinson, its first openly gay bishop, in 2003.[23] More than any event in recent years, this highlighted theological and practical differences between traditionalists and pro-gay revisionists, bringing those differences onto prime-time talk and news programs. The country was now engaged not just in a discussion over the legitimacy of homosexuality but in a debate over what the Bible does or does not say about the matter.

———

The pro-gay interpretation of Scripture has gained visibility and clout unimaginable—even to its own adherents—a decade ago. As of this writing, it is arguably the most divisive, emotionally heated issue the modern church faces. Our ability to address it effectively will be determined first by our willingness to teach, defend, and live up to the standards for sexual behavior that are clearly and emphatically spelled out in Scripture. Our stand will then be enhanced by our willingness to learn what the revisionists believe (and what they're asking us to believe as well), then develop a reasoned, biblically based response to their revisions.

The first requirement—standing by and living up to the standards we promote—warrants an entire book of its own. The goal of this book, an admittedly more modest one, is to better equip us to understand, and respond to, the growing challenge to traditional beliefs about homosexuality. And it is that goal we'll pursue in the following chapters.

PART TWO

Beliefs
and
Ideologies

5

PRO-GAY
THEOLOGY

---

*"For this cause God shall send them strong
delusion, that they should believe a lie."*

2 THESSALONIANS 2:11 KJV

Now that we have a general understanding of how both the gay-rights and gay Christian movements came about, we can begin to answer the larger questions: Exactly *what* do those who call themselves gay Christians believe? *How* did they come to believe it?

In the chapters that follow I hope to answer the first question which, frankly, will be much easier than answering the second. Explaining *what* a group believes isn't hard. Explaining *how* they came to believe it is another matter.

We can't read people's minds or motives. That, I am sure, is one reason Jesus warned us against judging others (Matthew 7:1). Unless we are given divine insight into another's motives (as Peter was given in Acts 8:20-23), we can't say for certain why people embrace false teachings.

We can be certain the teachings themselves are false; why people have accepted them is something we can't prove one way or another.

Yet the Bible offers us some clues on this issue. And testimonies from members of the gay Christian movement are also enlightening. Let's consider both as we try to understand what the gay Christian movement believes, and what personal and spiritual factors may have influenced those who hold to these beliefs.

The Pro-Gay Theology in Brief

Just as the Athanasian and Nicene Creeds sum up most of the foundational Protestant beliefs,[1] the pro-gay theology is the cornerstone of the gay Christian movement. The movement is diverse. Some of its spokespersons, such as Robert Williams, Bishop John Shelby Spong, and Jane Spahr, promote blatantly heretical ideas. But most groups within it ostensibly subscribe to traditional theology. (The "Statement of Faith" of the UFMCC, for example, is based on the Apostles' and Nicene Creeds.[2])

Discuss basic Christianity with a member of the gay Christian movement and you will be in agreement on many points: the Godhead, the work of Christ, the inerrancy of the Bible, the final judgment, and so forth. This is one reason the pro-gay theology is so seductive. Like many errors, it contains major portions of truth.

Yet in my conversations with gay spokesmen, both as one who embraced pro-gay theology and now as one who opposes it, I have noticed departures from sound doctrine that keep arising.

Ambiguity About the Bible

The first has to do with biblical authority. Gay Christian leaders are quick to say they believe in it, but at times their definition of what it is can be disturbing.

Troy Perry's assertion that "scientific information, social changes, and personal experience are the greatest forces for change in the way we interpret the Bible" is unsettling.[3] Social change and personal experiences are relevant, but they don't determine truth. Jesus Christ, who is the same yesterday, today, and forever (Hebrews 13:8), is not known to follow social trends. John Boswell's remarks about the inadequacy of Scripture to answer life's problems (also mentioned earlier) betray ambiguity about biblical authority as well.

I have found this ambiguity to be fairly common. During a radio debate I had with a gay minister, when he was asked how he discerned God's truth, he said there were three sources he relied on, each having equal authority: the Bible, the witness of his own heart, and the witness of his community. I responded that I had no such confidence in either my heart or my community—the Bible was the ultimate authority in all matters.

In a discussion at a Presbyterian church in Washington, DC, I was challenged by the local representative of the Lesbian and Gay Concerns Committee. "You keep talking about the Bible," he complained. "But I want to know what you think about the Holy Spirit!" His remark was meant to steer the conversation away from the objective Scripture and into the more subjective realm of personal experience and spiritual revelation.

Now, I think the Holy Spirit is wonderful, and I said as much. But I also said that when it came to matters of doctrine, I could not trust my ability to discern the Spirit's voice. That, I argued, was exactly why God gave us a written standard (inspired by the Spirit)—so we need not guess at what He requires of us.

My opponent disagreed; and there, I'm sure, was our main difference. He felt that matters such as sexuality could be decided by what one subjectively thinks the Spirit is saying to the individual. I contend we have to objectively rely on the written Word alone. (In that vein, I can't count the number of people who've said to me, "I've prayed earnestly on this issue, and I really feel I'm doing what God has told me to do!" The implication, of course, is that earnest prayer or an attempt to discern God's voice can somehow override Scripture's plain teaching.)

Sexual Ethics

Another problem the gay Christian movement faces has to do with sexual ethics. The Bible provides clear guidelines for sexual behavior:

Intercourse before marriage is forbidden, marriage must be monogamous, and divorce is permissible only in the event of fornication or abandonment by an unbelieving spouse. Any serious believer has to recognize these standards—and therein lies the problem.

During my involvement with the gay church, we made virtually no effort to abide by these standards. Among gay men (religious or not) it was unheard of to wait until marriage (or a "union ceremony," as it was called then) before having sex. Indeed, sexual relations within days or even hours of meeting were not uncommon, and they were never, in my experience, criticized from the pulpit.

Monogamy, though usually held up as an ideal, was seldom (to my knowledge) adhered to. And the dissolution of a relationship required far less than abandonment or adultery. Most couples I knew broke up because of incompatibility or one partner's interest in a third party.

Of course, problems like these are common among heterosexuals and take place in all churches, but most churches at least hold to a standard of chastity before marriage and monogamy during it. Though things may have changed since the onset of the AIDS epidemic, I saw no such standards being consistently upheld in the gay Christian movement.

Still, the gay Christian movement claims a conservative theological base, and in most gay churches, I found that to be true. But some additions were made to the basic tenets of the faith—additions vital to the pro-gay theology.

One of these convenient additions is that homosexuality is viewed as being God-ordained and God-created. As such, it is seen as being on a par with heterosexuality. "If you don't see that premise," Mel White points out, quite accurately, then "gay marriage looks ridiculous, if not insane."[4]

Discrediting the Bible

For homosexuality to be seen as created by God, the traditional understanding of it must be discredited. This is done in several basic ways within the gay Christian movement.

First, prejudice against homosexuals is blamed for the understanding most Christians have of the biblical references to it. John Boswell emphasizes this point throughout *Christianity, Social Tolerance, and Homosexuality.* Troy Perry repeats this point early in his book as well:

> To condemn homosexuals, many denominations have intentionally misread and misinterpreted their Bibles to please their own personal preferences.[5]

So, according to Perry and others, not only are most Christians wrong about homosexuality, but many or most are *intentionally* wrong, deliberately reading their prejudice against gays into the Bible.

Others within the movement contend that the Scriptures we understand to condemn homosexuality have actually been mistranslated. Wainwright Churchill and Roger Biery insist on this; John Boswell, of course, expounds on it considerably. Thus, according to this view, the Bible should be taken literally in its original language; the problem with most Christians, these authors say, is that they do not know biblical Greek and Hebrew well enough to realize that our modern translations on homosexuality are all wrong.

Another claim pro-gay theorists make is that the verses that seem to prohibit homosexuality (Leviticus 18:22; 20:13; Romans 1:26-27; 1 Corinthians 6:9-10; 1 Timothy 1:9-10) have actually been yanked out of context from their original meaning. Or, as Boswell, Perry, and author Robin Scroggs argue, they only applied to the culture existing at the time they were written. (For example, in the book *The New Testament and Homosexuality,* Scroggs

Discrediting Motives

Mel White goes to an extreme, stating that major leaders in the Christian community—Jerry Falwell, James Kennedy, and Pat Robertson—take public stands against the gay-rights movement for the sake of raising funds and increasing their visibility.[6] Casting doubt on the motives of conservative leaders and numerous denominations makes it easier to discount their Bible-based objections to homosexuality. No wonder this tactic is so common in the gay Christian movement.

claims that "biblical judgments about homosexuality are not relevant to today's debate."[7])

Skeptical Reactions

These arguments do not sit well with most Bible-believing Christians. The Scriptures cited above are so clear and specific that they defy misinterpretation of any sort. "Thou shalt not lie with a man as with a woman" is just as clear as "Thou shalt not kill." It is intellectually dishonest to say that conservatives "interpret" such verses out of prejudice against homosexuals. Those same "prejudiced" conservatives (Falwell, Kennedy, Robertson, and others) also take Scriptures against heterosexual sins quite literally. If they only prohibit homosexuality out of their own prejudice, why on earth do they, as heterosexuals, also condemn heterosexual sins?

Neither does the "mistranslation" argument make sense. We can allow some discrepancy in minor areas of translation. On something as important as sexual ethics, however, are we really to believe that the Bible translators we rely on got it wrong five different times, in two different testaments? And only on the Scriptures regarding homosexuality? (Pro-gay apologists seem to have no problem with other scriptures condemning sins such as adultery and child abuse.)

Equally hard to swallow is the "out of context" argument. The fact is, in Leviticus, Romans, 1 Corinthians, and 1 Timothy, homosexuality is mentioned *in* the context of sexual and immoral behavior! The context is quite clear—a variety of behaviors are prohibited. Homosexuality, along with adultery, fornication, and idolatry, is one of them.

The "cultural" argument fares no better. In some cases, a scripture may seem culturally bound. (Examples sometimes cited include injunctions against long hair on men, or women speaking to their husbands during church.) But again—five times? Five different scriptures, from both testaments, addressed to highly different cultures (including the Hebrew and the Roman), are obviously not culturally bound. The cultures these verses are addressed to are just too different.

All of this leaves conservatives highly skeptical of the gay Christian movement's claim to respect biblical authority. It takes mental gymnastics to accept these arguments, and those not having a stake in accepting them are unlikely to do so.

Choosing to Abandon Truth

However, those who have a personal interest in the pro-gay theology are another matter. Deciding to believe what you *want* to believe (as I once did) is the first step. The next is to make the Bible agree with you. That's nothing new; people have been doing it for years.

Twenty years ago, for example, I was informed by a rather libertine Christian that smoking marijuana was permissible and, in fact, biblical.

"Where did you get a notion like that?" I gasped.

"From Genesis 1:29," he said, confidently turning to the Old Testament. "Right here, see?" His finger rested on the verse, "And God said, Behold, I have given you every herb bearing seed" (KJV).

No, he wasn't kidding. Neither was the Christian couple I once knew who justified their passion for nude beaches by reminding me of Adam and Eve's original state. "Ought we not to be as they were?" they asked innocently. "Naked and unashamed?"

Twist the Scriptures hard enough and you can make them appear to say anything you please. It's not that hard to do. I remember, having already decided to express myself homosexually, how I read the Bible through the eyes of my decision, rather than objectively. Paul Morrison sums up the issue in this way:

> If I were a Christian homosexual, I think this one question would disturb me most: Am I trying to interpret Scripture in the light of my proclivity; or should I interpret my proclivity in the light of Scripture?[8]

A disastrous pattern of doing the former can be seen in the gay Christian movement's testimonials. Troy Perry writes about having already decided that homosexuality was acceptable and then searching the Bible to equip himself to answer conservatives. In his book, Mel

White alludes to some earlier studies of the destruction of Sodom, but his turning point seems to have come not from a careful, prayerful study of Scripture, but from a psychologist who encouraged him to accept his homosexuality and find a lover![9]

Lesbian musician Marsha Stevens, one of the pioneers in contemporary Christian music, gives a lengthy account of her acceptance of lesbianism without once explaining how she reached the point of believing that homosexuality was scripturally acceptable. (The closest she comes is in telling how she prayed one night for confirmation that lesbianism was okay; the next morning someone gave her a pin saying, "Born Again Lesbian."[10]) For someone like Stevens, who was spiritually raised under the teachings of conservative Bible teacher and founder of the Calvary Chapel church's Chuck Smith, who always emphasizes the Word of God over experience, that is astounding.

Or maybe it isn't. A sign of the end times, according to the apostle Paul, will be an abandonment of truth for the sake of personal fulfillment:

> In the last days perilous times shall come. For men shall be lovers of their own selves (2 Timothy 3:1-2 KJV).

> The time will come when they will not endure sound doctrine; but after their own lusts shall they heap to themselves teachers, having itching ears; and they shall turn away their ears from the truth (2 Timothy 4:3-4 KJV).

Self over truth, man over God—can a Christian be so deceived? Evidently so, since Paul referred to the Galatian church as having been "bewitched" (Galatians 3:1), and Jesus warned that a prominent sign of the days before His coming would be an increase in deception (Matthew 24:4).

To confront the pro-gay theology, then, is to confront a deception of our time—the tendency to subjugate objective truth to subjective experience.

That's one reason that confrontation is not enough to change a heart. Being knowledgeable enough to dismantle all the gay Christian movement's claims won't be enough to persuade a homosexual to repent. The heart, having been hardened through deception or rebellion or both, has to be softened. And that is the work of God alone. Ours is to simply speak the truth, trusting Him to make it alive to our hearers. With that in mind, having grasped a general definition of pro-gay theology, let's move on to a description of common pro-gay arguments and a response to each.

6

PRO-GAY ARGUMENTS ON THE NATURE OF HOMOSEXUALITY

"But when a man's fancy gets astride on his reason,
When imagination is at cuffs with the senses,
And common understanding, as well as common Sense,
Is kicked out of doors;
The first Proselyte he makes, is Himself."

JONATHAN SWIFT

In the early 1980s, I faced a dilemma as a gay Christian: Most of society believed I was wrong.

That could not be ignored. Every day I saw or heard something that reminded me homosexuality was abnormal, immoral, unequal to heterosexuality. But having struggled so hard to accept my new identity, I was not about to reject it again, so the tension between society and me had to be resolved. One of us had to be wrong, and I had already decided it wasn't going to be me. So I needed to convince myself that society erred in its beliefs about, and treatment of, homosexuals.

It wasn't too hard finding evidence to support my belief. Prejudice against gays would crop up occasionally—a "fag" joke overheard in the lunchroom at work, graffiti scrawled on the walls of my favorite gay bar, newspaper accounts of yet another gay man assaulted. All I needed to do was convince myself that prejudice was more than occasional—that it was everywhere, lurking behind every negative view of homosexuality, no matter how reasonably that view was expressed. Thus all objections to homosexuality were, in my mind, born of bigotry or misunderstanding. That made those objections easy to write off as "prejudice," and my comfort with myself would stay intact.

The "bigotry" argument is effective because bigotry makes us queasy. It reminds us of man's dark side, documented in photos from Nazi Germany and history books describing slavery in America. We recoil from it, partly out of disgust and partly, I believe, out of collective guilt. We are ashamed to recall our country's institutionalized racism; we're all too aware that the disease still thrives, both here and abroad. So when charges of discrimination are thrown around, we duck. The last thing we want to be accused of is bigotry.

This puts us in a bind when charges of bigotry against homosexuals are leveled against us. We have heard of people protesting gay parades, waving signs saying "God Hates Fags" and similar nonsense; naturally, we distance ourselves from them. But in doing so, we risk being silent altogether on the subject of homosexuality, for fear of being lumped into the "extremist" category.

Pro-gay arguments are not unanswerable, however; answered properly and politely, unbiblical ideas can be challenged in the secular arena. Paul proved that with the Athenian citizens at Mars Hill (Acts 17:22). But the Christian challenger needs to be aware that often, because of his position, he will be seen as the bad guy. And that is all the more reason to speak with equal measures of clarity and politeness.

Thomas Schmidt, in his excellent critique of the pro-gay theology, minces no words on this point:

> Christians who cannot yet deal with the issues [pertaining to homosexuality] calmly and compassionately

should keep their mouths shut, and they should certainly stay away from the front lines of ministry and public policy debate—not to mention television talk shows.[1]

Let's take a look, then, at the common myths used by the gay Christian movement to gain acceptance. The following four pro-gay arguments—"Homosexuality is inborn"; "Homosexuality is unchangeable"; "Psychology says it's normal"; and "Ten percent of the population is gay"—deal with the nature of homosexuality. To answer them, the challenger must dismantle pro-gay assumptions (gays are victims; conservative Christians and their beliefs are persecutors) by pointing out when and how those assumptions are either illogical, misleading, or exaggerated. We will look for at least one of those three elements when responding to these pro-gay arguments.

Argument One: "Homosexuality Is Inborn"

As the gay-rights movement has evolved, the notion of homosexuality being something that one is born with—like gender or hair color—has gained wide approval, especially among gays themselves. In the 1940s, when sexologist Alfred Kinsey asked homosexuals how they "got that way," only 9 percent claimed to have been born gay. In 1970, nearly the same percentage of 979 gays in San Francisco answered the same way. But 13 years later, when the gay-rights movement had become more politicized, 35 percent of 147 homosexuals said they were born that way. And today, most gay leaders, especially in the gay Christian movement, would agree with Mel White's assertion that homosexuality is "a gift from God to be embraced, celebrated, lived with integrity."[2]

The "inborn theory" takes on special significance when viewed religiously. It implies that if something is inborn, God must have created it. And who are we to argue with the Creator?

No doubt many homosexuals sincerely believe they were genetically determined to be gay. But the emergence and growth of that belief, along with the emergence and growth of the gay-rights movement, cannot be a coincidence. It's clearly politically expedient to view sexual orientation as inborn; many people who would otherwise consider homosexuality immoral will support gay rights if they can be convinced it is an inherited trait.

The words of William Cheshire, editorial page editor for the *Arizona Republic,* form a good example. "My feelings about gays and lesbians were dominated by religious beliefs," he said in a 1993 interview with *U.S. News and World Report.* But after reviewing certain studies purporting to prove that homosexuals were born that way, he "did a complete reversal in [his] attitude toward gays and lesbians," and he began actively promoting, through his paper, antidiscrimination laws for gays.[3]

Those in the gay Christian movement may find extra reassurance in studies alleging to prove that their sexual preference is inborn:

> "I felt in my heart that this [homosexuality] is something
> I was born with," one gay man enthused. The "born gay"
> studies, he added, "made me feel good about myself. They
> made me feel less a sinner."[4]

People tend to view homosexuality more favorably when they think it is inborn. No wonder gay leaders (not all, but most) push the born-gay theory; it furthers the cause. Responding to the "born gay" argument is crucial, then, and our response should concentrate on two facts:

1. As of now—2006—homosexuality has still not been proven to be genetic or biological in origin.

2. Even if someday it is proven to be inborn, that will not make it normal or morally desirable.

To further develop our response, let's look at two of the studies most often cited when people insist that homosexuality has been proven to be inborn.

The Simon LeVay Study

In 1991 Dr. Simon LeVay, a neuroscientist at the Salk Institute of La Jolla, California, examined the brains of 41 cadavers—19 allegedly homosexual men, 16 allegedly heterosexual men, and 6 allegedly heterosexual women. His study focused on a group of neurons in the hypothalamus structure called the *interstitial nuclei of the anterior hypothalamus,* or the INAH3.

He reported this region of the brain to be larger in heterosexual men than in homosexuals; likewise, he found it to be larger in heterosexual men than in the women he studied. For that reason he postulated homosexuality to be inborn, the result of size variations in the INAH3, and his findings were published in *Science* magazine in August 1991.[5] This is the study most often quoted when people insist that homosexuality has been "proven" to be inborn.

However, that conclusion is exaggerated and misleading for six reasons.

1. *LeVay did not prove homosexuality to be inborn; his results were not uniformly consistent.* On the surface it appears that *all* of LeVay's homosexual subjects had smaller INAH3s than his heterosexual ones; in fact, three of the homosexual subjects actually had *larger* INAH3s than the heterosexuals. Additionally, three of the heterosexual subjects had *smaller* INAH3s than the average homosexual subject. Thus, as Dr. John Ankerberg of the Ankerberg Theological Research Institute notes, six of LeVay's 35 male subjects—17 percent of his total study group—contradicted his own theory.[6]

2. *LeVay did not necessarily measure the INAH3 properly.* The area LeVay was measuring is quite small—smaller than snowflakes, according to scientists interviewed when his study was released. His peers in the neuroscientific community cannot agree on whether the INAH3 should be measured by its size and volume or by its number of neurons.[7]

3. *It is unclear whether brain structure affects behavior or behavior affects brain structure.* Dr. Kenneth Klivington, also of the Salk Institute, points out that neurons can change in response to experience. "You could postulate," he says, "that brain change occurs throughout life, as a consequence of experience."[8] In other words, even if there is a significant difference between the brain structures of heterosexual and homosexual men, it's unclear whether the brain structure

caused homosexuality, or if homosexuality affected brain structure.

In fact, one year after LeVay's study was released, Dr. Lewis Baxter of UCLA obtained evidence that behavioral therapy can produce changes in brain circuitry, reinforcing the idea that behavior can and does affect brain structure.[9] So, even if differences do exist between the INAH3s of homosexual and heterosexual men, it's possible that the diminished size of the homosexual's is caused by his behavior, rather than his behavior being caused by the INAH3's size.

4. *LeVay was not certain which of his subjects were homosexual and which were heterosexual.* He admits this represents a "distinct shortcoming" in his study. Having only case histories on his subjects to go by (which were by no means guaranteed to provide accurate information about the patient's sexual orientation), he could only assume that, if a patient's records did *not* indicate he was gay, he must have been heterosexual.

Yet 6 of the 16 reportedly heterosexual men studied had died of AIDS, increasing the chances that their sexual histories may have been incompletely recorded.[10] If it is uncertain which of LeVay's subjects were heterosexual and which were homosexual, how useful can his conclusions about "differences" between them really be?

5. *LeVay did not approach the subject objectively.* LeVay, who is openly homosexual, told *Newsweek* magazine that, after the death of his lover, he was determined to find a genetic cause for homosexuality or he would abandon science altogether. Furthermore, he admitted that he hoped to educate society about homosexuality, affecting legal and religious attitudes toward it.[11] None of this diminishes his credentials as a neuroscientist. But his research cannot be said to have been unbiased.

6. *The scientific community did not by any means unanimously accept LeVay's study.* Comments from other scientists in response to LeVay's work are noteworthy. Dr. Richard Nakamura of the National Institute of Mental Health says it will take a "larger effort to be convinced there is a link between this structure and homosexuality." Dr. Anne Fausto-Sterling of Brown University is less gentle in her

response: "My freshman biology students know enough to sink this study."[12]

Dr. Rochelle Kliner, a psychiatrist at Medical College of Virginia, doubts we will "ever find a single cause of homosexuality." And *Scientific American* sums up the reason many professionals approach the INAH3 theory with caution: "LeVay's study has yet to be fully replicated by another researcher."[13]

Pillard and Bailey's Twin Studies

Another study frequently cited is the twin study released around the same time as LeVay's. Psychologist Michael Bailey of Northwestern University (a gay-rights advocate) and psychiatrist Richard Pillard of Boston University School of Medicine (who is openly homosexual) compared sets of identical male twins to fraternal twins (whose genetic ties are less close). In each set, at least one twin was homosexual. They found that, among the identical twins, 52 percent were both homo-sexual; among the fraternal twins, only 22 percent shared a homosexual orientation.[14] Pillard and Bailey suggested that the higher incidence of shared homosexuality among identical twins meant that homosexuality was genetic in origin. However, this argument is misleading and exag-gerated for four reasons.

1. *Pillard and Bailey's findings actually indicate that something besides genes must account for homosexuality.* If 48 percent of identical twins, who are closely linked genetically, do *not* share the same sexual orientation, then genetics alone *cannot* account for homosexuality. Bailey admitted as much: "There must be something in the envi-ronment to yield the discordant twins."[15]

2. *All the twins Pillard and Bailey studied were raised in the same house-hold.* If the sets of twins in which both brothers were homosexual had been raised in *separate* homes, it might be easier to believe that genes had played a role in their sexual development. But since they were all raised in the same households, it is impossible to know what effect environment played, and what effect, if any, genes played. Dr.

Anne Fausto-Sterling commented that "in order for such a study to be at all meaningful, you'd have to look at twins raised apart."[16]

3. *Drs. Pillard and Bailey, like Dr. LeVay, did not approach their subject objectively.* Their personal feelings about homosexuality, like LeVay's, certainly do not disqualify them from doing good research on the subject. But their feelings must be, at the very least, considered. Pillard said, in fact, "A genetic component in sexual orientation says, 'This is not a fault,'" and both he and Bailey stated they hoped their work would "disprove homophobic claims."

4. *A later study on twins yielded results different from Pillard and Bailey's.* In March 1992, the *British Journal of Psychiatry* published a report on homosexuals who are twins (both fraternal and identical) and found that only 20 percent of the homosexual twins had a gay co-twin, leading the researchers to conclude that "genetic factors are insufficient explanation of the development of sexual orientation."[17] Not only has Pillard and Bailey's work not been replicated; when a similar study was conducted, it yielded very different results.

Subsequent studies have been released suggesting homosexuality may be inborn, and no doubt for years to come new research will be touted as "proof" of a gay gene or hormonal influences that create homosexuality. The underlying message continues to be, "If it's inborn, it must be right."

Response

Rather than track each study down as it comes out, I find it more effective to challenge the assumptions these studies seem to make, which is that if something is inborn, it's, therefore, normal or even God-ordained. And this assumption is faulty for three reasons.

1. *"Inborn" and "normal" are not necessarily the same.* Even if homosexuality is someday proven to be inborn, *inborn* does not necessarily mean *normal.* Any number of defects or handicaps, for example, may be inborn, but we would hardly call them normal for that reason alone. Why should we be compelled to call homosexuality normal just because it may be inborn?

2. *Inborn tendencies toward certain behaviors (such as homosexuality) do not make those behaviors moral.* Studies in the past 15 years indicate that a variety of behaviors may have their roots in genetics or biology. In 1983, the former director of the National Council on Alcoholism reported on a number of chemical events that can produce alcoholism. In 1991, the City of Hope Medical Center found a certain gene present in 77 percent of their alcoholic patients. Obesity and violent behavior are also now thought to be genetically influenced. Even infidelity, according to research reported in *Time* magazine, may be in our genes![18]

Surely we are not going to say that obesity, violence, alcoholism, and adultery are legitimate because they were inherited. So it is with homosexuality. Whether inborn or acquired, it is still, like all sexual contact apart from marriage, immoral. And immoral behavior cannot be legitimized by a quick baptism in the gene pool.

3. *We are a fallen race, born in sin.* Scripture teaches that we inherited a corrupt sin nature that affects us physically and spiritually (Psalm 51:5; Romans 5:12). We were born spiritually dead (John 3:56) and physically imperfect (1 Corinthians 15:1-54). We cannot assume, then, that because something is inborn, it is also God-ordained. There are mental, psychological, physical, and sexual aspects of our beings that God never intended us to have. In short, inborn does not mean "divinely sanctioned."

Argument Two: "Homosexuality Is Unchangeable"

"Sexual orientation simply cannot be changed," a gay psychiatrist says confidently. He warns that "there may be severe emotional and social consequences in the attempt to change from homosexuality to heterosexuality."[19]

This argument draws heavily from the social sciences, as it must; the Bible supports no such claim. Indeed, the apostle Paul makes the opposite clear, stating that homosexuals can change, when he asserts,

> Neither fornicators, nor idolators, nor adulterers, nor homosexuals...will inherit the kingdom of God. And such *were* some of you. But you were washed, but you were

sanctified, but you were justified in the name of the Lord
Jesus (1 Corinthians 6:9-10).

Of course, the gay Christian apologist does not believe this verse refers to homosexuality, which brings us to the crux of the issue—whether
or not homosexual behavior is, according to the Bible, a sin. If it is,
there's no argument over whether or not it can be changed. Christ frees
us from the power of sin (Romans 6:14) as we become new creatures
in Him (2 Corinthians 5:17). By this we are certain that any sin condemned in Scripture can be overcome by God's grace.

But if gay apologists really believe homosexuality is not a biblically
forbidden sin, why do they bother arguing, vehemently, that they cannot
change? If something is not a sin, after all, then it doesn't matter if it's
inborn or chosen, immutable or changeable.

Allow me, if I may, to make a frivolous comparison. I believe it was
all right, in God's sight, for me to marry an Italian woman. I have always
thought olive-skinned, dark-haired women are particularly beautiful,
and I think that's perfectly okay. I don't care whether my taste for dark
hair and olive complexions is inborn or acquired, nor do I see any need
to prove that it's "unchangeable." Maybe it is, maybe it isn't—but since
I feel good about it, who cares?

Now, if someone came along and told me that the Bible condemned
my attraction to dark hair, I would ask them to show me where the
Bible condemned it. If I was convinced their biblical interpretation was
wrong—as I'm sure I would be—then I would leave it at that. I certainly
wouldn't bother explaining any psychological or biological roots that
may have influenced my attractions.

If I felt right about these attractions before God, they would need no
explanation. Which begs the question: Aren't gay Christian spokesmen
betraying a certain self-doubt when they try so hard to prove their
sexuality is inborn and unchangeable?

At any rate, the "unchangeable" argument plays a major role in
gay Christian thinking. Mel White repeats it throughout his book; his
former wife, in fact, takes it on herself to speak for all homosexuals

when she says, "After all those decades of trying, we discovered that no one can choose or change his or her sexual orientation."[21]

Troy Perry is just as adamant:

> There is no "cure" [for homosexuality]. Those who make claims to the contrary are charlatans, or are inadequately informed persons who for any of many possible reasons try to delude themselves or their associates.[22]

Scanzoni and Mollenkott make light of Christians who "believe" they have been cured from homosexuality. And Sylvia Pennington scoffs at the very notion of "ex-gay."[23]

One former homosexual, quoted in Thomas Schmidt's book, makes a point I've always suspected when he explains why many gays feel so strongly about the change issue:

> Homosexual activists want to convince not only the public, but *themselves* that change never occurs, because if *I* exist, each of them must be haunted by the possibility that they, too, might find the power to change.[24]

But if pro-gay apologists insist there is no such power and then rely on clinical authorities to support their position, then that position can be answered by other clinical authorities who disagree.

Response

The "unchangeable" argument is misleading because, while many mental-health authorities believe homosexuality is unchangeable, others declare it is amenable to change, whether in small or greater degrees.

In 1970, the Kinsey Institute reported that 84 percent of the homosexuals they studied had shifted their sexual orientation at least once; 32 percent of them reported a second shift; and 13 percent reported five changes during their lifetime in their sexual orientation![25]

The director of the New York Center for Psychoanalytic Training, no doubt aware that such changes occur, remarked on the "misinformation spread by certain circles that homosexuality is untreatable," saying this assertion did "incalculable harm to thousands." And Dr. Irving Bieber concluded, after treating more than 100 homosexuals, that "a heterosexual shift is a possibility for all homosexuals who are strongly motivated to change."[26]

Sex researchers Masters and Johnson (hardly a pair of standard-bearers for conservative virtues) said that the "homosexuality cannot be changed" concept was "certainly open to question." Drs. Wood and Dietrich, writing about the effectiveness of treatment for homosexuality, confirmed that "all studies which have attempted conversions from homosexuality to heterosexuality have had significant success." And the "New Report of the Kinsey Institute" explains that people do not "necessarily maintain the same sexual orientation throughout their lives," and then explains that "programs helping homosexuals change report varying degrees of success."[27]

But no one has said it better than Stanton Jones, Chair of Psychology at Wheaton College:

> Anyone who says there is no hope [for change] is either ignorant or a liar. Every secular study of change has shown some success rate, and persons who testify to substantial healings by God are legion.[28]

A further consideration is that the "unchangeable" argument is illogical: It assumes that if a condition is unchangeable, it is, therefore, desirable.

For the sake of argument, suppose it could be proven that homosexuality, as a condition, *is* unchangeable—that no amount of prayer, counseling, or efforts of any sort could make a homosexual become attracted to the opposite sex. What then? Should that change our view of homosexual behavior as being sinful?

No. There is no "contingency factor" in any scriptural reference to any kind of sin, in either the Old or the New Testament. We never read anything like, "Thou shalt not do thus and so! (Unless, of course, you tried hard to change, went for prayer and counseling, and found you just couldn't stop wanting to do thus and so. If that's the case, then thus and so is no longer a sin. It's an inborn, immutable gift, and you can darn well indulge in it!)"

The apostle Paul's thorn in the flesh, whatever it may have been, was unchangeable. Despite his prayers for deliverance, God allowed it to remain. But it certainly was not desirable (2 Corinthians 12:7-9). Other conditions—alcoholism, for example, or various other addictions—are widely believed to be unchangeable and to require daily coping. That hardly makes them desirable, natural, or God-ordained.

Sexual-Orientation Change Is Not Always an Issue

For many people the subject of change is not critical. When I repented of homosexuality in 1984, I didn't have a change of sexual feelings in mind. I'd come to realize that homosexual sex was wrong, and I was determined, by God's grace, to abstain from it, whether my attractions to men continued or diminished. I'd always had attractions to women as well, so I knew that marriage and a normal sex life were a distinct possibility. So it was obedience, not a change in orientation, that I was seeking.

Even so, to this day I'm aware that, under the right conditions, I could be sexually aroused by a potential partner of the same sex. If I were to put myself in an environment where men were being overtly sexual with each other—a gay bar, for example, or a gym where sexual activity between men commonly occurred—I think I'd be strongly tempted back to my old patterns with men. For obvious reasons, then, I keep myself away from environments like that.

Nor can I be sure that, at some point, involuntary homosexual feelings couldn't arise in me again, even without the "right environment." I'm convinced we could all be pulled back toward whatever sins we've abandoned. Should that happen, I can't imagine abandoning my present life as I know it or assuming I'd experienced no worthwhile change just because old temptations arose. In this life, after all, is it really smart to expect them not to? As always, the question isn't what we feel or don't feel, or to what extent our feelings may fluctuate or change. The question is what we do with them: how successfully we resist them when they pull us toward what's immoral, and how healthy we are when indulging feelings when they pull us toward what's right.

I can respect the skepticism some hearers feel about the personal stories of people claiming a change in their sexual orientation. Sometimes these claims are made too quickly, or a proper definition of *change* isn't made. Change in *behavior,* for example, is a very legitimate change that many people have experienced while still experiencing no significant change in the direction of their sexual feelings. Others have experienced degrees of change in their sexual attractions, with heterosexual desires awakening and homosexual ones diminishing, without a complete "cure" of their homosexual temptations. While in all such cases a change has inarguably occurred, what changed and what didn't need to be clarified.

Argument Three: "Psychology Says It's Normal"

This argument draws its strength from the American Psychiatric Association's 1973 decision to delete homosexuality from its list of disorders. (The APA Board of Trustees determines what conditions are listed in the *Diagnostic and Statistical Manual,* which is the official list of mental and emotional disturbances used by all mental-health professionals. Obviously, the association's definition of "normal" has tremendous impact on American life.)

During discussions on homosexuality, the APA's decision to "normalize" same-sex attraction is often referred to as the bottom line. "If the APA decided homosexuality is normal, then it's normal!" is a common remark.

Response

Saying the APA decided one day to normalize homosexuality is a bit like saying General Lee randomly decided one day to meet with General Grant and negotiate a surrender. A long, bloody war was fought before Lee's decision was reached; to ignore that is to misrepresent history.

A war was likewise fought within the APA before its landmark decision was reached. The details have been recorded by Dr. Ronald Bayer in *Homosexuality and American Psychiatry: The Politics of Diagnosis.* The story has been retold several times, most notably by Kenneth Lewes and William Dannemeyer.

The key events. Following are the main points of Bayer's description:

1. The American Psychiatric Association had traditionally viewed homosexuality as a disorder prior to 1973. The *Diagnostic and Statistical Manual,* originally compiled in 1952, listed homosexuality as a sociopathic personality disturbance in its first version. The second version—*DSM II*—moved homosexuality from the category of personality disturbances to that of sexual deviations in 1968.[29]

2. Gay leaders began protesting at the annual conventions of the APA, demanding a reconsideration of homosexuality's diagnostic status and further demanding that they be included in any future discussions within the APA on the subject.[30] The APA consented; intense discussion and debate followed.

3. On December 15, 1973, the Board of Trustees of the APA, concluding months of negotiations with gay activists, voted to delete homosexuality altogether from the *DSM*. Opposition from several psychiatrists immediately followed. A referendum on the board's decision was called, and in the spring of 1974, the entire membership of the APA was polled for their support or rejection of the board's decision.[31]

4. Out of 10,000 voting members, nearly 40 percent opposed the board's decision to normalize homosexuality.[32] Though the 40 percent were clearly a minority and the decision was upheld, it showed how deeply divided the APA was on the matter.

5. The American Psychiatric Association, like the American Psychological Association, has since aligned itself heavily with gay causes,[33] furthering the impression that psychiatrists and psychologists in America generally view homosexuality as normal.

For these reasons, leaders within the gay Christian movement look to psychiatry for support when they claim that their orientation and behavior are normal.[34]

Why it's misleading. The "psychology says it's normal" argument is misleading for three reasons:

1. *The APA decision was not made under normal circumstances,* but instead under remarkable duress in an intimidating environment. In fact, it was made in the heat of grueling conflict under threats of disruptions and intimidation, and the methods by which it was reached are questionable to this day.

   Recounting the events, Ronald Bayer comments,

   > The entire process, from the first confrontation organized by gay demonstrators to the referendum demanded by orthodox psychiatrists, seemed to violate the most basic expectations about how questions of science should be resolved. Instead of being engaged in sober discussion of data, psychiatrists were swept up in a political controversy. The result was not a conclusion based on an approximation of the scientific truth as dictated by reason, but was instead an action demanded by the ideological temper of the times.[35]

   Considering Bayer's pro-gay sympathies, which are obviously displayed throughout his writing, this admission on his part is remarkable.

2. *The APA did not state that homosexuality is normal.* The resolution that the APA Board of Trustees voted for in 1973 agreed that only clearly defined mental disorders should be included in the *DSM,* and that if homosexuals felt no "subjective distress" about their sexuality and experienced no "impairment in social effectiveness or functioning," then their orientation should not be labeled as a disorder. In fact, the psychiatrist who authored the resolution, flatly denied that the APA was thereby saying homosexuality was normal.[36]

3. *The APA decision did not necessarily reflect the views of American psychiatrists.* A survey conducted by the journal *Medical Aspects of Homosexuality* in 1979 (six years after the APA decision) asked 10,000 psychiatrists if they felt homosexuality "usually represented a pathological adaptation." Of the respondents, 69 percent said

"yes," and 60 percent said homosexual men were less capable of "mature, loving relationships" than heterosexual men.[37] Obviously, there remained a huge discrepancy between the American Psychiatric Association's official position and the views of many of its members.

The "psychology says it's normal" argument is also illogical in that it assumes that the APA definition of mental health and the biblical definition of righteousness are one and the same.

Even if all members of the APA *had* agreed from the beginning that homosexuality was normal, and even if all psychiatrists currently in practice viewed it as healthy, that would have no bearing on the Christian position on the subject. The Bible speaks of homosexuality (as well as other sexual sins) in moral, not psychological, terms. In developing a sense of ethics, the Christian cannot take his cues from the mental-health profession. What is deemed mentally sound by man may not be morally viable to God.

Argument Four: "Ten Percent of the Population Is Gay"

This argument has been so roundly disproven it may be unnecessary to even mention it. But on the chance there is a need to confront it, we will briefly review what is commonly called the "ten percent myth" and how to respond to it.

In 1948, sex researcher Alfred Kinsey published *Sexual Behavior in the Human Male,* which listed his findings after taking the sexual histories of 5300 American men. The findings, especially on homosexuality, shocked American sensibilities: 37 percent of the subjects admitted having at least one homosexual experience since their adolescence, and ten percent claimed to have been homosexual for at least three years.[38]

The word was out—ten percent of the male population was homosexual! Knowing there is power in numbers, pro-gay theorists and spokesmen repeated the statistic relentlessly until it became a given: One out of every ten males was gay; therefore, homosexuality was much more common than anyone had previously thought. The concept was extremely useful to activists when, decades later, they'd ask how anyone could believe ten percent of the population was abnormal, immoral, or just plain wrong.

Response

This argument is exaggerated. Kinsey did not claim ten percent of the male population was homosexual.

Kinsey's wording was plain—ten percent of the males surveyed claimed to have been homosexual for at least three years. They had not necessarily been homosexual all their lives, nor would they necessarily be homosexual in the future. Future studies by the Kinsey Institute, in fact, would confirm that sexual orientation is not necessarily fixed, and may change throughout a person's lifespan. The 1990 *New Kinsey Report* states, "Some people have consistent homosexual orientation for a long period of time, then fall in love with a person of the opposite sex; other individuals who have had only opposite sex partners later fall in love with someone of the same sex."[39]

The "ten percent" argument is also very misleading for two reasons:

1. Kinsey's data was not taken from a population accurately representing American men. Dr. Judith Reisman, in her book *Kinsey, Sex and Fraud: The Indoctrination of a People,* has soundly discredited Kinsey's conclusions and methods. One of her important findings was that 25 percent of the men he surveyed were prisoners, many of whom were sex offenders.[40] Naturally, a higher incidence of homosexuality would be found among prisoners, especially sex offenders, many of whom may have been in prison for sexual offenses.

2. Subsequent studies have disproven the "ten percent" claim. On April 15, 1993, *USA Today* reported a new survey of 3321 American men indicating that 2.3 percent of them had engaged in homosexual behavior within the previous ten years; only 1.1 percent reported being exclusively homosexual.

This was only the latest in a series of studies proving Kinsey wrong. In 1989 a United States survey estimated that no more than 6 percent of adults had had any same-sex contacts and only 1 percent were exclusively homosexual. A similar survey in France found that 4 percent of men and 3 percent of women had ever had homosexual contacts, while only 1.4 percent of the men and 0.4 percent of the women had done so within the past five years. The article concluded, not surprisingly, that the "ten percent" statistic proposed by Kinsey was "dying under the weight of new studies."

A candid remark by a lesbian activist explains how the "ten percent" figure stayed in the public's awareness for so long:

> The thing about the "1 in 10"—I think people prob-
> ably always did know that it was inflated. But it was a nice
> number that you could point to, that you could say "one
> in ten," and it's a really good way to get people to visualize
> that we're here.[41]

If what she's saying is true, gay spokesmen were willing to repeat something they knew to be false for the sake of furthering their cause. With that in mind, one wonders what other "facts" on homosexuality (for example, "gays are born gay"; "gays cannot change") will someday be disproven as well, exposed as propaganda that people "always knew was inflated" but promoted anyway because the end justified the means.

We can accept some parts of these pro-gay arguments. We can allow, for example, the possibility of genetics someday being found to play a role in the development of homosexuality. We can agree that, in many cases, the homosexual condition—sexual attractions to the same sex rather than the opposite one—begins very early in life. And while it's common knowledge that ten percent of the population is not, nor ever has been, gay, we will admit there are probably far more homosexuals in the population than we're aware of. Homosexuals' claim of not having asked for their orientation is, in most cases, true; we ought to feel genuine compassion for people struggling with, or mistreated for, something they never chose. Stanton Jones of Wheaton College puts it well:

If you cannot empathize with a homosexual person because of fear of, or revulsion toward, them, then you are failing our Lord.[42]

But where we must part company with promoters of the pro-gay theology is in the conclusions they have drawn. We cannot rewrite Scripture, as they have, to accommodate a sin simply because some believe it to be inborn, unchangeable, or common. On this point, we might well borrow a quote from the liberal playwright Lillian Hellman: "I cannot and will not cut my conscience to suit this year's fashions."

Let's Talk About Pro-Gay Arguments on the Nature of Homosexuality

Pro-gay argument: "How can you say it's wrong to be gay when it's been proven gays are born that way? Do you think God made a mistake when He made me gay?"

Response: "Of course God didn't make a mistake when He made you, but why assume He made you gay?"

Pro-gay argument: "Well, *I* sure didn't choose these feelings!"

Response: "Maybe not, but we *all* have feelings we don't choose. We all feel angry sometimes, or jealous, or we feel like lying or having a sexual relationship with someone outside of marriage. Those *feelings* aren't a choice, but we do choose whether or not to *act* on them."

Pro-gay argument: "But these aren't just minor temptations like the ones you just named. I've had them all my life. I was born with them, in fact!"

Response: "I beg to differ. I really don't believe homosexuality is inborn, but even if it is, that doesn't mean God intended it."

Pro-gay argument: "You're saying my deepest feelings are wrong!?"

Response: "I'm saying we all have feelings—deep ones, at that—which aren't necessarily right, and which we shouldn't give in to."

Pro-gay argument: "But I read a study that said my sexual feelings come from some variation in the hypothalamus. I can't do much about that, can I?"

Response: "I read that study too, but no one's sure if it's accurate."

Pro-gay argument: "Why do you say that?"

Response: "First, the study has never been replicated. And second, the researcher wasn't really sure which of his subjects were gay and which ones weren't, and he admits he doesn't know if the differences he found in brain sizes were the cause *of* homosexuality, or if they were caused *by* homosexuality. The scientific community isn't at all convinced he's proven anything."

Pro-gay argument: "But there's another study on twins that seems to prove gays are born that way."

Response: "That one isn't too conclusive, either. Nearly half the identical twins studied *didn't* have the same sexual preference. Don't you think the percentage should have been higher if the cause is genetic? And none of those twins were raised apart, so who can tell what made them gay? Besides, none of the twin studies have been replicated, either. In fact, other twin studies have had completely different results."

Pro-gay argument: "Well, I've felt gay all my life, so I must have been born this way!"

Response: "Maybe, or maybe it started so early you can't even remember it. Anyway, who says that 'inborn' means 'ideal'?"

Pro-gay argument: "So you think God might have given me these feelings and then expected me to resist them?"

Response: "Just because we've got feelings doesn't mean God gave them to us. I've got feelings too that I have to resist. And I feel like I've had them all my life. It's not easy for me, either."

Pro-gay argument: "Well, maybe you can do something

about those feelings, but homosexuality can't be changed. All the psychologists agree on that."

Response: "Actually, they don't. Did you know there have always been, and still are, plenty of psychologists who think homosexuality can be changed, if the patient really wants that sort of change?"

Pro-gay argument: "But I don't! Besides, even if I did, the only people who would do a thing like that would be right-wing fanatics."

Response: "There are plenty of credible therapists, non-Christian as well as Christian, who would help you if you wanted it."

Pro-gay argument: "You're trying to say I'm sick. But I'm not. Didn't the American Psychiatric Association say homosexuality is normal over 30 years ago?"

Response: "That's not exactly what they said. They *did* decide homosexuality wasn't a disorder, but they didn't quite say it was normal, either. Truthfully, politics played more into that decision than anyone realizes."

Pro-gay argument: "Maybe so, but ten percent of the population couldn't possibly be mentally ill!"

Response: "I never said you're mentally ill. The Bible says homosexuality isn't natural; it doesn't say homosexuals are crazy. But if you're saying ten percent of the population is gay, I'm afraid that's way off. Every study done on the gay population, both here and abroad, shows it's much smaller than ten percent."

Pro-gay argument: "Well, I don't believe God wants me to deny something I've had all my life—something I've tried to change, and something so many other people have too. That just doesn't sound like God to me!"

Response: "That's funny. It sounds *exactly* like God to me. And it sounds like He requires of you the same things He requires of all of us. He asks us to deny something we've had all our lives—our *selves*—and take up our crosses daily to follow Him. He knows we've tried to change ourselves, and He knows we can't! But Jesus never said we had to change ourselves. He told us to follow Him and to live obediently. The inward change is up to Him, but the obedience is up to us. Plenty of other people have 'selves' too, by the way.

They may choose to indulge their selves, but as Christians, we're called to something different. We're not here to satisfy our selves. We're here to lose them! In the long run, that's the only way to really find ourselves anyway."

7

PRO-GAY ARGUMENTS
FROM SOCIAL ISSUES

*"The purpose of [gay] victim imagery is
to make straights [heterosexuals] feel very uncomfortable—
gays should be portrayed as victims of prejudice.
Straights must be shown graphic pictures of brutalized
gays, dramatizations of job and housing insecurities,
loss of child custody, public humiliation, etc."*

MARSHALL KIRK AND HUNTER MADSEN
*After the Ball: How America Will Conquer
Its Fear and Hatred of Gays in the '90s*

No decent person can be indifferent to victims of prejudice. And when gays are seen as "brutalized," who wants to criticize their behavior? That alone can intimidate us into compromising our stand on homosexuality—or taking no stand at all.

That is the power of many pro-gay arguments. They call for fair treatment and recognition of past injustices, along with assurances that those injustices will not be repeated. They also put anyone who disagrees with the "victims" on the defensive, discrediting their arguments and painting them in the worst possible light.

They're also effective because they sound so good. They demand an end to homophobia and insensitivity; who wants to say that they're against such goals? But just as the question "When did you stop beating your wife, Mr. Jones?" assumes (without proof) that Mr. Jones *has* been beating his wife, so the pro-gay social-justice arguments assume (without proof) that gays are victims, and that the conservative church is largely responsible for their victimhood.

The following social arguments—"Homophobia's the problem" and "Anti-gay teaching incites violence"—are most effective in secular discussions—talk shows, interviews, university debates—where listeners are unlikely to judge them by biblical standards. Instead of discerning which side is theologically correct, non-Christian audiences tend to side with whoever seems "nicest." Usually, that means the gay spokesman asking for antidiscrimination laws or support clubs for gay teenagers. The person against these things—usually a conservative Christian—doesn't seem "nice," no matter how nice he may truly be.

Argument One: "Homophobia's the Problem"

Some words have a chilling effect—*sexist* or *racist,* for example. In their original use, they described attitudes we should abhor. Today, though, their meaning changes to suit the agenda of whoever is using them. A man defending abortion may label pro-lifers as "sexist" for wanting to deny a woman's "right to choose." A woman opposed to affirmative-action programs may find herself accused of being "racist." Negative labels stick. The person they're stuck to loses credibility, even when he or she has something important to say. Who, after all, values a bigot's opinion?

In this manner, the label "homophobia" has been used to tarnish any objection to homosexuality. The word itself is relatively new, coined in 1972 by psychologist George Weinberg, referring to the "dread of being in close quarters with homosexuals." Its meaning has expanded to include, according to Dr. Joseph Nicolosi, "any belief system that values heterosexuality as superior to and/or more natural than homosexuality."[1] By that standard, no conservative Christian escapes the "homophobia" label; neither do most other people, religious and nonreligious alike.

Still, when the term is used in discussions today, it is seldom defined. People throw it at their opponents, judging them guilty of homophobia without telling them exactly what homophobia is and exactly how they are guilty of being whatever it is. So instead of simply denying I am homophobic (which usually gets me nowhere), I've found it helpful to discuss the word itself, making an intelligent discussion of it more likely. So once "homophobia" is pointed to as the "problem," it's best to begin with a response to the term itself.

Response

The "homophobia" argument is misleading for two reasons.

First, *it implies a phobic condition that the accused most likely does not really have.* A phobia, according to the *Diagnostic and Statistical Manual* of the American Psychiatric Association, is defined as "an irrational dread or fear of object or activity, leading to significant avoidance of the dreaded object."

In the comedy movie *What About Bob?* a psychiatric patient is beset with phobias, claustrophobia being one of them. When approaching a small space, such as an elevator or crowded bus, he psychs himself up, mutters under his breath, and tries (usually unsuccessfully) to endure being in a small space for even a short time.

Assuming that homosexuality is the "object or activity" the homophobe dreads, shouldn't all of us "homophobes" be like Bob? When seeing a homosexual, if we are truly homophobic, shouldn't we too have to psych ourselves up, muttering under our breath, barely enduring the presence of a homosexual even for a short time?

Yet we don't. The Christian woman or man who speaks face-to-face with homosexuals—whether in confrontations or discussions—or works alongside them, or relates to them in any way, could hardly be said to have a "phobic response" to them. In the literal sense, then, few people can truly be called "homophobic." Their feelings toward

Phobias, Prejudices, and Convictions

My admiration for one of my favorite actors has helped me understand the difference between a phobia, a prejudice, and a conviction. There is no one I enjoy watching more on the screen than Spencer Tracy. In all his films, he exudes a combination of integrity, cynicism, dry wit, and kindness. He was a rare breed—a true gentleman with a "don't even think of messing with me" attitude. I love his films; I respect his work.

I also know he was an adulterer. For years he carried on an affair with Katharine Hepburn, even though he was married. And knowing adultery is biblically condemned, I make no bones about the immorality of Tracy and Hepburn's relationship.

Does that make me "Tracy-phobic"? Hardly! I couldn't enjoy watching someone I had a phobic response to, any more than an arachnophobe could enjoy watching a spider.

Perhaps, then, it makes me guilty of prejudice, having an opinion about Tracy without adequate basis? Again, no. There is a specific basis for my belief about adultery, but that in no way interferes with my respect for the man in other areas. I have a conviction about adultery: It's wrong. Tracy committed it, so in that area, I say he was wrong. I also say he was terrific in other ways.

homosexuals may be negative, but that in itself does not constitute a phobia.

Second, *the argument prematurely assumes that negative reactions to homosexuality are phobias.* I have come to believe that most negative reactions to homosexuality stem not from homophobia, but from one of two sources: prejudice or convictions.

Webster defines *prejudice* as an "opinion against something without adequate basis." By that definition, there's a great deal of prejudice against homosexuals. They are automatically disliked—despised, even—by people who have formed opinions about them with no rational basis. Prejudice hurts; it's unfair and mean-spirited in the extreme. But it's not a phobia, as in a "dread" or "fear." It is a sin—and a vile one, at that.

By contrast, *conviction*, according to Webster, "is a state of being convinced; a strong belief." It is entirely possible to have a strong belief about homosexuality without prejudice or phobia. That, I believe, is the case with most Christians. Even Mel White, who throughout his book condemns homophobia in the church, agrees that "thoughtful students of the Scriptures may disagree on the subject of homosexuality."[2]

Andrew Sullivan, the well-known gay journalist, goes even further:

> Perhaps the most depressing and fruitless feature of the current debate about homosexuality is to treat all versions of this [conservative Christian] argument as the equivalent of bigotry. They are not. At its most serious, it [the Christian prohibition against homosexuality] is not a phobia; it is an argument.[3]

In truth, the term *homophobia* can be used accurately in very few cases. Rather, *prejudice* describes unfounded negative attitudes toward homosexuals, while *conviction* describes the beliefs of people holding the conservative Christian view of homosexuality.

Argument Two: "Anti-Gay Teaching Incites Violence"

In Roger Biery's *Understanding Homosexuality: The Pride and the Prejudice,* a devastated parent describes the death of his gay son during an altercation with a policeman:

> The cop said that he flashed a badge and that my son flashed a knife, a switchblade. They fought and my son was killed. If all this was true, why was our son carved up like a turkey? Our son never had a knife. He never hurt anyone. That Anita Bryant witch and her mob helped kill him. She spread enough hate to kill lots of kids. Gave the crazies an excuse to witch hunt.[4]

It's not for us to explore the allegations this man makes against the police, but his allegations against Anita Bryant—and by extension, all of us taking a public stand against the gay-rights movement—need to be taken seriously.

Does teaching that homosexuality is wrong, or preaching against homosexual behavior, or speaking publicly against pro-gay laws as Anita

Bryant did, really "help kill," "spread hate," and give "crazies" an excuse to go on a witch hunt? I'm convinced it does not. But this argument deserves careful consideration. If we care at all about homosexuals, we cannot be indifferent to charges that we are in any way harming them.

Still, I'm convinced this argument is misleading and illogical because it assumes that religious teaching is responsible for violent behavior. There are three reasons for believing it is *not*.

First, *there is a difference between belief and bigotry.* Teaching and preaching moral beliefs simply does not incite violence. If it did, every time a pastor preached on the evils of lying, cheating, or fornicating, his parishioners would leave the sanctuary and attack the first liar, tax-evader, or fornicator they ran into. Logic tells us, then, that preaching or speaking against a certain sin cannot in itself move people to attack the person committing the sin.

Second, *violent bigotry needs no teaching or preaching in order to survive.* Racists on the prowl for minorities to attack don't need a sermon to get them going; their hatred is motivation enough. Likewise, "gay bashers" (people who commit acts of violence against homosexuals) need no sermon on the evils of homosexuality to motivate their actions. Seldom if ever have gay bashers approached a victim saying, "We just came from church and heard you're a sinner, so we're going to assault you."

Third, *religious beliefs* can *be used as a cover for bigotry and as an excuse for violence.* White supremacists mangle the Bible to justify their hate. Nazis referred to Jewish people as "Christ-killers," giving them yet another excuse for their anti-Semitism. This is also true of people who assault homosexuals—they may use religious beliefs as a cover for their hatred, but it's their hatred, not their beliefs, that incites their violence.

Gay activist Mel White provides a good example of this, perhaps unintentionally, in his book *Stranger at the Gate.* Criticizing the Christian community as "the nation's primary source of antigay bigotry and discrimination," he then relates the story of an author who, in writing about the murder of a homosexual, interviewed young men who had been found guilty of hate crimes against gays and lesbians.

"In far too many cases," he says, "those young men came from

Christian homes and families." Citing another study on violence against gays, he continues, "Available studies show that those who attend church more regularly and are more 'orthodox,' 'devout,' or 'fundamentalist' tend to be more disapproving [of gay and lesbian people]."[5]

Response

Though it seems that White is attempting to show how religious disapproval of homosexuality leads to violence against homosexuals, in fact he makes a good case for the opposite position. The studies he mentions seem to prove that such teaching does not, by itself, incite violence.

If it did, these young "gay bashers" from Christian homes would not have been convicted of hate crimes against homosexuals alone; they'd have also been found guilty of hate crimes against adulterers, gossips, drunks, idolators, rebellious teenagers, and believers who didn't carefully examine their hearts before taking Holy Communion. Why? Because all of these things are also preached against in church and in Christian homes.

Furthermore, if fundamentalist, devout, orthodox Christian teaching on homosexuality inspires violence against homosexuals, shouldn't the majority of children raised in Christian homes be out assaulting homosexuals? To be sure, even one person attacking one homosexual is one too many. But why are the youths cited in White's book the exception rather than the rule? If Christian teaching against homosexuality has the result White maintains it does, then the majority of people raised in Christian homes should both hate and assault gays.

But they don't. Those raised in Christian homes who do attack homosexuals are seriously disturbed. Their beliefs are incidental; they may use them as an excuse, but their illness, not their religion, fuels their behavior. There is no reason to believe they would behave any differently if they'd never heard religious teaching on homosexuality, just as there is no reason to assume Nazis would hate Jewish people any less if they didn't have the "Christ-killer" teaching to hang their hatred on. John Boswell provides a relevant quote on doctrine being used as a mask for pre-existing hate:

> We can easily reduce our detractors to absurdity and show them their hostility is groundless. But what does this prove? That their hatred is real. Intolerance itself will remain finally irrefutable.[6]

But that doesn't leave us blameless. Standing for biblical values has by no means contributed to the death or emotional damage of homosexuals. But the *way* in which we have stood for those values may be another matter. Regardless of how often we claim to "hate the sin but love the sinner," many of us need to ask ourselves just how that "love for the sinner" has been expressed.

In 1981, Professor Richard Lovelace at Gordon-Conwell Theological Seminary commented in *Christianity Today* magazine,

> Most of the repenting that needs to be done on the issue of homosexuality needs to be done by straight people, including straight Christians. By far the greater sin in our church is the sin of neglect, fear, hatred.[7]

Of course, many Christians and many churches have opened their doors and hearts to homosexuals. They have loved them without compromising the Bible's standards, and by speaking the truth in love, they've seen gays and lesbians won into the kingdom of God.

But not all pastors and congregations can say the same, which brings us to a crucial point: If homosexuals have found rejection and isolation in society, and then they've come into our sanctuaries only to find no sanctuary at all but more rejection, then the judgment we so eagerly pronounce on them for their perversion of sex will no doubt fall on us as well—perhaps a hundredfold—for our perversion of the gospel.

Pro-Gay Arguments from Social Issues

Pro-gay argument: "When you say homosexuality is wrong, you're really expressing the same old problem: homophobia."
Response: "What exactly is *homophobia?*"

Pro-gay argument: *"Homophobia* is the unreasonable fear or hatred of gays, and it's everywhere. Our whole society is saturated with it."
Response: "That sounds horrible. And if people have hated or feared you, I'm sorry to hear it. No one should be treated that way. But tell me, exactly how have *I* done that to you?"

Pro-gay argument: "By using the Bible verses to condemn me whenever you talk about homosexuality!"
Response: "But I believe the Bible. You say, as a gay Christian, that you believe it too. Doesn't that mean we both take our moral guidance from Scripture?"

Pro-gay argument: "Yes."
Response: "Then what's wrong with quoting it when I explain why I believe homosexuality is wrong?"

Pro-gay argument: "Because most people who quote the Bible to gays are homophobic, and they're using the Bible as an excuse to hate us."
Response: "That's a strong accusation. Am I acting like I hate you? I believe homosexuality's wrong, sure. But that's a belief, not a phobia. If I were homophobic, could I be sitting here talking to you? After all, if I had a phobia about gays, I'd be afraid to be anywhere near you!"

Pro-gay argument: "But you think homosexuality's a big sin or something."
Response: "I think it's a sin, no worse or better than some of my own sins. But thinking something is a sin—and having a phobia about it—are two very different things."

Pro-gay argument: "But don't you know how many lesbians and gays get beaten up because people like you go around saying it's a sin?"
Response: "I'm against anyone getting hurt, and I'll speak out against gay bashing as much as I'll speak out against gay practices.

But nobody gets beat up just because I, or any other Christian, says homosexuality is a sin."

Pro-gay argument: "Oh, yes, they do! Studies show that gay bashers come from religious homes just like yours."

Response: "Some do, but it's their own craziness, not religion that makes them do those terrible things. Some murderers and rapists also come from Christian homes, but that doesn't mean their religious upbringing made them commit their crimes. Thinking homosexuality is wrong doesn't make you beat up homosexuals. I think it's wrong, but I'm not beating you up, am I?"

Pro-gay argument: "No, but it does happen!"

Response: "Yes, and we should work together to prevent it. But silencing the Christian view of homosexuality isn't the way to do it. The fact is, you and I have a completely different view of homosexuality. I can live with that. But I would ask, with all due respect, that you not accuse me of things I've never done—things like hurting gays or spreading prejudice. Because when you do that, you're guilty of the very thing you say conservative Christians do to you. You're spreading myths and stereotypes. We may not agree on homosexuality, but I'm sure we both agree on the need to be truthful, even when we disagree."

8

RELIGIOUS PRO-GAY ARGUMENTS

"What is being depicted to individuals is a 'user-friendly'
God who will smile benignly down upon their lifestyles
of choice, as they continue to live as they like."

GREG LAURIE
The Great Compromise

We'd rather be nice.

That's a strange tendency creeping into the church—niceness is taking precedence over truth. Immorality—even among Christian leaders—is often going unconfronted; doctrinal lines are fuzzier than ever; and many churches seem more concerned with making people comfortable than arousing in them a sense of their need for God. In these "seeker-friendly" times, we're in danger of believing that if people like us, then we've reached them and done our job.

This loss of balance in the church needs to be acknowledged before we confront the gay Christian movement. And much of the criticism we level at them needs to be sent our way, as well.

For example, while reading Mel White's *Stranger at the Gate,* I was struck by his description of the conversation he had with the pastor of the Metropolitan Community Church he had begun attending: "When I asked Ken why he never preached about sin or judgment, but only about God's love and grace, he smiled and answered without hesitation, 'The people who come to this church have heard enough about sin and judgment.'"[1]

How typical of a gay church, I thought. *No preaching on sin—just grace without responsibility.*

Not three days later, though, I ran across information proving that this pastor's unbalanced approach wasn't unique to gay churches. Reluctance to discuss sin—much less confront it—is widespread among Christians. Truth is taking a backseat to accommodation.

A recent poll showed that 66 percent (two-thirds) of Americans no longer believe there is such a thing as "absolute truth." More distressing, though, was the fact that 53 percent of those not believing in absolute truth identified themselves as being born-again Christians—75 percent of whom were mainline Protestants.[2]

If absolute truth no longer exists, even in the minds of half the born-again population, it logically follows that doctrine, and the Bible itself, are given less credence. As pollster George Gallup Jr. put it,

> While religion is highly popular in America, it is to a large extent superficial. There is a knowledge gap between America's stated faith and the lack of the most basic knowledge about that faith.[3]

In short, today's self-identified Christians are biblically ignorant. Doctrine has become less important than good feelings; indeed, a *USA Today* survey found that, of the 56 percent of Americans who attend church, 45 percent did so because "it's good for you," and 26 percent went for peace of mind. Specific doctrines, the pollster noted, seemed unimportant.[4]

If the notions of "truth" and "doctrine" are becoming unimportant to Christians, can the idea of "sin" hope to survive? Probably not.

Twenty-five percent of Christians polled in 1993 believed sin to be "an outdated concept."[5]

"The awareness of sin used to be our shadow," writes Cornelius Plantinga. "Christians hated sin, feared it, flew from it. But now the shadow has faded. Nowadays, the accusation *you have sinned* is often said with a grin."[6]

But the gospel truth is never so accommodating. John the Baptist was ferocious with the Pharisees (Matthew 3:7-8); Jesus trounced Peter when he tried to interfere with His mission (Matthew 16:22-23); and Paul was willing to publicly rebuke hypocrisy, even when committed by a respected disciple (Galatians 2:11-14). To be sure, there is a place for gentleness. But never at the expense of truth.

Today, the gap between truth and modern practice has been large enough to allow any number of false (albeit "nice") ideas to enter the church, creating a mentality that says, *Let's all get along without conflict, shall we?* Author J. Stephen Lang attempts to explain this phenomenon: "Love is understandable—warm and fuzzy. Doctrine, on the other hand, sounds cold, difficult, and demanding."[7]

A desire for "warm and fuzzy" without a commitment to truth makes the general religious arguments of the pro-gay theology all the more palatable. Unlike the arguments of the previous chapters, these arguments are more "religious"—that is, they appeal to general religious themes of harmony and goodwill while bypassing issues of the fallen nature, sin, and obedience. To the biblically ignorant they can pass for truth; in the light of Scripture, though, they don't stand up well.

Since those arguments are more religious in approach than the social arguments, they can be answered almost exclusively in biblical terms. Remembering that members of the gay Christian movement say they believe in biblical authority, the best answers are a call to return to the objective truth of the Bible instead of relying on the subjective winds of human experience and understanding.

Argument One: "I'm a Born-Again Gay"

This argument is most often promoted in the form of a declaration: "I'm gay and Christian, which is living proof you can be both!" Mel White, upon his installation as dean of America's largest gay congregation, made a similar affirmation: "Now, thank God, after 30 years of struggle, I can say at last who I really am. I am gay. I am proud. And God loves me without reservation."[8] The message, then, is that if a person is truly born again and homosexual, the two must be compatible.

Response

This argument is illogical in that it assumes that if one is a Christian, and, therefore, loved by God, then what one does—no matter what it is—must be all right in God's sight.

We can assume Dr. White's assertions are true: He is gay, he says he is proud (and no one is in a position to say otherwise), and God loves him. But does God's love for him, or White's pride in being gay, justify homosexuality itself?

Not at all. Let's remember that Christians do not automatically become non-Christians just because they're sinning. The fact that they are sinning—even if they don't realize it—does not automatically nullify their salvation.

But neither does their salvation legitimize their sin. A Christian may indeed be openly homosexual. But that's no proof that homosexuality and Christianity are compatible. In fact, a Christian may be openly sinning; that's no proof that sin and Christianity are compatible either.

Ananias and Sapphira, a husband and wife mentioned in Acts 5, were evidently believers. Yet their sin of hypocrisy (pretending to give more money to the church than they actually did) cost them their lives. They were Christians, and they were in serious error. Their error didn't mean they weren't Christians; their Christianity, however, did not legitimize their error.

On at least one occasion, the apostle Peter was afraid to be seen associating with Gentiles for fear of reprisals from Jews who felt that Jews and Gentiles should never mix. So when Jewish people were not around, he was willing to eat with Gentile friends; when Jews were present, he avoided Gentiles (Galatians 2:11-13). His hypocrisy in the face of prejudice was wrong, yet no one doubts he was a Christian. That still in no way justified his hypocrisy.

In other words, being a Christian is no indication in itself that your life is pleasing to God. Any honest believer knows that.

Most of the people I knew while working at the pro-gay Metropolitan Community Church were from conservative backgrounds like mine. They had come from Baptist, Pentecostal, or fundamentalist churches where they'd had a genuine conversion experience. Yet we all had decided that homosexuality was acceptable, and, to the best of my knowledge, we did not become non-Christians the moment we made that decision. (I will leave it to others to speculate at what point we might have lost our salvation, if that is possible.) For all intents and purposes, we were Christians, and we were homosexual.

We were also wrong. Deceived, rebellious, or ignorant, the fact remains we were wrong. That's where the discussion should focus—on ethics, not experience. Instead of arguing whether or not a Christian can be homosexual or vice versa, the primary question should be whether homosexuality itself is right or wrong.

It's a waste of time to argue intangibles, such as whether or not a "gay Christian" is truly born-again, or "saved." We may argue that if he continues in sin, he risks hardening his heart toward God or reaping corruption, since God is not mocked. But we cannot see inside his soul to determine how hardened, backslidden, or deceived he may be.

For that reason I find it more useful to focus the discussion on the Bible instead of on the spiritual state of the person I'm arguing with. No matter how proud, confident, or loved by God a person is, he can be walking in darkness without knowing it. That's exactly why we have an objective standard against which we can judge our actions. "Take heed unto thyself," Paul told Timothy, "and unto the doctrine; continue in them: for in doing this thou shalt both save thyself, and them that hear thee" (1 Timothy 4:16 KJV).

Saying "I'm Christian and gay" proves nothing. The question

shouldn't be, *Can a person be homosexual and still belong to God?* but rather, *Is homosexuality right or wrong according to God's Word?*

Argument Two: "We Feel the Spirit Too!"

When Reverend Sylvia Pennington attended her first gay church, she still believed homosexuality was wrong. But something happened to change her mind:

> I became aware of the Holy Spirit's presence hovering around, about and within me. They [gay Christians] were sensing the same Spirit that I sensed and loving God back as I was. They were actually worshipping God. And God was there—undeniably there![9]

Her sense of the presence of God in a gay church convinced Pennington that homosexuality was acceptable to Him. What else could it have meant? If He was there, He must approve.

Response

From Reverend Pennington's above description of a gay church, we can assume one of three things: Either God's presence was not there at all and what she felt was just emotion; or what she (and the others) felt was a demonic counterfeit; or, in fact, God's presence *was* there.

I find it useless to argue over whether or not the presence of God can actually be found in gay churches. Instead it's best to ask, "So what?" Even if God is present in gay churches and His gifts are manifested there, does that prove He condones homosexuality?

Not at all. God's presence, wonderful as it is, and His gifts, valuable as they are, are given freely. They are neither a reward for, nor evidence of, righteousness.*

To illustrate this, consider the Corinthian church. No one could doubt they were genuine believers. Paul opened his letter to them addressing them as "sanctified in Christ Jesus" (1 Corinthians 1:2). Further, the

---

* Please note: I am not arguing that God *is* present in gay churches—I am only saying that, like the "I'm gay and Christian" argument, it is best to stick to the bottom-line issue: *Is homosexuality right or wrong?*

gifts of the Spirit—teaching, preaching, prophetic words, and so forth—were manifest there. Paul spent all of chapters 12 and 14 teaching them how to manage these gifts. So God's presence and His gifts were clearly a part of the Corinthian church's life.

And the Corinthian church was a mess. They were, by Paul's own account, carnal and full of divisions (1 Corinthians 3:3-4). Incest was openly committed among them (5:1-5). They were hauling each other to court over lawsuits (6:13). And they were getting drunk at the communion table (11:21).

Yet God's presence was at Corinth. Because He approved of their behavior? Of course not. But His gifts and calling, as Paul said in Romans 11:29, are "without repentance." God would not remove them, even when the church was in serious error.

Blessing vs. Approval

I recall discussing with a lesbian friend of mine my own doubts about the gay Christian movement when I was still a part of it. I had been active with the gay church for at least two years by then, but I had never gotten past a certain gnawing at my conscience. I was not convinced, and I told her as much.

"But Joe," she said earnestly, "if we were wrong, God wouldn't be blessing our church with His presence. We wouldn't see people coming forward for altar calls, we wouldn't see the gifts of teaching and preaching manifest themselves, and we wouldn't feel His presence the way we do every Sunday." That helped still my conscience a little, but *only* a little. And only for a little while. Eventually, I had to recognize that this argument is misleading, in that it assumes that God's gifts and presence are an indication of His approval.

Modern examples abound. By now we have all heard of evangelists or preachers whose ministries thrived even when, unfortunately, they were involved in sexual immorality. For years, in some cases, God's presence and blessing was on their ministry efforts even as they continued their secret sin. Yet none of us would assume that God approved of their behavior.

What *can* we assume then? Two things: First, if God has given someone a gift of the Spirit, that gift may continue to operate even if the person is willfully sinning. Second, the gift, or God's presence, is a sign of grace, not approval. It cannot be said that because the gifts are operating in a church, all the church's activities are legitimate. Legitimacy is determined by Scripture, not spiritual dynamics.

Argument Three: "How Can Love Be Wrong?"

As the gay-rights and gay Christian movements have evolved, increasing emphasis has been put on the quality of homosexual relationships. Initially, gay apologists argued for sexual freedom. Today, they argue for legitimacy.

"God is ecstatic that I'm so happy in a relationship with a woman," a lesbian member of the Metropolitan Community Church gushed on a news program.[10] A stable relationship, then, is viewed as evidence of God's blessing. And if true love is involved, so the argument goes, it must be right.

Response

This argument is misleading because it assumes that love sanctifies a relationship.

It's hard these days to say that love is not the final standard for right and wrong. Love is nice, after all; in our culture, it's been nearly deified as something so intense and beautiful that it justifies almost anything done in its name. And with all the hatred and violence in the world, why knock a loving relationship between any two people?

Because love, in itself, does not make a relationship right. In fact, contrary to the touchy-feely wisdom of the times, love is not always such a good thing. An essay on homosexuality and ethics puts it well:

> One of the most popular errors in the realm of Christian ethics has been the effort to make love an omnipotent spiritual quality which has the power to sanctify anything that is done in its name.[11]

The wrong kind of love can, according to Jesus, interfere with God's plan for an individual. In Matthew 10:37, for example, He warns His followers that love for anyone, no matter how legitimate the relationship, becomes sin when it surpasses our love for Him. We can learn an important lesson from King Solomon in this regard. Solomon loved his foreign wives. The problem was, they turned his heart away from God (1 Kings 11:3-4). In his case, love became a snare.

Love is not enough to justify a relationship. An unmarried Christian couple may be very much in love; if they become sexually involved before marriage, it will still be fornication, no matter how much love went into it. And it will *still* be wrong. A married man can fall deeply in love with a woman other than his wife; that will never sanctify adultery.

Likewise two men, or women, may be in love. Their love may run very deep, and they may pledge fidelity to each other and live as happily as any married heterosexual couple. But again, that will not in itself justify a homosexual relationship. Scripture places boundaries on human relationships, offering no compromise even if love is present. If a form of sexual relating is wrong, it remains wrong no matter what degree of love goes along with it.

Pro-gay religious arguments have a nice tone to them. Like the quaint sayings "God helps those who help themselves," "All roads lead to God," and "It doesn't matter which religion you choose as long as you're sincere" (none of which are biblical), they're religious enough to sound good, yet unscriptural enough to be dead wrong. Viewed in light of Scripture, they can be answered and corrected.

Let's Talk About
Religious Pro-Gay Arguments

Pro-gay argument: "If you think homosexuality is wrong, how do you explain me? I'm born again and I'm gay, and I take my Christian life just as seriously as you do!"

Response: "Are you saying that whatever a Christian does is okay because he's a Christian?"

Pro-gay argument: "Of course not, but I know God loves me just as I am."

Response: "Sure He does. But that doesn't mean He approves of every part of your life."

Pro-gay argument: "He hasn't told me that!"

Response: "What's to tell? We've got His Word in writing. And no matter how much He loves and accepts you, if His Word says your behavior is wrong, then He's already told you what He thinks of it."

Pro-gay argument: "But if He thinks badly of it, why do I feel His presence every week at my church? Our whole congregation is gay, and He knows it. So why is He blessing us?"

Response: "I'm not sure He is. We can sometimes think we're feeling God's blessings when in fact we're having an emotional, or even a demonic, experience. But just for the sake of argument, let's say you're right—God's presence is in your church. God's presence isn't quite the same as His approval. I can think of lots of ministers who had God's blessing on their lives but who weren't living right."

Pro-gay argument: "If you're talking about my being gay, there's no reason He wouldn't condone what I do. I'm in a long-term relationship. My lover and I care very much about each other. God doesn't have any problem with that."

Response: "Because you love each other? That's a shaky foundation. The Bible doesn't say any kind of relationship is okay if there's love in it. What about adultery? Or fornication? Are those okay too, as long as both people involved love each other?"

Pro-gay argument: "You don't understand. People involved in adultery have a choice. I don't! I've been gay ever since I can remember, and I've tried to change more times than I can count. So I've finally accepted who I am, and I'm sure it's okay with Him."

Response: "Because it's okay with you?"

Pro-gay argument: "Not just me. Plenty of other gay Christians too! We tried to change because people like you tell us we're sinners, but we don't have a choice over our sexual orientation. I've known so many people who tried to go straight, and all of them are back in the gay community now."

Response: "That doesn't make it right. I know it's hard to change. I know some Christians who have to resist homosexual temptations nearly every day. But then, doesn't every Christian have to resist temptations every day? That's what sanctification is all about—growing daily to become more like Him! When we're born again, our sinful feelings don't just vanish. Some of them, in fact, stay with us our whole lives.

"And I know, in your case, those feelings are very deeply ingrained. It would probably be harder for you to resist them than people in the church realize. But God isn't going to change His standards to accommodate ours. Please don't decide something is right just because it's hard to get over. That's tampering with the Word of God. I think you'll find it's better, in the long run, to obey God's Word than to try to change it."

PART THREE

Issues with the Bible

9

THE NATURE
AND USE
OF THE BIBLE

*"The Christian homosexual position when carefully
examined can be exposed for what it is at its very
core: an attack upon the integrity, sufficiency, and
authority of Scripture, which for the Christian church
is an attack upon the very nature of our Holy God."*

UNITED CHURCH OF CHRIST, 1979
"Issues in Sexual Ethics"

Even the most vocal critics of conservative Christians, televangelists, and the "Religious Right" adhere to an unspoken rule: It's not kosher to directly attack Jesus Christ or the Bible. Seldom if ever will a mainstream journalist say, "Jesus was a kook," or "The Bible is hogwash!" Instead, modern attacks on the person of Christ and Scripture come in the form of revisions, rather than direct thrusts.

So today's Jesus is often a socially conscious pacifist or a non-judgmental rebel; He speaks of love and peace, but never of eternal damnation, self-denial, or of Himself as being the *only* way to God (as the original Jesus did). He is too nice for that sort of thing.

"If Jesus were alive, He'd be marching here with us!" a well-known actress once said during a gay-pride rally, feeling free to interpret the actions of someone she didn't even profess to believe in.

Likewise, even the most theologically liberal person will acknowledge that the Bible is a good book, though not one to be taken as a literal guide for life. Instead of saying they outright reject its teachings, modern critics just diminish its authority. Respect for the Bible is so deeply ingrained in our culture that no one wants to denigrate it; instead, they settle for revisions.

I found this to be true in the gay Christian movement as well. We had too deep a respect for the Bible to ignore it. But in my opinion, we weren't willing to obey it either. So revising it was the next best thing.

The pro-gay theology's scriptural arguments are, therefore, basic revisions of the biblical texts traditionally understood to forbid homosexuality.*

While showing a measure of respect to the Bible, gay Christians generally negate its authority or its sufficiency, or they claim it has been mistranslated, and thus misunderstood, in modern times. The following arguments about the nature and use of the Bible, then, could be categorized as "the Bible is a good book, but..." arguments, which diminish the authority and sufficiency of Scripture.

Which Jesus?

An example of the "new" Jesus hit me full force when I finished speaking at a church conference one time. "You should be ashamed of yourself for calling homosexuality a sin!" a furious gay man huffed, charging down the aisle toward me. "Jesus never called people sinners, and He never judged anyone!"

Jesus WHO? I wondered as he stomped away. Certainly not the Jesus of the Bible, who was unsparing in denouncing sin, and not at all shy about pronouncing judgment (Matthew 23:13-39).

---

* I borrow the term *revision* from Dr. Stanton Jones, who refers to pro-gay theology as "revisionist" in his excellent article "The Loving Opposition."[1]

While claiming the Bible is divinely inspired, many pro-gay theologians also offer five ways to diminish it.

Argument One: *"The Bible is a good book, but its authors knew nothing of the homosexual orientation when they condemned homosexual behavior."*

"The idea of a lifelong homosexual orientation or 'condition' is never mentioned in the Bible," Scanzoni and Mollenkott allege. "The Bible writers assumed that everyone was heterosexual." Roger Biery agrees: "The concept of sexual orientation did not exist in biblical times." Mel White echoes the belief, arguing that the authors of biblical passages against homosexuality "knew nothing of sexual orientation."[2]

Thus Scripture, uninformed about "sexual orientation," is an insufficient guide on sexual matters. "The Scriptures are not self-interpreting," a liberal spokesman insists. "You have to make judgments about how to use today what was written long ago."[3]

Baptist minister George Williamson, pastor of the First Baptist Church of Granville, Ohio, is even more specific when he declares the Bible to be irrelevant to the subject of homosexuality: "We're taking the old book and applying it to the new world in which gay and lesbian people have found themselves."[4]

Response

This argument is misleading because it assumes that orientation justifies behavior. It's audacious to think a behavior is legitimate just because a person is naturally inclined toward it. As shown earlier, recent studies indicate there may well be such a thing as an "orientation" toward drunkenness and violence. Are we to assume that if the Bible's authors knew nothing of these conditions either, that we should revise our view of alcoholism or violent behavior?

Nowhere in the Bible is any behavior condemned with a qualification, as in, "Thou shalt not do this thing unless thou hast an orientation toward it." Nor does the context of a "loving relationship" justify any sexual sin mentioned in Scripture, as pro-gay spokesmen would have us believe. The love between two homosexuals cannot make homosexuality normal or legitimate, any more than the love of two people committing adultery justifies the breaking of marital vows.

Besides, if orientation justifies sexual behavior, why stop at homosexuality? Pedophilia, as mentioned earlier, is believed by some experts to be an orientation; bestiality may be seen the same way in the future. Does biblical ignorance of these conditions nullify biblical injunctions against the actions they result in?

Not if Scripture is truly inspired—and there's the crux of the issue. If the Holy Spirit indeed moved the biblical authors to write under His guidance, as 2 Timothy 3:16 asserts, then it's insulting to think the third person of the Trinity was ignorant of the human condition. Joseph Gudel, writing in the *Christian Research Journal,* underscores the point:

> It is ludicrous to believe that the Creator of the universe, in guiding the biblical authors, was ignorant concerning the things we now know about homosexuality through modern biology, psychology, sociology, and so forth. To deny scriptural statements about homosexuality on these grounds is to completely deny God's superintendence in the authorship of Scripture.[5]

If the Bible prohibits certain behaviors only because its authors were ignorant of the "orientations" leading to them, then it is not, as it claims to be, "profitable for doctrine, for reproof, for correction, for instruction in righteousness" (2 Timothy 3:16). Rather, it is outdated, uninformed, and irrelevant. There is no middle ground.

Argument Two: *"The Bible is a good book, but it has been used in the past to justify bigotry."*

Gay activist and pastor Troy Perry likes to remind us of early American believers who used the Bible to justify slavery. Authors Letha Scanzoni and Virginia Mollenkott refer to the Nazi use of Scripture to legitimize anti-Semitism.[6] By comparing the past abuses of Scripture to today's objections to homosexuality, they place the homosexual in the same category as the persecuted, and the conservative Christian in the role of the bigot. "The church was wrong in the past," they seem to say. "Therefore, you must be wrong in the present when you condemn us."

Response

To have been wrong in the past is not proof that one is wrong in the present.

There is no question that the church has erred at different times, but common sense tells us that past errors are not proof of errors in the present. They *are* proof that we are fallible, and that we can, if we ignore our past mistakes, repeat sins of prejudice or mistreatment. But Christians cannot be assumed to be committing these errors *now* simply because some Christians committed them *before*.

Additionally, there is a difference between calling a behavior sinful and calling for the persecution of a group of fellow citizens. A conservative stand against gay rights cannot be compared with the Inquisition or the Holocaust. Conservative Christians are not calling for the imprisonment or death of homosexuals; we do not wish them to be denied the right to vote or hold citizenship. In fact, we are against their mistreatment in any form.*

There is a clear difference between taking a moral stand on an issue and calling for the mistreatment of people you disagree with. To suggest the two are the same is misleading and unfair.

Argument Three: "The Bible is a good book, but its original language cannot be understood by the average layman. It takes an expert to understand what the authors said about homosexuality."

This argument casts doubt on the average person's ability to comprehend the Bible. More to the point, it suggests an inability to take a

---

* Just as the pro-life movement has its lunatic fringe, who call for the death of abortionists, so there are few (very few, thank God) who really would advocate violence against gays. They are clearly a minority; it would be just as unfair to hold them up as typical conservatives as it would be to hold the wildest gay activists up as typical of all gays and lesbians.

stand on biblical issues. After all, if we can't be certain what the Bible's authors meant when they referred to homosexuality, how can we take a stand against pro-gay theology and legislation?

"Normally, it is impossible to understand the meaning of a passage by merely reading it," Roger Biery warns us. "The passage of thousands of years obscures, sometimes beyond recovery, the exact meanings of words," adds John Boswell.[7]

Response

Oddly enough, this inability to understand the Bible seems to apply only to references to homosexuality. Read virtually any gay Christian material and you will find the generous use of other Scriptures, with nary a concern for their original Greek or Hebrew meaning. But on the subject of same-sex contact, gay Christians show a deep, sudden concern for historical, linguistic, or contextual accuracy. Yet, as Elodie Ballantine Emig points out, this argument "fails to account for the fact that the Bible has not been translated by modern English speakers with little knowledge of classical languages."[8] Rather, large numbers of experts and highly qualified scholars have put their best efforts into most Bible translations.

In fairness, certain portions of the Bible *are* difficult; both laymen and experts wrestle with some passages. But it takes neither a rocket scientist nor a scholar to grasp the meaning of most Bible verses. To cast doubt on one part of a translation without scrutinizing the rest of it in a similar manner is inconsistent; it must be taken as a whole, or not at all.

Argument Four: *"The Bible is a good book, but conservative Christians pick and choose which of its verses they take literally."*

Troy Perry describes an encounter he had with a Bible-quoting woman:

> She said, "Young man, do you know what the Book of Leviticus says?"
> I told her, "I sure do! It says that it's a sin for a woman to wear a red dress, for a man to wear a cotton shirt and

woolen pants at the same time, for anyone to eat shrimp, oysters, or lobster—or your steak too rare."

She said, "That's not what I mean."

I said, "I know that's not what you mean, honey, but you forgot all those other dreadful sins, too, that are in the same book of the Bible."[9]

The point is clear—quoting verses against homosexuality is like picking and choosing which Scriptures to stand by and which ones to ignore. Elsewhere Perry expresses it even more strongly:

To condemn homosexuals, many denominations have intentionally misread and misinterpreted their Bibles to please their own personal preferences, remembering only Scriptures that suit themselves, forgetting or ignoring many other Scriptures.[10]

In short, quoting Scripture against homosexuality is a form of inconsistency—hypocrisy, even—since other Scriptures are not taken literally.

Response

This argument is misleading in that it assumes prejudice is the reason for the conservative position. A commonsense approach to the Bible shows that certain ceremonial and dietary laws in the Old Testament, such as those quoted by Perry, aren't necessary to follow today. Christians are not, thankfully, under the Mosaic law (Galatians 3:17-25). But the biblical commandments against homosexual conduct do not appear in the same sections as the dietary and ceremonial laws; in Leviticus (the book Perry's argument centered on) they appear alongside other sexual sins forbidden in both the Old and New Testaments (Leviticus 18:22; 20:13).

Besides, if Perry is to be believed when he says "many denominations" pick and choose which Scriptures suit us, "forgetting or ignoring" those that do not, an obvious question arises: Why do heterosexual conservatives still preach against heterosexual sins? Why don't we just ignore all references to heterosexual lust, adultery, and fornication? For that matter, why do we still preach against lying and stealing, since we are all tempted toward those sins to some degree?

Listen to any conservative preacher who stands against homosexuality, and you will also hear him standing against heterosexual sins. So if we're indeed picking and choosing verses according to our personal preferences, why do we insist on choosing Scriptures that so obviously go against our preferences? Why not make it easy on ourselves and choose only the Scriptures condemning *homosexual* sins, while ignoring the ones condemning *heterosexual* sins?

The fact is, we aren't picking and choosing to suit our prejudice. Our scriptural position on homosexuality is based not on one or two obscure verses yanked out of context. Rather, it is drawn from five specific verses—two found in the Old Testament and three in the New—as well as on a general overview of the only form of sexual expression consistently commended throughout Scripture: heterosexual union.

Argument Five: *"The Bible is a good book, but its verses are used to clobber gays and lesbians."*

"Clobber" is a term that Mel White, and authors Scanzoni and Mollenkott use to describe the way conservatives quote scriptures on homosexuality.[11] In fact, the five verses that mention same-sex contact are often referred to, in the gay Christian movement, as "the clobber passages." That cleverly puts the person using them in a negative light; he's not just quoting the Bible—he's clobbering people with it.

I remember discussing theology with a gay author on a radio program, when a woman called in and quoted some Bible verses against homosexuality.

"Well, congratulations, honey," the author sneered. "You've got all the clobber passages down just right."

Of course, that effectively shut down any rational discussion of the Bible. Decent people don't want to clobber anyone; when they know they'll be accused of doing so, they're less likely to speak up. And that, I suspect, is the reason the "clobber" argument is used so effectively.

Response

This argument is inaccurate in that it equates "quoting" and "clobbering."

Actually, Bible verses *have* been used to "clobber" people in the past; that is, they've been implemented in harsh, even cruel, ways. In Puritan times, for example, if a person was found guilty of gossip, he would be tied onto a chair attached to a long beam. The chair would then be swung out over a lake or pond and, with the person tied to it, dunked underwater for up to a minute. Likewise, if a person missed church services without good reason, he would be placed in wooden stocks or in the pillory (a device clamped around head and hands) and left in public to be humiliated. And unwed mothers, during their pregnancies, might find themselves chained in front of the church, where those passing by would throw rotten fruit at them.

What was wrong here? Was it the fact that the church preached against gossip, neglecting fellowship, or sex outside of marriage? Not at all. The problem was the harsh way these scriptures were being enforced.

So it is with quoting Scripture against homosexuality. There are those who do so in a harsh, unloving manner; there are those who would, given the chance, implement them in an equally harsh way. Both groups are wrong.

But to simply *quote* a Scripture is not to clobber anyone, as gay spokespersons well know. Perry, after all, has no problem using Bible verses to back his complaints against Anita Bryant, while White feels free to use Scripture when criticizing Pat Robertson.[12] When conservatives quote Bible verses against homosexuality it's called "clobbering," yet when gays quote Scripture while arguing against conservatives, it's just—well, quoting Scripture.

Let's Talk About the
Nature and Use of the Bible

Pro-gay argument: "Whatever reasons you have for objecting to homosexuality, you won't find any of them in the Bible. It's been badly mistranslated; the fact is, it doesn't condemn gays and lesbians the way you think it does."

Response: "I never said it condemns gays and lesbians, any more than it condemns anyone else. The Bible says we've all sinned, and we're all in need of redemption."

Pro-gay argument: "Fine, but I mean it also doesn't condemn loving sexual relationships between men or between women. Those men who wrote the Bible didn't even know what homosexuality was. It's only in the last hundred years that we've come to understand what sexual orientation is. Biblical writers didn't know anything about people who felt they were gay from the time they were young—and who are in lasting, responsible lesbian and gay relationships."

Response: "But there's no contingency in the Bible for homosexuality. It doesn't say, 'Thou shalt not lie with man as with woman, unless that's your orientation.' The biblical authors probably weren't concerned about what *caused* certain behaviors—they were concerned with the behaviors themselves. By the way, it's quite an insult to God and His Word to ignore what the Bible says about homosexuality just because its authors never heard of 'sexual orientation.' They may never have heard about alcoholism, either, but don't you think they knew what they were talking about when they prohibited drunkenness? Orientation, in itself, doesn't justify behavior."

Pro-gay argument: "But the Bible has always been used to back prejudice; haven't you noticed that? The KKK does it, the Nazis did it, and now the Religious Right's doing it to gays and lesbians!"

Response: "So many people use the term 'Religious Right' nowadays that I'm not even sure what it is. But if you mean conservative Christians, then you're wrong. Sure, bigots have twisted the Bible in the past, but the fact that some Christians were wrong in the past doesn't automatically mean they're wrong in the present. It only means we should be careful before we take a stand on something, and believe me, I am."

Pro-gay argument: "Don't you think Christians of colonial times said the same thing while they bought and sold their slaves?"

Response: "That's a bad comparison. Gays have never been bought and sold in America; you've never been denied the right to vote; there are no gay and straight classrooms or drinking fountains; and you've always had the right to hold property and participate in the political process. In fact, you've always had the same rights all Americans have had. The same sure can't be said about African-Americans."

Pro-gay argument: "But bigotry is bigotry, no matter who it's directed against."

Response: "You're right about that. But is taking a biblical stand a form of bigotry? I'm saying homosexuality is wrong. I'm not saying homosexuals are less than human and should be treated as such. It's unfair and inaccurate when you confuse a moral position with bigotry."

Pro-gay argument: "But you're way too sure of yourself. You're not a language expert, so how can you be so sure the Bible really does condemn homosexuality? It's written in ancient languages."

Response: "But it's been translated by experts who know a lot more about language than either one of us. Check the credentials of these guys before you write their translations off. They knew what they were doing."

Pro-gay argument: "Maybe so, but you fundamentalists sure do pick and choose what Scriptures you want to believe in. You yank out the passages on gays and say how terrible we all are, but you don't seem half as concerned about other Bible verses."

Response: "That's true, to a point. Sometimes Christians do get more excited about homosexuality than other sins. But they also preach against sins they're guilty of. Face it, if I wanted to pick and choose which Bible verses to take seriously, I'd only choose the ones that applied to your sins and never mention the ones that apply to mine. But I don't do that; I admit I've got struggles too. Most other fundamentalists do the same."

Pro-gay argument: "But when you quote verses on homosexuality, you clobber us with them!"

Response: "I've heard you quote Scriptures; you don't seem to think you're hitting someone with them just because you're quoting them. When I quote Scriptures on homosexuality, I'm only doing so to back my belief that homosexuality is a sin. That's not clobbering; it's talking. So can we talk?"

10

GENESIS AND HOMOSEXUALITY

———⊗———

"Biblical authority is not tyranny: We read, reflect and
reconcile ourselves with scripture; but we never simply
remake it or reject it if we affirm its authority."

MARION SOARDS
Scripture and Homosexuality

So far we've discussed general points about the nature of homosexuality—whether or not it's inborn and unchangeable, and how prevalent it really is. We've also discussed common objections homosexual people raise when we refer to homosexuality as sin, as well as the nature and use of the Bible in this discussion.

Now we get to the Bible itself. These next four chapters will examine the specific verses that mention homosexuality, or that are usually referred to when the subject's addressed. For many of us, this is the heart of the matter because it addresses what the Bible does or does not say. This is also where pro-gay theologians try to make their strongest case, as they argue that these verses do *not* condemn same-sex coupling and, in most cases, are not even referring to it.

This, then, is the boldest part of pro-gay theology—the revised interpretation of specific Bible verses. For many Christians, it's also the most difficult to respond to, because the revisionist gay apologist will take what seems obvious in the relevant scriptures and claim to have discovered a different, heretofore hidden, meaning in them.

To illustrate, let's take a fairly straightforward scripture. Jesus said, "I am the light of the world." That seems plain, both in wording and context, so it doesn't need much analysis. Its meaning is clear.

Now suppose someone tells you that they have done an extensive word study on this verse, and have discovered that Jesus was really saying, "I am a hair dryer." That seems ridiculous; the context so clearly points to something else. But if you haven't taken the time to study the original Greek in this verse, you can't technically refute the "hair dryer" idea, though common sense tells you it's nonsense.

That's the power of the pro-gay theology. It takes scriptures we're all familiar with, gives them an entirely new interpretation, backs its claims with the words of well-credentialed scholars, and gives birth to a new sexual ethic. Common sense may reject it, but until it's examined more closely, it's difficult to refute.

Two Excellent Resources

Thankfully, the Scripture issue has been examined, with admirable scholarship and clarity, in two books I highly recommend: *Straight and Narrow?* by Thomas Schmidt and *The Bible and Homosexual Practices: Texts and Hermeneutics* by Robert Gagnon.* Both of these authors examine the original language, historical interpretations, and cultural contexts of these scriptures much more thoroughly than we will in these chapters. Anyone interested in a more comprehensive analysis should refer to these.

To approach this portion of the pro-gay theology, we will review each Scripture verse referring to homosexuality, establish the *traditional* view of the verse, cite the *pro-gay arguments* against that view, and offer a *response* to each.

---

* Published, respectively, by InterVarsity Press, 1995; and Abingdon Press, 2002.

Created Intent: Genesis 1:27-28; 2:18-24

God created man in his own image, in the image of God He created him; male and female He created them. And God blessed them, and God said unto them, "Be fruitful, and multiply, and replenish the earth, and subdue it" (Genesis 1:27-28 KJV).

The LORD God said, "It is not good that the man should be alone; I will make a help meet for him."...And Adam said, "This is now bone of my bones, and flesh of my flesh: she shall be called Woman, because she was taken out of Man." Therefore shall a man leave his father and his mother, and shall cleave unto his wife: and they shall be one flesh (Genesis 2:18,23-24).

TRADITIONAL VIEW

God's intention for human sexual relationships is limited to heterosexual union between one man and one woman in marriage.

Argument: "The creation account is irrelevant."

The Genesis account does not forbid homosexuality; it simply doesn't refer to it, for obvious reasons. A gay couple could hardly begin the population process. But these verses cannot be seen as a model for all couples. Many heterosexual couples are childless or unable to have sexual relations. Are they in sin because they do not conform to the Genesis account?

Response One

While it's true that this passage does not "forbid" homosexual relations, it does provide the primary model for sexuality by which other forms of sexual expression must be judged. Thomas Schmidt puts it well, saying that Genesis

provides a basis for biblical commands and for subsequent reflection on the part of those who wish to construct a sexual ethic to meet changing situations...It is appropriate for us to explore the relevance of biblical commands about marriage and to evaluate modern homosexuality in light of Genesis.[1]

Stanton Jones, in regard to creation as a model for sexuality, adds,

> The heart of Christian morality is this: God made sexual union for a purpose—the uniting of husband and wife into one flesh in marriage. God uses sexual intercourse, full sexual intimacy, to weld two people together.[2]

Response Two

The male-female union, introduced in Genesis, is the only model of sexual behavior consistently praised in both Old and New Testaments. Though other forms of behavior—polygamy and the use of concubines, for example—are introduced and even allowed in the Old Testament, a monogamous relation between husband and wife is the standard upheld in Scripture as the ideal. While the often-used phrase "God created Adam and Eve, not Adam and Steve" seems flippant, it's a fair assessment of created intent: Whereas heterosexuality is commended throughout the Bible, not once is a homosexual relationship mentioned in anything but negative terms.

The Destruction of Sodom: Genesis 19:4-9

> Before they [the angels visiting Lot to judge the wickedness of Sodom and determine whether or not to spare it] lay down, the men of the city, even the men of Sodom, compassed the house round, both old and young, all the people from every quarter. And they called unto Lot, and said unto him, "Where are the men which came in to thee this night? Bring them out unto us, that we may know them." And Lot went out at the door...and said, "I pray you, brethren, do not so wickedly. Behold now, I have two daughters which have not known man...do ye to them as is good in your eyes: only unto these men do nothing."...And

they said, "...Now we will deal worse with thee, than with them" (Genesis 19:4-9 KJV).

TRADITIONAL VIEW

The men of Sodom were attempting homosexual contact with Lot's visitors. Sodom was subsequently destroyed for its great wickedness.

Argument One: "Inhospitality was the sin of Sodom."

Sodom was destroyed because of the inhospitality of its citizens, not because of homosexuality. Both John Boswell and Derrick Bailey support this view, basing it on two assumptions: 1) Lot was violating Sodom's custom by entertaining guests without the permission of the city's elders,[3] thus prompting the demand to bring the men out "so we may know them"; and 2) the words "to know" do not necessarily have a sexual connotation.

The Hebrew word *yada* means "to know," and it is used here when the men said they wanted to know Lot's guests. Since *yada* appears 943 times in the Old Testament but carries a sexual meaning in only perhaps 10 of those 943 occurrences, the argument, then, is that the men of Sodom had no sexual intentions toward Lot's visitors.

Response

This argument makes little sense in light of Lot's responses to the men. His first response—"Brethren, do not so wickedly"—could hardly apply to a simple request to "get to know" his guests. His second response is especially telling: He answered their demands by offering his two virgin daughters, another senseless gesture if the men wanted only a social knowledge of his guests. And why, if these men had innocent intentions, was the entire city destroyed for inhospitality? Whose rudeness was being judged—Lot's, or that of Sodom's citizens?

This theory raises more questions than it answers. While Boswell and Bailey are correct in pointing out the seriousness of inhospitality in biblical times, inhospitality alone cannot account for the severity of Lot's response to the men, or for the judgment that soon followed.

Argument Two: "Rape, not homosexuality, was the sin of Sodom."

This argument, proposed by Scanzoni and Mollenkott, Troy Perry, and others, is more common and is far more plausible than the "inhospitality" theory. "Violence—forcing sexual activity upon another—is the real point of this story," Scanzoni and Mollenkott assert.[4] Accordingly, homosexuality had nothing to do with Sodom's destruction. Had the attempted rape been heterosexual in nature, judgment would have fallen just the same. Violence, not homosexuality, was being punished when Sodom fell.

Response

This argument is partially true; the men of Sodom certainly were proposing rape. But for such an event to include "all the men of the city, both young and old," homosexuality must have been commonly practiced. Scanzoni and Mollenkott make a persuasive case for the event being much like a prison rape, or the kind of assault conquering armies would commit against vanquished enemies.[5] But their argument is weakened by Thomas Schmidt's citations from early literature that connect Sodom with more general homosexual practices:

> The second century BC Testament of the Twelve Patriarchs labels the Sodomites "sexually promiscuous" (Testimony of Benjamin 9:1) and refers to "Sodom, which departed from the order of nature" (Testament of Naphthali 3:4). From the same time period, Jubilees specifies that the Sodomites were "polluting themselves and fornicating in their flesh" (16:5, compare 20:56). Both Philo and Josephus plainly name same-sex relations as the characteristic view of Sodom.[6]

Argument Three: "General wickedness, not homosexuality, was the sin of Sodom."

The real sins of Sodom, according to Ezekiel 16:49, were "pride, fullness of bread, and abundance of idleness...neither did she strengthen the hand of the poor and needy." These sins have nothing to do with homosexuality.

Response

Again, this argument is partially true. When Sodom was destroyed, homosexuality was only a part—or symptom—of its wickedness. Romans 1 gives a similar illustration, describing the generally corrupt condition of humanity, while citing homosexuality as a symptom of that corruption. But Ezekiel also says of the Sodomites, "And they were haughty, and committed abomination before me." The sexual nature of these "abominations" is suggested in 2 Peter 2:6-7, which says that God, "turning the cities of Sodom and Gomorrah into ashes, condemned them to destruction…And delivered righteous Lot, who was oppressed by the filthy conduct of the wicked."

In Jude 7 we similarly read, "Likewise, Sodom and Gomorrah and the surrounding cities, which, in the same manner as they, indulged in sexual immorality and pursued unnatural lust, serve as an example by undergoing a punishment" (NRSV).

Dr. Bruce Metzger of Princeton Theological Seminary mentions other references to Sodom's sexual immorality. In the apocryphal book of 3 Maccabees, we read of "the people of Sodom who acted arrogantly" and "who were notorious for their vices" (2:5). Reference is also made in Jubilees 16:6 to "the uncleanness of the Sodomites."[7]

The pro-gay interpretation of Sodom's destruction has merit. Homosexual rape was attempted, and the Sodomites were certainly guilty of sins other than homosexuality. But in light of the number of men willing to join in the rape, and the many other references—both biblical and extrabiblical—to Sodom's sexual sins, it's likely that homosexuality was widely practiced among the Sodomites. It's also likely that the sin for which they are named was one, but only one, of the many reasons judgment finally fell on them.

Let's Talk About Genesis and Homosexuality

Pro-gay argument: "So exactly which Scriptures do you think condemn homosexuality?"

Response: "Well, Genesis, for example, makes God's intent for sexual relationships pretty clear when it describes the first couple."

Pro-gay argument: "There's nothing about gays in those verses!"

Response: "My point exactly. The story of Adam and Eve doesn't say anything about homosexuality, only heterosexuality. It gives a very clear picture—a standard—of God's intention for men and women. Throughout the Bible, only that standard is upheld."

Pro-gay argument: "So you're saying all of us should, like Adam and Eve, be married and have kids? And that those who don't perfectly fit that model are in sin?"

Response: "Not at all. People have different callings and situations in life. Some are single; some married. Some are widowed; some celibate. All are valid. But the only standard for sexual expression that you'll find consistently praised in both Testaments is that of heterosexual monogamy."

Pro-gay argument: "Then I'd say a lot of Christians are doing a lousy job keeping that standard!"

Response: "And I'd agree with you. But when people aren't living up to a standard, the solution is to change the behavior of the people, not the standard itself. Besides, it's not just the Creation account that comes to mind when I think of the Bible and homosexuality. There's the story of Sodom, later in Genesis, which makes a very strong statement."

Pro-gay argument: "But not against homosexuality. The men in Sodom were condemned for trying to rape Lot and his visitors."

Response: "That, among other things. But you've got to admit that homosexuality must have been practiced pretty commonly in Sodom, or all the men of the city wouldn't have tried to participate in the rape. Besides, several other Scriptures refer to Sodom's sins as being sexual, as well as idolatrous and prideful."

Pro-gay argument: "Then you admit Sodom wasn't destroyed because of gays."

Response: "Sodom was destroyed because of wickedness, period. You know, lots of modern cities around the world are full of people practicing all sorts of sin, sexual sins as well as nonsexual. If judgment were to fall on any of them, I'd never say it was because of the sexual sins alone. It would no doubt be because of the cumulative effect of the many sins. And that, to my thinking, is what happened in Sodom. Besides, thank God, we don't have to figure out who's getting judged or for what reason. That's in God's hands. Our responsibility is to determine what He wants from us and, to the best of our ability, mold our lives to His will. On that point, I hope we agree."

11

MOSES AND HOMOSEXUALITY

"A man is justified by faith without the deeds of the law....Do we then make void the law through faith? God forbid: yea, we establish the law."

ROMANS 3:28,31 KJV

An episode of the popular television show *The West Wing* that aired in 2000 showed how far-reaching pro-gay theology's influence has become, even in mainstream secular media.

In this episode, the character President Bartlet castigates a conservative talk-show host who has stated publicly that the book of Leviticus condemns homosexuality. Intent on humiliating her, he peppers her with loaded, sarcastic questions based on a rigid interpretation of the Mosaic law:

> I wanted to ask you a couple of questions while I have you here. I wanted to sell my youngest daughter into slavery, as sanctioned in Exodus 21:7. What would be a good place for her to be?

My chief of staff insists on working on the Sabbath.
Exodus 35:2 clearly says he should be stoned to death. Am
I morally obligated to kill him myself? Or is it OK to call
the police?

Here's one that's really important because we've got a
lot of sports fans in this town. Touching the skin of a dead
pig makes one unclean, according to Leviticus 11:7. If they
promise to wear gloves, can the Washington Redskins still
play football?[1]

That's a common and often effective way of silencing anyone who
quotes the verses from Leviticus that prohibit homosexuality. You'll
hear this approach on talk shows and debates. It usually goes something
like this:

If you say that *one* verse from Leviticus applies to us
today—for example, the verse that forbids sex between
men—then you have to say that *all* verses from Leviticus
apply, including those that command us to stone adulterers,
refrain from touching footballs, and sell our children into
slavery. Otherwise you're picking and choosing which scriptures you want to take seriously.

This brings up two questions: 1) Does the book of Leviticus really
condemn homosexual behavior? and 2) If it does, is that condemnation
relevant to us today? In this chapter we'll address both questions and
offer responses to each.

What Is the Abomination?: Leviticus 18:22; 20:13

Thou shalt not lie with mankind, as with womankind:
it is abomination (Leviticus 18:22 KJV).

If a man also lie with mankind, as he lieth with a woman,
both of them have committed an abomination: they shall
surely be put to death (Leviticus 20:13 KJV).

TRADITIONAL POSITION

Under Levitical law, homosexuality was one of many abominable
practices punishable by death.

Argument One: "Idolatrous homosexuality is the problem."

The practices mentioned in these chapters of Leviticus have to do with idolatry, not homosexuality. The Hebrew word for *abomination,* according to Boswell, has less to do with something intrinsically evil and more to do with ritual uncleanness. The Metropolitan Community Church's pamphlet *Homosexuality: Not a Sin, Not a Sickness,* makes the same point: The Hebrew word for *abomination* found in Leviticus "is usually associated with idolatry."[2]

Roger Biery agrees, associating the type of homosexuality forbidden in Leviticus with idolatrous practices. Pro-gay authors refer to the heathen rituals of the Canaanites—rituals including both homosexual and heterosexual prostitution—as reasons God prohibited homosexuality among His people.

They contend that homosexuality itself was not the problem, but its association with idolatry and, at times, the way it was practiced as a part of idol worship. In other words, God was not prohibiting the kind of homosexuality we see today; He forbade the sort that incorporated idolatry.

Response One

The prohibitions against homosexuality in Leviticus 18 and 20 appear alongside other sexual sins—adultery and incest, for example—which are forbidden in both the Old and New Testaments, completely apart from the Levitical codes. Scriptural references to these sexual practices, both before and after Leviticus, show God's displeasure with them whether or not any ceremony or idolatry is involved.

Response Two

Despite the UFMCC's contention that the word for *abomination—toevah—*is usually associated with idolatry, it in fact appears in Proverbs 6:16-19 in connection with sins having nothing to do with idolatry or pagan ceremony:

> These six things doth the Lord hate: yea, seven are
> an abomination *[toevah]* unto him: a proud look, a lying

tongue, and hands that shed innocent blood, an heart that deviseth wicked imaginations, feet that be swift in running to mischief, a false witness that speaketh lies, and he that soweth discord among brethren (KJV).

Idolatry plays no part in these Scriptures; clearly, then, *toevah* is not limited to idolatrous practices.

Response Three

You can't have it both ways—if the practices in these chapters are condemned *only* because of their association with idolatry, then it logically follows that they would be permissible if they were committed apart from idolatry.

But that would also mean that incest, adultery, bestiality, and child sacrifice (all of which are listed in these chapters) are also only condemned when associated with idolatry; otherwise, they are allowable. No serious reader of these passages could accept such a premise.

Argument Two: "You're picking and choosing!"

Revisionists often ask, "Even if these scriptures in Leviticus do condemn homosexuality, what's that got to do with us today? Paul clearly said that we, as Christians, are not under the Law."

Because of what Paul wrote, some people assume that even if these verses *do* condemn homosexuality, that condemnation is not relevant to us today. So unless you want to start living under *all* the prohibitions and commandments of the Law, you can't apply these verses to homosexuals. You can't just pick and choose which parts of the Law you want to abide by—it's all or nothing.

Response

A proper reading of the Bible in its entirety shows us the relationship Christians have with the Law. A few points about this need to be made:

1. The Law is good. We as believers are not under the Law, and in fact, we cannot keep it no matter how hard we try. Nonetheless, the

Law itself is good, and the New Testament in no way nullifies it. Paul described the Law as "holy and good" (Romans 7:12) and as a "schoolmaster" that makes us aware of our need for salvation (Galatians 3:24). Jesus Himself said He did not come to destroy the Law, but to fulfill it (Matthew 5:17). So whatever role we assign the Law, we must begin with the premise that it is perfect, just, and good.

2. The New Testament clarifies portions of the Law that are no longer binding to the Christian. When portions of the Law are specifically mentioned in the New Testament as no longer binding, then we are not obliged to keep them. Far from "picking and choosing," this is simply a matter of taking the Bible as a whole. So for example, when Hebrews chapter 12 tells us that we are not bound to sacrifice animals to atone for sin, because Christ's sacrifice is sufficient, we are not ignoring the Law's earlier commandments to make sacrifice. We're simply recognizing that the final sacrifice has been made—so the verses commanding sacrifice are no longer binding.

The same can be said of dietary and ceremonial laws, which were binding to Israel but are not to modern Christian believers, according to Galatians 3:10-13.

3. Some commandments are *contained* in the Law; some also *transcend* the Law. In Leviticus 18 and 20, incest, bestiality, adultery, and homosexuality are prohibited. And these prohibitions are repeated in the New Testament as well, making them not only a part of the Law, but the broader biblical ethic as well. In fact, according to Leviticus 18:27, all the abominations practiced and prohibited in this chapter (adultery, homosexuality, incest, and bestiality) defiled the land when they were committed by the land's inhabitants. God also stated He "abhorred" the people who inhabited the land before Israel did because they practiced these behaviors (Leviticus 20:23). Clearly, these practices offended God no matter who practiced them, or in what context.

In other words, there are some commandments *contained* in the Law that are not binding to believers; others are both *contained* in the Law and also *transcend* the Law.

The commandment to love God, for example, is spelled out in the Law, but it is repeated throughout both Testaments as well. The same is true of the commandments to love one's neighbor, speak the truth, and deal justly with all people. Although these rules are contained in the Law, they're also stressed in the Gospels, the epistles, and the books of wisdom and poetry.

If the commandment to abstain from any form of homosexual behavior was a minor technicality only applicable to Israel during a specified point in history, then it would hardly be worth our attention today. But when a commandment is contained within the Law, then repeated and reiterated throughout Scripture, then it is binding not only today; it is also binding to all.

Let's Talk About
Homosexuality and Leviticus

Pro-gay argument: "The holiness code in Leviticus had to do with Israel, not us. It was necessary for them to procreate to keep their race alive, so of course homosexuality would be looked down on. Besides, we're not under the Law, so why even mention it?"

Response: "You're right about the Law, thank God. We're not under it, and I, for one, am glad, because I'd never be able to keep it. But the chapters in which the Levitical prohibitions against homosexuality appear also contain other sexual sins—adultery and incest, for example—that are condemned in the New Testament as well."

Pro-gay argument: "But homosexuality was associated with idol worship back then. That's why God condemned it."

Response: "Not necessarily. Sure, there were rituals that heathen nations practiced, including all sorts of sexual orgies, homosexual or heterosexual or both. But it's quite a stretch to assume that's the only form of homosexuality practiced at the time. More important, though, is the contingency you seem to be putting into these chapters. Are you saying that if the other sins in those chapters—incest, adultery, and bestiality—weren't associated with idol worship, then they'd be okay too?"

Pro-gay argument: "Of course not!"

Response: "Then you can't have it both ways. Either all the sins in those chapters were condemned because of their association with idolatry, or none of them were."

Pro-gay argument: "So you're saying you believe what Leviticus says about homosexuality being a sin? And that you think homosexuality is wrong?"

Response: "I do."

Pro-gay argument: "Then to be consistent, you also have to believe I should be stoned to death, because that, as you know, is the penalty those verses in Leviticus call for if someone commits a homosexual act."

Response: "Interesting point. Do you believe these chapters also condemn adultery? And do you believe adultery is wrong?"

Pro-gay argument: "Obviously they condemn it, and yes, I believe it's wrong."

Response: "Then to be consistent, you also have to believe that Bill Clinton, Jim Bakker, and Franklin D. Roosevelt should have been stoned to death, because they all committed that sin. And as you know, stoning is the penalty those verses in Leviticus call for if someone commits adultery."

Pro-gay argument: "Nonsense! Just because I think adultery's wrong doesn't mean I think people who commit it should be put to death! If Bill Clinton, Jim Bakker, or Franklin D. Roosevelt had lived in Israel's camp at that time, death would have been their punishment. That's what those verses mean. Adultery's wrong, sure, but in the New Testament, we're certainly not told that adulterers have to be put to death."

Response: "Thank you. I couldn't have said it better myself. If a homosexual was found guilty of that behavior in Old Testament times, death would have been his punishment, as it would have been for the adulterer. But though both are still sins, neither one warrants the death penalty today. That doesn't legitimize them, though. It's possible, as you just said so well, to believe something's wrong without believing the person doing the wrong needs to be penalized in a significant way. And that, to my thinking, is a proper approach to the Old Testament's position on homosexuality."

12

JESUS
AND HOMOSEXUALITY

―――――

*"While some work to clothe Jesus in the silk suit
of a televangelist or the khaki fatigues of a revolutionary,
the harder and humbler task is to hold ourselves
accountable to the truth that was given
two thousand years ago."*

THOMAS SCHMIDT
Straight and Narrow?

Although the Gospels don't contain any account of Jesus speaking directly against homosexuality or dealing with openly homosexual people, the question of what Jesus thought about this behavior is being asked more frequently, with a variety of answers being volunteered. Three in particular have become prominent in gay Christian circles and are being promoted more aggressively.

So in this chapter, we'll look at what pro-gay spokesmen are saying about Jesus and homosexuality, with an emphasis on the common pro-gay arguments about Christ, which are presented to prove the revisionist position:

- Jesus said nothing about homosexuality.
- Jesus mentioned homosexuals favorably when referring to "eunuchs."
- Jesus healed a centurion's male lover, thus offering tacit approval of their homosexual relationship.

Let's look at, and respond to, each of these.

Argument One: *"Jesus said nothing about homosexuality."*

This one is a favorite at gay parades. Invariably, among the representatives of the gay Christian movement, someone will hold up a sign like this:

> ## HERE'S WHAT JESUS SAID ABOUT HOMOSEXUALITY:
>
> _____

The idea, of course, is that if Jesus did not specifically forbid a behavior, then the behavior must not have been important to Him. Stretching the point further, this argument assumes that if Jesus was not manifestly concerned about something, we shouldn't be either.

Troy Perry is typical of gay Christian leaders in making much out of this argument:

> As for the question "What did Jesus say about homosexuality?" the answer is simple. Jesus said nothing. Not one thing. Nothing! Jesus was more interested in love.[1]

So, according to the argument from silence, if Jesus didn't talk about it, neither should we.

Response

This argument is misleading and illogical for four reasons:

First, *the argument assumes that the Gospels are more authoritative than the rest of the books in the Bible.* The idea of a subject being unimportant just because it was not mentioned by Jesus is foreign to the Gospel writers themselves. At no point did Matthew, Mark, Luke, or John say their books should be elevated above the Torah or, for that matter, any writings yet to come. In other words, the Gospels—and the teachings they contain—are not more important than the rest of the Bible. *All* Scripture is given by inspiration of God (2 Timothy 3:16). The same Spirit that inspired the authors of the Gospels also inspired the men who wrote the rest of the Bible.

Second, *the argument assumes that the Gospels are more comprehensive than they really are.* Not only are the Gospels no more authoritative than the rest of Scripture, they're not comprehensive either. That is, they do not provide all we need to know by way of doctrine and practical instruction.

Some of the Bible's most important teaching, in fact, does not appear in the Gospels: the doctrine of man's old and new nature, outlined by Paul in Romans 6; the future of Israel and the mystery of the Gentiles, hinted at by Christ but explained more fully in Romans 9 through 11; the explanation and management of the spiritual gifts, detailed in 1 Corinthians 12 and 14; the priesthood of Christ as illustrated in Hebrews—all of these appear after the Gospel accounts of Christ's life, death, and resurrection. (And we're not even mentioning the entire Old Testament!) Would anyone say these doctrines are unimportant simply because they weren't mentioned by Jesus?

Or, put another way, are we really to believe that Jesus didn't care about wife-beating or incest just because He said nothing about them? Aren't the prohibitions against incest in Leviticus and 1 Corinthians, as well as Paul's admonition to husbands to love their wives, enough to instruct us in these matters, without their being mentioned in the Gospels? There are any number of evil behaviors Jesus did not mention by name; surely we don't condone them for that reason alone!

Likewise, Christ's silence on homosexuality in no way negates the very specific prohibitions against it which appear elsewhere in both the Old and New Testaments.

Third, *this argument is inaccurate in that it presumes to know all of what Jesus said.* The Gospels do not profess to be complete accounts of Jesus' life and teachings. Whole stretches of His early years go undescribed; much of what He did and said remains unknown.

Luke wrote his Gospel so Theophilus would "know the certainty of those things, wherein thou hast been instructed" (1:4 KJV). John's motives are broader: "These are written, that ye might believe that Jesus is the Christ, the Son of God; and that believing ye might have life through his name" (20:31 KJV). But none of these authors suggested they were recording *all* of Christ's words.

John, in fact, said that would have been an impossibility:

> There are also many other things which Jesus did, the which, if they should be written every one, I suppose that even the world itself could not contain the books that should be written (John 21:25 KJV).

If that's the case, how can we be certain He said nothing about homosexuality? No one can say. But we know there are other equally important subjects left undiscussed in the Gospels but mentioned in detail in other books of the Bible. Homosexuality, while absent from Matthew, Mark, Luke, and John, is conspicuously present in both testaments; and, just as conspicuously, it is forbidden.

Fourth, *this argument wrongly assumes that because Jesus said nothing specifically about homosexuality, He said nothing about heterosexuality as a standard.* In Mark 10:6-9, Jesus spoke in the most specific terms about God's created intent for human sexuality:

> From the beginning of the creation God made them male and female. For this cause shall a man leave his father and mother, and cleave to his wife; and they twain shall be one flesh…What therefore God hath joined together, let not man put asunder (KJV).

In this passage, Jesus had been presented with a hypothetical question: Was divorce lawful? Instead of giving a simple "yes" or "no," He referred to the Genesis account and, more specifically, to created *intent* as the standard by which to judge sexual matters. By citing Genesis, He emphasized several key elements of God's created intent for marriage and sexual relating: *Independence* was one—a man was to leave his own home to establish his own family with his wife; a "one flesh" *sexual union* (between male and female—man and wife) was another; and, of course, *monogamy.*

Argument Two: *"Jesus mentioned homosexuals favorably when referring to 'eunuchs.'"*

In his book *Jonathan Loved David,* Episcopal priest Tom Horner suggests that Jesus was referring to homosexuals in Matthew 19:12:

> There are eunuchs who were born thus from their mother's womb, and there are eunuchs who were made eunuchs by men, and there are eunuchs who have made themselves eunuchs for the kingdom of heaven's sake. He who is able to accept it, let him accept it.

Horner stretches the definition of the term *eunuch,* which is traditionally understood to mean a man who is castrated or without reproductive organs, to also include homosexuals,[2] thus bringing homosexual men not only under the umbrella of this passage but also the blessings pronounced in Isaiah, where God promises,

> To the eunuchs…I will give them an everlasting name
> that shall not be cut off (56:4-5).

With this revisionist understanding of *eunuch,* we could assume that eunuchs were and are a special class of individuals, some of whom were born homosexual, and who suffer outcast status but are favored by God much as the meek and the downtrodden, who Jesus described as blessed in the Sermon on the Mount. And of course, we would conclude that Jesus singled them out and recognized that at least some of them are homosexual, implying that, to Him, homosexuality was a nonissue.

Response

This argument is misleading and inaccurate, as it distorts the meaning of the term *eunuch*.

The most glaring contradiction in Horner's use of the term *eunuch* and his application of it to homosexuals lies in the word itself. The Hebrew word used in each Old Testament references to eunuchs is *cariyc*, taken from a root word meaning "to castrate." Eunuchs were, as Jesus said and as is commonly understood, either castrated deliberately to be put into service guarding women without the threat of sexual interaction, or else they were born without testicles. In the New Testament, the term *eunouchos*—"a castrated person, or an impotent man"—is used in both Jesus' and Luke's references to eunuchs (Acts 8:26-40). Either way, the unambiguous meaning of the term had nothing to do with sexual preference and everything to do with sexual function.

Eunuchs were often seen as pitiable, outcast, or second-rate because of their inability to reproduce. And, as always, God expressed a special tenderness to the outcast. Thus the special promises and comfort offered eunuchs in Isaiah's promise. But an unbiased look at the scriptural references to eunuchs would never have yielded Horner's conclusion that homosexuals were included in their ranks.

This is not to say that homosexual eunuchs—men who were sexually attracted to the same sex but were unable to perform sexually—did not exist. It is only to say that homosexuality, or any sexual orientation for that matter, cannot be read into the meaning and concept of *eunuch*.

Argument Three: *"Jesus healed a centurion's male lover, thus offering tacit approval of their homosexual relationship."*

In Matthew 8:5-13, we see a Roman centurion approach Jesus in distress over his servant, who he clearly loved and who was seriously ill:

> When Jesus entered Capernaum, a centurion came to Him, imploring Him, and saying, "Lord, my servant is lying paralyzed at home, fearfully tormented." Jesus said to him, "I will come and heal him." But the centurion said,

"Lord, I am not worthy for You to come under my roof. But just say the word, and my servant will be healed. For I also am a man under authority, having soldiers under me. And I say to this one, 'Go,' and he goes, and to another, 'Come!' and he comes, and to my servant, 'Do this!' and he does it." Now when Jesus heard this, He marveled and said to those who were following, "Truly I say to you, I have not found such great faith, with anyone in Israel"…And his servant was healed that very moment.

Clearly Jesus was pleased with the faith of this centurion and, true to form, He was moved with compassion and healed his servant from a distance. That much we can all agree on.

But in recent years a pro-gay slant to this story has gained popularity. Promoted by Horner and frequently cited on Web-site postings,* this interpretation of Christ's healing of the centurion's servant suggests that the servant and his master had a sexual relationship. Thus, the centurion's concern for the servant was born not of brotherly but romantic love, and Jesus was fully aware they had a same-sex relationship. So, by healing the servant, He offered an endorsement of their love.

The justification for sexualizing the centurion-servant relationship comes from the Greek word *pais,* the word Matthew used when referring to the servant and which, according to Horner, was often a term used to describe the younger partner in a male homosexual union.

Response

This argument is misleading for two primary reasons:

First, while the centurion's love for his *pais* was unquestionable, the knee-jerk conclusion that their love was sexual is very questionable. Other words for a homosexual lover were available at the time Matthew recorded this event, words that would have made a sexual relationship between men much clearer. And while it is true that *at times* there were sexual relations between servants and masters, as there are today between

---

* Such as on the Cathedral of Hope Metropolitan Community Church Web site at www.cathedralofhope.com.

employers and employees, the leap from *at times* to *all the time* is too large. We can no more assume that a slave-master relationship in Christ's time *had* to be sexual just because *some* slave-master relationships were, than we can assume an employer-employee relationship today *has* to be sexual just because *some* employer-employee relationships are.

More important to this discussion, though, is the implication that if Jesus healed someone, He approved of their life in general. This requires a broader leap in logic than the previous assumption because it requires that we accept the idea that Christ endorsed the sexual and moral behavior of every person He healed. And that's too much to require.

It's too much because it first presumes healing to be a reward for merit, rather than an act of grace. Yet nothing in any Gospel, historical, or epistle account of healing implies this. In fact, when Christ healed, it was out of compassion, not obligation.

It's also too much to assume because we know from the Gospels that Christ healed hundreds, perhaps thousands, of individuals in mass settings (see Matthew 4:23-24; 8:16), curing all who were present. Are we really to assume that every sick individual who came to Jesus for healing was living a righteous life, which would make His touch a stamp of approval? The pro-gay interpretation of this story requires that we do make such an assumption, because its strength rests not only on the notion that the centurion and his servant were lovers (a possibility, though unprovable), but also on the assumption that Christ's healing indicated Christ's approval. And that's an assumption nowhere to be found in Scripture or common sense.

But what about the centurion's faith? Jesus declared He'd never seen anything like it, making the pro-gay argument more compelling if indeed the centurion and his servant had a sexual relationship—a possibility, however remote, that we have to allow. Suppose they were lovers. Would that not make Jesus' remarks on this man's faith an endorsement of him and, by extension, his homosexual relationship?

If that were the case, we'd have to concede the point to Horner and other revisionists. But even if we stretch this story to make it one in which Jesus heals a man's male lover while commending the man's faith, we're still left without a confident foundation for the "Jesus approved of homosexuality" approach. Why? Because a person's faith, while laudable, doesn't legitimize his behavior.

Rahab the harlot and her role in Israel's conquest of Jericho illustrate this. When Joshua's spies needed a place to hide while surveying the city, she provided it, striking a bargain with them that they would spare her and her family's lives when they took the city. She feared them and their God, and in honor of that, not only was she spared when Jericho fell, but her name appears in the book of Hebrews' "hall of faith" (11:31).

And she was a harlot. Is anyone really going to suggest that, because she was practicing prostitution at the time God spared her and honored her faith, He somehow approved of her behavior? Her sin didn't nullify her faith, but neither did her faith legitimize her sin. And if indeed the centurion of Matthew 8 was involved in homosexuality when Jesus healed his servant, we would say the same of him as well.

We are left, then, with some general conclusion about the Gospels and pro-gay theology.

1. It's true that homosexuality may not have been mentioned by Jesus, but many other sexual sins weren't either. But He couldn't have spelled out the standard for sexual expression more clearly: male to female, joined as God intended them to be. Jesus can't be assumed to have approved of anything less.

2. Jesus reiterated the place eunuchs, and indeed all outcasts, have in God's heart, but to read *homosexual* into *eunuch* is akin to reading *sexual orientation* into the word *castration*. The two are simply worlds apart.

3. While there's a remote, though unlikely, possibility Jesus was healing a man's homosexual lover when He healed the centurion's servant, *healing* and *approval* are two very different things as well. Likewise,

commendation of a man's faith can't be construed as a blessing on a man's behavior.

Let's Talk About Jesus and Homosexuality

Pro-gay argument: "How come you're so against homosexuality? Jesus didn't say a word against it."

Response: "I'm no more against homosexuality than any other sin. And frankly, whether or not Jesus mentioned it is a secondary point. It's plainly condemned in other scriptures."

Pro-gay argument: "But His teachings are the foundation of the faith!"

Response: "Not exclusively. Paul said *all* Scripture—that means the whole Bible—is profitable for instruction in righteousness. Christ's teachings are very important, sure. But they're not meant to be our only source of guidance. If that were the case, we wouldn't need a 66-book Bible; we'd just use the four Gospels. But there's plenty of important doctrinal and historical information in the other books as well. They carry as much weight as the Gospels."

Pro-gay argument: "Still, if Jesus thought homosexuality was important, don't you think it's strange He said nothing about it?"

Response: "Who's to say He didn't? He might have said quite a bit on the subject but it never got recorded. But even if He didn't, that's no proof it wasn't important to Him. He didn't explicitly say anything in the Gospels about wife-beating or child abuse either, but I'm sure they were important to Him."

Pro-gay argument: "Wrong! He held up a standard of love for children and respect for women, so it's obvious He did not approve of abusing them."

Response: "Exactly. He also held up a standard for sexual relationships when He referred to the marriage of a man and a woman as being God's intention. So even if He didn't say anything about homosexuality, it's obvious He didn't approve of it—just as

He didn't approve of anything short of God's intention for the sexual experience, which He clearly said was marriage."

Pro-gay argument: "That's an argument from silence."
Response: "So is yours. You see? You can't prove Jesus condoned something just because He didn't mention it. I can't prove what He said or didn't say about it either. But I do know what He upheld as a standard, and it certainly wasn't homosexuality."

Pro-gay argument: "Yet He taught that eunuchs have a place in the kingdom, and that would include gays."
Response: "A eunuch was a man who'd either been castrated or who'd been born without reproductive organs. Surely you don't think that's the definition of the average homosexual."

Pro-gay argument: "Eunuchs were outcasts. So are gays and lesbians. And it looks like, in some cases, eunuchs were gay."
Response: "Perhaps, but what made them eunuchs wasn't their orientation, but the fact they were unable to reproduce. Lesbian women and gay men can, by and large, reproduce, and in most cases their organs are intact. So the word *eunuch* really doesn't apply to them."

Pro-gay argument: "But if Jesus Himself approved of a gay relationship, you'd have to concede He approves of homosexuality, wouldn't you?"
Response: "I suppose. What relationship are you referring to?"

Pro-gay argument: "The relationship between a centurion and his servant, who Jesus healed. The Gospel says he loved his servant, and in those days, centurions often had sexual relationships with their servants. And not only did Jesus heal this man's lover, but He openly commended the man's faith! How could that be, if He disapproved of their relationship?"
Response: "Your question makes several assumptions, so let me answer each of them. First, we don't know that these two had a sexual relationship. Yes, at times, centurions had relations with their slaves. That doesn't mean every centurion did. Bosses sometimes have affairs with their assistants too, but we don't assume every boss and assistant are involved. So right off the bat your argument

unravels, because you've no way of knowing that the relationship between the servant and the centurion was sexual.

"Second, even if they *did* have a sexual relationship, do you really think Jesus approved of the lifestyle of every person He healed? Healing is an act of grace, not a stamp of approval, and nothing in Scripture indicates He granted it as a reward.

"Finally, if in fact they were homosexual, Jesus could well recognize someone's faith and even commend it without necessarily condoning their behavior. Does Rahab the harlot come to mind? She was clearly a woman of faith, and there were parts of her life that sure didn't square with God's will."

Pro-gay argument: "But God is love—and that, after all, is what Jesus taught: that we're to love each other. That's what He was all about."

Response: "Not quite. Yes, He taught us to love one another, and we sure could do a better job of it. But He also taught obedience, repentance, and the need to conform our lives to God's will, not ours. So when you say, 'All He taught is love,' you oversimplify both Him and His teachings. And that's something none of us, I'm sure, wants to do."

13

PAUL AND HOMOSEXUALITY

"Arguments about the genetic or sociological origins
on homosexuality, about genuinely loving homosexual
relationships—none of these would impress Paul. He would
simply understand the use of such information in arguments
for the acceptance of homosexual behavior as further
evidence of the blindness of humanity in bondage to sin."

MARION SOARDS
Scripture and Homosexuality

Three pointed condemnations of homosexuality can be found in the New Testament, and all of them come from the apostle Paul. In the book of Romans, he refers to both the behavior and the internal attractions; he references the behavior apart from the orientation in 1 Corinthians and 1 Timothy. A key point is, in each case he cites homosexuality as either a symptom of larger problems, or as one of many sexual and nonsexual immoral behaviors. He consistently treats the matter as something his readers no doubt recognized as being wrong—as a "given"—so he spends no time arguing the point.

Compare this to the way he condemns legalism in the book of Galatians and then spends whole chapters explaining and defending his condemnation of it. Here, as at other times, Paul not only condemns a thing; he then tries to persuade his readers to share his condemnation, in case they're still unconvinced. In contrast, Paul mentions homosexual sin much as he mentions adultery, deceit, or fraud—things inarguably wrong, their wrongness requiring no explanation. He cites it as an example of things commonly understood to be ungodly. In all three books, he includes it in a list of vices, though in Romans it begins the list and is given more descriptive detail than the other sins included.

In short, Paul clearly understood homosexuality to be wrong and unnatural, and he wrote as though he assumed his readers shared his views, though he did not single it out as a sin graver than others. And he viewed it as a symptom of the fallen nature, one that should never appear among Christians, and one that at least some of his readers had themselves at one time been involved in (see 1 Corinthians 6:9-11).

Let's look specifically at the books and verses in question.

"Natural" vs. "Unnatural": Romans 1:26-27

> For this cause God gave them up unto vile affections: for even their women did change the natural use into that which is against nature: And likewise also the men, leaving the natural use of the woman, burned in their lust one toward another; men with men working that which is unseemly, and receiving in themselves the recompence of their error which was meet (KJV).

TRADITIONAL VIEW

Paul begins Romans by describing humanity in its unredeemed, rebellious state. His goal is not to pick out any particular sin and condemn it, but rather to prove that all people—whether Gentile or Jewish—are lost until they are redeemed by Christ. He starts with the human race in general, stating that all people have a consciousness of God but, in their fallen state, deliberately ignore both it and Him and live as they please (1:18-21). This is not a limited, select group of people Paul is describing here—he's providing a wholesale view of all people born in sin. Accordingly, their hearts and minds became "darkened" and idolatrous (verses 21-23).

He then cites homosexuality as a symptom of the problem, describing it as unnatural and unseemly, then cites several other sins that, along with homosexuality, are common. (However, of all the sins listed here, only sexual relations between members of the same sex are described as "unnatural.")

Chapter 1 ends with a summation that anyone practicing these sins is worthy of death, thus placing all Gentiles under a death sentence. Paul doesn't assume everyone is guilty of committing *all* the sins he names, but he does assume those sins are commonly practiced, and that no one could hear or read this chapter without finding a few of his own transgressions on the list.

Then in chapter 2, Paul turns to his Jewish audience and tells them, essentially, not to assure themselves that they also are not under a death sentence, since sinful practices are found among all people, Jewish and non-Jewish. In short, Paul opens Romans with a sweeping condemnation of everyone and an appeal to trust in Christ's atonement, not themselves or their own righteousness.

Argument One: "In these verses, Paul is not describing true homosexuals, but heterosexuals who practice homosexuality, thus 'changing their nature,' which is something God abhors."

The real sin here, according to this argument, is in changing what is natural to the *individual*. Boswell takes this argument up:

> The persons Paul condemns are manifestly not homosexual: what he derogates are homosexual acts committed by apparently heterosexual persons. The whole point of Romans 1, in fact, is to stigmatize persons who have rejected their calling, gotten off the true path they were once on.[1]

Scanzoni and Mollenkott agree:

> What Paul seems to be emphasizing here is that persons who are heterosexual by nature have not only exchanged the

true God for a false one but have also exchanged their ability to relate to the opposite sex by indulging in homosexual behavior that is not natural *to them.*[2]

In short, Paul in Romans 1 describes *heterosexuals* who have deliberately committed *homosexual* acts, thus violating their true nature. This, they maintain, has nothing to do with lesbians and gays who are in loving, committed relationships and to whom these relationships come naturally. Homosexuality, they contend, if committed by true homosexuals, is, therefore, not a sin and is not referenced here.

Response

Paul is not speaking nearly so subjectively in Romans 1 as this argument would suggest. There is nothing in his wording to imply he even recognized such a thing as a "true" homosexual versus a "false" one. He simply describes homosexual *behavior* as unnatural, no matter who it is committed by.

In fact, his wording is unusually specific. When he refers to "men" and "women" in these verses, he chooses the Greek words that most emphasize physiology: *arsenes* and *theleias.* Both words are rarely used in the New Testament; when they do appear, they appear in contexts meant to emphasize the gender of the subject, as in a *male* child *(arsenes).* Here, Paul is very pointedly saying that the homosexual behavior committed by these people was unnatural to them as males and females *(arsenes* and *theleias);* he is not considering any such thing as sexual orientation. He is saying, in other words, that homosexuality is biologically unnatural—not just unnatural to heterosexuals, but unnatural to *anyone.*

Additionally, the fact that these men "burned in their lust" for each other makes it highly unlikely that they were heterosexuals experimenting with homosexuality. Their behavior was born of an intense inner desire. Suggesting, as Boswell and Mollenkott do, that these men were heterosexuals indulging in homosexual behavior requires mental gymnastics.

Besides, if verses 26 and 27 condemn homosexual actions committed by people to whom they did not come naturally, but don't apply to people to whom those actions do come naturally, then doesn't consistency compel us to apply the same logic to *all* the practices mentioned in this chapter? We would have to say that it's not only homosexuality that is not condemned in these verses—if practiced by someone to whom it comes naturally and in the context of a loving relationship. We would have to say that *all* of these behaviors—if practiced by someone to whom they come naturally and in the context of a loving relationship—are not condemned in these verses.

Read Romans chapter 1 again, and you'll notice that between verses 20 and 31, Paul names 24 sins:

1. homosexuality	13. backbiting
2. unrighteousness	14. hating God
3. sexual immorality	15. violence
4. wickedness	16. pride
5. covetousness	17. boasting
6. maliciousness	18. inventing evil things
7. envy	19. disobedience to parents
8. murder	20. lack of discernment
9. strife	21. untrustworthiness
10. deceit	22. lack of love
11. evil-mindedness	23. lack of forgiveness
12. whispering	24. lack of mercy

Boswell, Mollenkott, and others suggest that sin number 1—homosexuality—is only a sin if it doesn't come naturally to you. But I doubt any pro-gay apologist would apply the same contingency to sins numbers 2 through 24. But why not? Since they're all lumped together in the same passage, wouldn't logic require it? Bishop Bennett Sims points this out in an interview with *Christianity Today* magazine:

> The logical effect of the exemption argument is to suggest that, given the proper motivation, there are loving ways to be "full of envy, murder, strife, malignity"…this is moral absurdity.[3]

To which I would add, as in the case of the prohibitions against homosexuality in Leviticus and the pro-gay contingencies applied to them, you simply cannot have it both ways.

Argument Two: "These verses only apply to people given over to idolatry, not gay Christians who worship the true God."

Verse 23 in Romans 1 describes people as having "changed the glory of the incorruptible God into an image like corruptible man—and birds and four-footed animals and creeping things." Based on this, some pro-gay apologists argue that this chapter can only be applied to people who blatantly worship idols or false gods. Troy Perry, for example, declares,

> The homosexual practices cited in Romans 1:24-27 were believed to result from idolatry and are associated with some very serious offenses as noted in Romans 1. Taken in this larger context, it should be obvious that such acts are significantly different than loving, responsible lesbian and gay relationships seen today.[4]

Response

Idolatry certainly plays a major role in Romans 1. Paul begins his writing by describing humanity's rebellion and decision to worship the creation rather than the Creator. The pro-gay theorist seizes on this concept to prove that Paul's condemnation of homosexuality does not apply to him. He does not worship idols; he is a Christian.

Thomas Schmidt cautions against this line of thought:

> Paul is not suggesting that a person worships an idol and decides therefore to engage in same-sex relations. Rather, he is suggesting that the general rebellion created the environment for the specific rebellion. A person need not bow before a golden calf to participate in the general human denial of God or to express that denial through specific behaviors.[5]

A commonsense look at the entire chapter bears this out. Consider again the 24 sins listed in this chapter. Will the "idolatry" interpretation, applied to homosexuality, also apply to numbers 2 through 24 on this list? Are they also sinful only if practiced in the context of idolatry, but legitimate if practiced, as Perry argues, in a "loving, responsible" way?

This, of course, is ridiculous. Like homosexuality, these sins are not born just out of idol worship; they are symptomatic of a fallen state. If we are to say homosexuality is legitimate so long as it's not a result of idol worship, then we also have to say these other sins are legitimate as well…so long as they too are not practiced as a result of idolatry.

Argument Three: "Paul is describing excessive, irresponsible sexual behavior based on lust and promiscuity. This has nothing to do with responsible, committed, loving homosexual relationships."

Though none of the major pro-gay theorists mention this in their writings, I've heard the above idea often enough to feel it warrants inclusion here. Often, when my gay friends and I would have candid conversations about the Bible, we'd get stuck on Romans 1. We'd begin wondering if there was any way to get around it. That's when someone in the group would say, "Well, I don't go around 'burning in lust' for people, or jump in bed with just anyone. So I really don't see myself in Romans 1." And that, at first glance, seemed good enough to quiet our doubts.

Response

The people practicing homosexuality in this chapter were, according to Paul's wording, lusting after members of the same sex and engaging in same-sex erotic acts. Nothing in his phrasing or choice of words states, or even implies, that they were doing it with many people of the same sex, or that they were doing it frequently or randomly. In other words, Paul condemns the thing itself, without qualifying the condemnation to apply only to homosexuality practiced "irresponsibly" or with many partners. Like adultery or fornication, it's no less a sin if it's committed once in a lifetime with one partner; no more a sin if it's committed daily with several partners. The condemnation here is of the thing itself, not the way it's practiced.

Paul's Use of the Terms Malakos and Arsenokoite: 1 Corinthians 6:9-10 and 1 Timothy 1:9-10

> Know ye not that the unrighteous shall not inherit the kingdom of God? Be not deceived: neither fornicators, nor idolaters, nor adulterers, nor effeminate [Greek *malakos*], nor abusers of themselves with mankind [Greek *arsenokoite*], nor thieves, nor covetous, nor drunkards, nor revilers, nor extortioners shall inherit the kingdom of God (1 Corinthians 6:9-10 KJV).

> The law is not made for a righteous man, but for the lawless and disobedient, for the ungodly and for sinners, for unholy and profane, for murderers of fathers and murderers of mothers, for manslayers, for whoremongers, for them that defile themselves with mankind [Greek *arsenokoite*], for menstealers, for liars, for perjured persons, and if there be any other thing that is contrary to sound doctrine; according to the glorious gospel of the blessed God, which was committed to my trust (1 Timothy 1:9-11 KJV).

In Romans, Paul describes homosexuality in some detail. However, in these two books he simply mentions it, listing it with other behaviors while trying to make a point.

In 1 Corinthians, his point is that believers' personal conduct should be in sharp contrast to that of nonbelievers. Appealing to the need for a way of life separate from the world's, Paul writes in a way reminiscent of Moses' words in Leviticus 18 and 20, where Israel's leader points to God's commandments that the Israelites apply a different standard to their sexual behavior than that of other nations.

In 1 Timothy 1, Paul points out the rightful use of Old Testament Law (verse 8) and lists many of the sins it condemns. And, more pointedly, he cites people who practice these sins and are thereby convicted by the Law, which is one of its primary purposes (see also Romans 7:7-12).

In both passages, Paul uses the term *arsenokoite* when referring to male homosexuality (lesbianism is mentioned only once in Scripture, in Romans 1:26). This term is translated "abusers of themselves with mankind" (1 Corinthians) or "those that defile themselves with mankind" (1 Timothy) in the King James Version. The word is translated "sodomites" in the New King James Version; "homosexual offenders" in the New International Version.

In 1 Corinthians 6 Paul also mentions *malakos*, translated "effeminate" in the King James Version; "male prostitutes" in the New International Version; "homosexuals" in the New King James Version.

Everyone agrees Paul is condemning both sexual and nonsexual sins in these chapters. Disagreement arises between traditionalists and pro-gay apologists, though, over which particular sexual acts Paul was condemning.

TRADITIONAL VIEW

In his references to *arsenokoite*, meaning "homosexual," and *malakos*, meaning "homosexual prostitution" or possibly "pederasty" (sex between adult men and younger boys), Paul is saying that homosexuality, homosexual prostitution, and pederasty are vices excluding their practitioners from the kingdom of God, or which are soundly condemned in the Law.

Argument One: "Paul was referring to prostitution only, or immoral behavior in general, when he mentioned arsenokoite. *And* malakos *doesn't refer to gay men, but rather to men who prostitute themselves, probably dressed as females or at least assuming a feminine sexual role."*

John Boswell argues the above contention the most cogently, though it's a point raised by virtually every pro-gay apologist. *Arsenokoite*, they maintain, is a word coined by Paul. It had never appeared in Greek literature before he used it in these scriptures. However, at the time there were other words for "homosexual" available in Greek. Had Paul meant to refer to homosexuality, he would have used one of the words already in existence. This Boswell sees as one of his strongest selling points for pro-gay theology, one in which he comes into sharp conflict with traditionalists.

On the proper translation of *malakos* there may be less resistance

Precise Definitions

Strong's concordance translates *arsenokoite* to mean "a Sodomite," in obvious reference to Sodom. The *Arndt-Gingrich Greek Lexicon* defines it as "a male who practices homosexuality, pederast, sodomite" and cites Romans 1:27 as an example. *Thayer's Greek Lexicon* has the same take on the word; indeed, according to Timothy Dailey's book *The Bible, Church, and Homosexuality*, no lexicon can be found that doesn't equate *arsenokoite* with male homosexuality.[6]

Malakos is translated by Strong's concordance as "soft, fine clothing" and, figuratively, as "catamite" (a male religious prostitute, probably effeminate in nature and clothed as a woman). The *Arndt-Gingrich Greek Lexicon* says *malakos* refers to "men and boys who allow themselves to be misused homosexually," applying the term to either effeminate male prostitutes or to youths who provided sexual favors to older men. In both passages, then, Paul seems to be condemning both male homosexuality between consenting adult men and also homosexual prostitution—whether practiced between a man and an effeminate "call boy" dressed as a woman, or between older men and younger boys.

to Boswell. The word appears not only in these passages, but also in Matthew 11:8 and Luke 7:25, when Jesus describes those who are "gorgeously appareled and live in luxury." Whether in these verses He's referring to rather weak, indolent men, or to those who literally service kings as cross-dressed prostitutes, is unclear. What *is* clear is that such men, though obviously spoken of critically by Jesus and Paul, were not necessarily homosexuals. Whether homosexual or heterosexual in their desires, they most likely were men who engaged in homosexual sex for pay or reward. Thus they were never representative of most homosexuals. On this point we agree with Boswell and others: *malakos* is not a term condemning all forms of homosexuality.

But when traditionalists argue that *arsenokoite* does offer such a sweeping condemnation, Boswell points out the word is peculiar to Paul, suggesting he didn't have homosexuality in mind when he used it. Prostitution is Boswell's first choice:

Arsenokoite, then, means "male sexual agents," i.e. active

> male prostitutes, who were common throughout the Hel-
> lenistic world in the time of Paul…male prostitutes capable
> of the active role with either men or women.[7]

And if it wasn't male prostitutes who were the specific target of Paul's criticism, Boswell suggests he was condemning general immorality, rather than homosexuality per se.[8] At any rate, according to this argument, the term refers to some sort of immoral man, but not to a homosexual.

Response

Paul's coining of a new term isn't out of character—he coined 179 terms in the New Testament. Coined terms do not, simply because they are original to the "coiner," significantly change the context of the verses they appear in.

It's especially unremarkable that he would have coined *arsenokoite*, considering the Greek root words it employs and the source he seems to have drawn the phrase from.

Arsenokoite is a combination of the words *arsenos* and *koite*, both of which appear infrequently in the New Testament. *Arsenos* was mentioned earlier in this chapter as to its appearance in Romans 1. It refers to a male (or males—*arsenes*) with an emphasis on their gender. *Koite* appears only twice in the New Testament, and it means *bed* or *couch* used in a sexual connotation:

> Let us walk honestly…not in chambering [*koite*] (Romans 13:13 KJV).

> Marriage is honorable…and the bed [*koite*] undefiled (Hebrews 13:4).

The first striking point about Paul's use of these two words when creating the term *arsenokoite* is that there's nothing in the words *male* or *bed* implying trade, buying, or selling, making Boswell's guess that the term referred to prostitution an unlikely one. The two words, as Paul combined them, put *male* and *bed* together in a sexual sense, with no hint of prostitution involved. This is not to say that later writers could not use the word to mean something more general, such as a "base" or "lewd" man. They could, but in so doing, even if their intent was clear, it would be a technical misuse of the word.

For example, in modern English, the word *whore,* which technically means *prostitute,* is often used to describe a woman who is morally loose and promiscuous but doesn't actually sell herself for sex and is not, therefore, a true prostitute. Likewise, some may refer to a cruel, thoughtless man as a *bastard,* a term literally meaning someone born out of wedlock, but used figuratively to malign someone's character in general. In both cases, we may know the speaker's intent while recognizing that he's technically, linguistically in error.

The same may be said for *arsenokoite.* While Boswell correctly points out other authors' later use of it when referring to men who commit immorality—but not necessarily with other men—those authors too miss Paul's original, technical meaning.

Arsenokoite (males combined with *bed* or *couch)* is, as Timothy Dailey points out, the Greek counterpart to the Hebrew phrase *mishkab zakur.*[9] *Mishkab* is Hebrew for *bed* or *couch* with a sexual connotation; *zakur* in Hebrew means *male* or *males.* The phrase *mishkab zakur* is found in Leviticus 18:22 and 20:13, where sex between men is expressly forbidden. This makes it impossible to accept Boswell's suggestion that Paul meant anything other than homosexuality when using the term *arsenokoite,* considering that it's derived directly from the Hebrew prohibitions of that very thing!

Indeed, the Septuagint, which is the Greek translation of the Old Testament, uses the terms *arsenos* and *koite* when translating prohibitions against homosexuality in those same passages in Leviticus:

> Thou shalt not lie with mankind as with womankind (Leviticus 18:22 KJV).
> *meta* **arsenos** *ou koimethese* **koiten** *gyniakos*

> If a man also lie with mankind, as he lieth with a woman, both of them have committed an abomination (Leviticus 20:13 KJV).
> *hos an koimethe meta* **arsenos** **koiten** *gynaikos*

When Paul coined the term *arsenokoite,* he took it directly from the Greek translation of Leviticus's prohibitions against homosexual behavior. His intent couldn't be clearer. Though *arsenokoite* is unique to Paul, it refers specifically and unambiguously to sex between men.

One final point needs to be considered, though, before moving on from Paul's teachings. While his specific condemnations of homosexuality are evidence enough against the revisionist view, his statements about the nature of a Christian in general should be considered as well, especially in response to common pro-gay arguments about the cause and nature of homosexuality.

Paul describes an internal war we as believers experience on a regular basis: a relentless conflict between the desires of our flesh, which are invariably ungodly, and those of our new spiritual nature, which tend toward life and righteousness (Romans 7:15-25; Galatians 5:16-25). Nowhere does he suggest this struggle will end in this life. On the contrary, he virtually promises it will continue, sometimes ferociously, sometimes mildly. Because of this, he encourages us to put to death desires that may seem natural to us (Romans 6:12-14) and yield our bodies daily to God's will and service (Romans 12:1). If, in the process of doing this, we find our carnal desires diminishing, so much the better. But it's obedience, not absence of temptation, that God requires.

In this light we can sympathize with the deeply ingrained nature of homosexuality, no matter what its origins, as we realize our own deeply ingrained sinful desires. And since no human being chooses the inherited Adamic nature, we can concur that homosexuals, by and large, have not chosen their orientation. But we can and must declare that if they claim to belong to Christ, then they, like us, are required to put aside what seems natural, deeply ingrained, and even unchangeable within, and submit themselves as living sacrifices to God, yielding to His purposes instead of those passions. Only then can they, or any of us, find true peace.

Let's Talk About Paul
and Homosexuality

Pro-gay argument: "I know you think the New Testament has a lot to say against homosexuality, but actually, if you study its original language and intent, you'll find it doesn't."

Response: "That's certainly not true of the first chapter of Romans. Paul lists quite a few sins there—homosexuality included. Of course, homosexuality is not the major sin of Romans 1, any more than it's the main sin in Leviticus. But it's definitely there, condemned and forbidden."

Pro-gay argument: "But the people Paul described in Romans 1 weren't really gay. That's why it was a sin! God didn't want them changing their nature. They were heterosexuals indulging in homosexuality. What made it wrong was the fact that it wasn't natural to them. Otherwise, it would have been fine."

Response: "And what about the gossips, adulterers, and backbiters in Romans 1? Were they also people who weren't 'really' gossips, adulterers, or backbiters? It didn't come naturally to them—*that* was the problem? I don't think so. Nothing in Scripture says a certain sexual behavior is a sin unless it somehow comes naturally to you but not the rest of us."

Pro-gay argument: "But I don't think Paul had any idea what it was like to be truly gay."

Response: "Probably not, but he knew what it was like to wrestle with sin, and he said so plainly. Anyway, I don't think it would have mattered one bit whether or not he personally struggled with homosexual sin. It's the behavior he condemned, without even considering what factors might have led someone to that behavior in the first place."

Pro-gay argument: "But Paul lived in a time when they knew nothing about homosexuality as we know it today. At that time, it mainly meant sex between adults and minors—pederasty—or prostitution maybe. That's what Paul condemned, not homosexuality as we know it today."

Response: "Actually, you're both misrepresenting the times and underestimating Paul. The idea of adult, mutually consensual homosexuality wasn't so foreign at that time. Gay historian John Boswell himself claims the idea that people were born gay was prevalent in Hellenistic times and that Aristotle himself both understood and approved of the homosexual orientation.[10] And to suggest Paul was unaware of these prominent figures is as much of a stretch as suggesting that modern preachers would be unaware of Sigmund Freud. Besides which, don't you believe the Bible was divinely inspired?"

Pro-gay argument: "Of course!"

Response: "Then if the Holy Spirit, who is God, inspired its writers, surely God Himself was aware of everything we now know about homosexuality, and then some! By the way, it's not only in Romans that Paul mentions homosexuality. Later in the New Testament, in 1 Corinthians and 1 Timothy, he lists homosexuality as one of the many sins keeping people away from God."

Pro-gay argument: "But the word he uses for *homosexuals* in those Scriptures really means *male prostitutes.*"

Response: "Where did you get that idea?"

Pro-gay argument: "I've read it time and again. Theologians have done careful word studies on Paul, and that's what they've found. The word Paul used—the one we usually think of as meaning *homosexual*—didn't mean homosexual at all."

Response: "Well, it certainly didn't mean *prostitute.* The word you're talking about is *arsenokoite.* It's a Greek term Paul developed directly from the Greek translation of the Old Testament—in fact, from the Leviticus verses that specifically refer to homosexuality, not prostitution. So there's no way Paul could have meant it as anything but a reference to homosexuality. Besides, if you look at the word itself—a compound of the Greek words *arsenos,* meaning 'male,' and *koite,* meaning 'bed or couch,' you'll see there's nothing in the word even suggesting prostitution. It's sex between men, not sex for money, that Paul is writing against."

Pro-gay argument: "Well, I still believe the Bible doesn't say anything against my sexuality. God loves me as I am, and I stand on that."

Response: "And you have every right to. But at some point you've got to ask yourself, Do I believe the pro-gay theology because I really think it's true—or because, despite the majority opinion of Bible scholars as well as a commonsense reading of the Scriptures, I *want* to believe it? Is it *conviction* we're talking about here, or *convenience?* Only you can answer that."

PART FOUR

Putting Knowledge into Action

14

A TIME TO SPEAK

*"Have no fellowship with the unfruitful
works of darkness, but rather expose them."*

EPHESIANS 5:11

Corruption thrives in a fallen world, where so little goes according to God's plan and so much runs in opposition to it. Much as we may enjoy singing the old hymn "This Is My Father's World," Scripture indicates it is a world wholly at odds with its Creator.

When Satan tempted the Lord in the wilderness (Matthew 4:1-11), he showed Him all the kingdoms of the earth, then made an astounding offer: "All these things will I give thee, if thou wilt fall down and worship me" (verse 9 KJV).

Jesus refused the offer without challenging the indication that Satan had the right to "give" Him all the kingdoms of the earth. He knew, as did Satan, that in its present state the world runs as Paul said it does—"according to the prince of the power of the air, the spirit that now worketh in the children of disobedience" (Ephesians 2:2 KJV).

In such an environment it's no surprise to find sexual sin on display. In fact, Paul told the Corinthian church that if they wanted to avoid fornicators they would have to leave the world (1 Corinthians 5:9-10). And though it's important to take a moral stand even in this fallen world, it's more important to remember the priority issue—if people are without Christ, they are *dead;* their immorality is secondary. A public stand against their sins should include an invitation to grace and a recognition that their behavior is symptomatic of a larger problem.

Sin among Christians, or groups calling themselves Christians, is another matter. When it's being practiced without remorse, or redefined from a "vice" to a "gift," the church is called to confront it—not just as sin, but as behavior that no one naming the name of Christ should be involved in! Immorality is serious enough in anyone's life; it becomes doubly serious when practiced by professing believers.

When gays claim that homosexuality is God's gift and bring that claim into our churches, then confrontation is a mandate for three reasons. First, *the church's integrity is compromised when professing Christians misrepresent Christianity.*

When people claiming to follow Christ misrepresent Him through heresy or immorality, Christians need to protest. A number of years ago an unusually blasphemous movie, titled *The Last Temptation of Christ,* was released, outrageously misrepresenting Jesus. Christians around the country protested; truth was being perverted and passed off as gospel.

So it is with the gay Christian movement: Its claims pervert the truth about God's intentions, thereby misrepresenting Him. And Christians need to protest. If homosexuals are comfortable with their behavior, that is one matter; when they say it is done with the blessings of Christianity, then the church, indignantly, should insist as Paul did: "The Lord knoweth them that are his. And, let everyone that nameth the name of Christ depart from iniquity" (2 Timothy 2:19 KJV).

Second, confrontation is necessary because *the gay Christian movement asks us to confirm its members in their sin, when we are biblically commanded to do just the opposite.* As Christ's ambassadors on earth—and members of His body—we unfaithfully represent Him if a professing believer's ongoing sin has no effect on our relationship with that professing believer. This is, in essence, what Paul told the Thessalonians:

> We command you, brethren, in the name of our Lord Jesus Christ, that ye withdraw yourselves from every brother that walketh disorderly, and not after the tradition which he received of us…And if any man obey not our word by this epistle, note that man, and have no company with him, that he may be ashamed. Yet count him not as an enemy, but admonish him as a brother (2 Thessalonians 3:6,14-15 KJV).

Finally, *unrepentant sin among believers is like a disease; eventually it will spread and affect the entire body.* When Paul heard of a Corinthian church member's incestuous relationship with his stepmother, he ordered the man excommunicated (1 Corinthians 5:1-5). Then he explained the principle of confrontation and—if necessary—expulsion from the community of believers:

> Know ye not that a little leaven leaveneth the whole lump? Purge out therefore the old leaven (verses 6-7 KJV).

A healthy body purges itself of impurities; the body of Christ cannot afford to do less. Confrontation is messy business. It's unnerving and painful; if it isn't, there's probably something wrong with whoever's doing the confronting! And it certainly does not match the "nice" image, mentioned earlier, that so many people have of Christianity.

Yet the first New Testament figure to encourage confrontation among believers was Jesus Himself. "If thy brother trespass against thee," He instructed, "go and tell him his fault" (Matthew 18:15 KJV). He then outlined a plan for continued confrontation if the erring brother did not repent: The last step was to hale him in front of the church, and then, if he was still unrepentant, treat him as an outcast (verses15-19).

The same Jesus who was gentle and forgiving, never winked at sin.

He expected it to be dealt with among His followers. He still does. Consider His rebuke to the church of Thyatira:

> I have a few things against thee, because thou sufferest that woman Jezebel, which calleth herself a prophetess, to teach and to seduce my servants to commit fornication… Behold, I will cast her into a bed, and them that commit adultery with her into great tribulation, except they repent of their deeds (Revelation 2:20-22 KJV).

Jesus held the Thyatiran church responsible for allowing false teaching to seduce His people. Let the church stand warned: If the gay Christian movement goes unconfronted, its members won't be the only ones facing His displeasure in the end.

How to Confront

How we confront the gay Christian movement is crucial. Paul's instruction—"Yet count him not as an enemy but admonish him as a brother" (2 Timothy 3:15 KJV)—should be kept in mind. The members of the gay Christian movement are not our enemies. They claim Christ as their own. I, for one, am not going to judge whether or not they truly know Him. Most of those I knew personally had a genuine salvation experience before they joined the gay church. And who is to say if, and at what point, they may have lost the salvation they found years earlier?

The pro-gay theology is a strong delusion—a seductive accommodation tailor-made to suit the Christian who struggles against homosexual temptations and is considering a compromise. Some who call themselves gay Christians may be truly deceived into accepting it (I certainly was); others might be in simple rebellion. What compels them to believe a lie, we cannot say. What we *can* say is this: They are wrong—dead wrong.

When we confront them and their beliefs, we should do it wisely, understanding our motives and concerns and expressing them clearly. That's why chapters 1 through 4—explaining why we should be concerned about homosexuality in the church, then outlining the history of the gay-rights and gay Christian movements—were included. Confrontation is effective when we understand both why we need to confront and the backgrounds of the people we are confronting.

Then we need to begin with ourselves. Jesus warned His disciples, and us, against rebuking others without self-examination:

> Why beholdest thou the mote that is in thy brother's eye, but considerest not the beam that is in thine own eye?... Thou hypocrite, first cast out the beam out of thine own eye; and then shalt thou see clearly to cast out the mote out of thy brother's eye (Matthew 7:3,5 KJV).

It would take unusual arrogance to think that we can approach the gay Christian movement as righteous folks approaching degenerates. If the major scandals in the body of Christ over the past quarter-century—scandals involving televangelists, famous preachers, renowned authors, and internationally acclaimed Christian musicians—have proven anything, it's that the body of Christ is not immune to sexual sin. It's not just the gay Christian movement that's in error; *we* are in error, and seriously.

This prompted commentator Cal Thomas to pose the question, "Why should the majority accept something they have not seen fully lived out by those who profess to believe?"[1]

Thomas's words do not negate our responsibility to confront the gay Christian movement, but they do caution us to represent ourselves honestly when we approach them: as sinners approaching other sinners, nothing more. Reverend Andrew Aquino of the Columbus Baptist Association expressed this perfectly: "My message to the homosexual is: 'We love you. Come and struggle with us against sin. Don't give in to it.'"[2]

"If a man be overtaken in a fault," Paul said, "restore such an one in the spirit of meekness, considering thyself, lest thou also be tempted" (Galatians 6:1 KJV). Self-examination and a right attitude are prerequisites to confrontation; without them our words will ring hollow, or destructive, or both. Before confrontation, then, there should be self-examination and repentance.

There should also be wisdom. Going off half-cocked to the local gay church and shaking our fists at its members won't do much good. Tracking down pro-gay spokesmen and challenging them to public debates usually isn't very effective either. It drains away time and energy better spent elsewhere. A commitment to confront is not enough; we need to plan the time and place for it.

Confrontation Among Family and Friends

At a more personal level, you may confront homosexuality among friends or loved ones. Those confrontations, though, will be more about homosexuality in general than the specifics of the pro-gay theology. If a friend or family member has embraced the pro-gay theology, the arguments used in these chapters may be useful to you. But the larger questions—such as, "How do I relate to a gay loved one?"—are beyond the scope of this book. So if someone you love is gay, let me refer you to my book *When Homosexuality Hits Home.**

There are two general situations in which you are likely to confront the gay Christian movement: within your church (if your denomination is considering accepting the pro-gay theology); and in the public arena, through debates or the media.

Confronting the Gay Christian Movement in the Church

While preparing to write this chapter, I interviewed pastors from Anglican, Baptist, Reformed, Catholic, Episcopalian, and Lutheran churches, all of whom are debating (at some level) whether or not to accept the pro-gay theology. I asked each pastor or priest how their denomination got to the point where they could even consider such a thing. A couple reasons came up repeatedly.

- *The elite vs. the majority.* Each pastor noted that people in high denominational positions—the church hierarchy—are in danger of adopting an ivory-tower mentality, keeping them out of touch with grassroots concerns. In an academic,

---

* Harvest House Publishers, 2004.

somewhat elite atmosphere, there may be more of a tendency toward liberalism and a "critical" view of Scripture. From their position of authority, members of the church hierarchy may hand down policies entirely at odds with their congregations' beliefs, creating a tension between the laity and denominational leadership.

• *Special committees.* Two pastors said their denominations had established, years earlier, committees to study homosexuality. Their intentions seemed right; they hoped to develop more effective ministry to homosexuals. But gays and their supporters, having quite a bit at stake in the denomination's acceptance of homosexuality, often joined the committees—while conservatives, less enthused about these projects, did not participate. Naturally the committees were often lopsided in composition, with more liberal than conservative members.

Committee members then turned, in many cases, primarily to the social sciences for information on homosexuality. Receiving a wealth of pro-gay information, they also adopted the revisionist view of Scripture and came—not surprisingly—to the conclusion that the church should revise its view on homosexuality. The ordination of homosexuals, gay marriages, and a commitment to gay rights were then recommended. Then, at the denomination's general conferences, the committee proposals were voted on (and usually voted down) by the more mainstream, conservative members of the denomination; the committee's reports were tabled, to be studied further and voted on again at the next general conference, when the cycle would begin again. (Of course, this is an oversimplification. The details and events have varied in each denomination involved in these discussions.)

Getting Involved

Each pastor or priest I spoke with recommended increased lay involvement. "Most people in our churches don't want this!" one said, referring to the pro-gay theology. "But if they don't want it, they'll have to get more involved in their local congregations and do something."

A few ideas for getting involved and for confronting the pro-gay theology within denominations came up in these discussions.

1. *Know your denomination's official position.* If you aren't sure what it is, write to the general headquarters of the denomination and request a copy of their position statement on homosexuality and the Bible. In most cases, you will find that your church still officially holds to a conservative position. Remind people of that during every discussion you have on the subject. Church authority is still, in most cases, on your side.

2. *Know your pastor's position on homosexuality.* If he takes a pro-gay position, you will naturally have a hard time soliciting his support. Otherwise ask for his ideas on addressing the pro-gay theology in your denomination. Explain to him that you aren't asking him to do any more than he is already doing. Pastors are swamped, and they do not usually appreciate a congregant asking them to get involved in yet another cause! But tell him you want to get more involved in standing for truth within your church. Ask for his blessing and counsel.

3. *When possible, participate in your denomination's process.* Join committees your denomination has formed to study the issue of homosexuality and the Bible. Use the materials in this and the books listed under "Suggested Reading" (at the end of the book) to bolster your arguments. Be sure to contribute verifiable information proving that homosexuality is not innate, unchangeable, or biblically permissible. Also contribute ideas on how to lovingly minister to homosexuals in your community without compromising the truth.

4. *Invite speakers to address your church.* Ask speakers to your Sunday school classes, midweek services, and main church services on the subject of homosexuality and the Bible. Locate people in your area who take a traditional stand on this issue and support them.*

---

* If you don't know of anyone in your area who teaches on the subject, contact Exodus International (www.exodus-international.org) for referrals.

Encourage your church and pastor to consider the need for education on homosexuality; people are perishing for lack of knowledge.

- *Sponsor local seminars on homosexuality.* Seminars are great vehicles for delving into a topic from all angles. A well-balanced seminar on homosexuality will include workshops on gay-rights issues, the pro-gay theology, counseling homosexuals, responding when a loved one is gay, and how the church in general can better address homosexuality in America. This is an excellent way to serve and educate the Christian community in your area.

- *Ask your pastor about developing ministries in your church.* Establish counseling and support groups for people struggling against homosexuality and for families with homosexual loved ones.

Developing Ministries

A friend of mine, Pastor Ken Korver of Southern California, proved that any church can establish a strong ministry on this issue. Having read some books on homosexuality and feeling a desire to do something constructive about the problem, he invited several speakers to his church for a special seminar on the subject. He then made two announcements to his congregation: First, he said that if anyone in his church struggled with homosexuality, he wanted them to call him personally during the week, and they would begin meeting together weekly, and privately, for Bible study, accountability, and encouragement.

He then asked his congregation how many members would be willing to make themselves available to the people who contacted him during the week wanting help: "Will you be there for them when they're tempted, and will you walk with them through their process of overcoming homosexuality?"

More than 70 people responded. That was years ago. Pastor Korver's ministry to homosexuals is still thriving. If more churches followed his example, we would be far more effective when rebutting gay theology. The leaders of the conservative Ramsey Colloquium noted as follows:

> One reason for the discomfort of religious leaders in the
> face of this new [gay] movement is the past and continuing

failure to offer supportive and knowledgeable pastoral care to persons coping with the problems of their homosexuality.[3]

We cannot, with integrity, denounce a problem while doing little or nothing to solve it. Years ago we learned this when protesting abortion. For decades we railed against the crime of killing the unborn. Yet *Roe v. Wade* was upheld by the Supreme Court, and the abortion industry thrived. At some point we realized our approach was too limited. It wasn't enough to tell women what *not* to do—we also needed to come alongside them and help them do what was right.

So we established homes for women to carry their children to full term instead of aborting them. Christian counseling centers for crisis pregnancies sprang up. Support groups for women who'd had abortions became commonplace as well. We became a part of the solution, not just another voice denouncing the problem.

If our churches are going to effectively withstand the gay Christian movement, they will have to do more than argue against it. They will have to become safe havens for women and men struggling against homosexuality—places where these believers, like all others, can freely say, "I struggle; help me." If we fail them when they need our support, we have no excuse to be surprised when they abandon biblical ethics altogether and become our most boisterous critics.

Confronting the Pro-Gay Theology in the Public Arena

Some of you may sense a calling to publicly confront pro-gay theology, whether in media interviews or public discussions. I use the word *calling* very literally. Some people are called and gifted by God to debate in public, and many (perhaps most) are not. I have found this to be a crucial point. Many people are concerned about this subject. But concern, in itself, does not qualify a person for public speaking. The public arena is a harsh battlefield that no one should enter without calling and preparation. Before venturing into it, seek input and confirmation from your pastor and the people who know you best. Be sure you are commissioned and equipped; better not to go at all if you are uncertain.

Still, the public arena can be a great vehicle for truth. Since 1988 I have participated in an average of 40 radio and television shows per year, both secular and Christian. Not once, even during the most hostile interviews, has the time been wasted. Without exception, phone calls have always followed from people wanting help. Counseling appointments increased; relationships across the country were established by phone or correspondence. So, for me, speaking in the public arena has proved to be very effective.

Ideas for Effective Confrontation

The need for Christians who are taking a public stand on this issue is greater than ever. The truth about homosexuality won't be effectively set forth by a mere handful of Christian speakers. We need a variety of men and women, from all backgrounds, speaking to the press, the media, campuses, and professional conventions.

You may be one of them. If so, let me offer a few ideas on effectively confronting the pro-gay theology in the public arena:

1. *Do your homework.* Learn all the scriptures that refer to homosexuality, and understand the pro-gay interpretations of each. Make sure you have at least one response to each pro-gay interpretation memorized or on hand. Also, make sure you are aware of the general arguments the gay Christian movement sets forth (see chapters 9 through 13), and also be certain you can articulate a response to each of them.

2. *Do not assume that every opportunity to speak publicly is a calling.* Because there is so much media interest on this subject, once you've spoken publicly on it you may well find yourself deluged with interview requests, both secular and Christian. A good principle to keep in mind is this: The need always outweighs the availability. Opportunity and calling are two different things.

   I have learned to turn down almost as many requests for interviews as I accept. Stewardship requires it; we've got only so much energy to expend, after all. When invited to a debate or an interview, ask yourself the following questions:

- Will this be beneficial to the purposes I am trying to achieve?

- Will I be given enough time during this interview to make an impact so that it will be worth my time to accept this invitation?

- Am I the best one to do this, or is someone else available who could do it better?

By making sure each opportunity passes this threefold test, you'll avoid the burnout that inevitably comes when people don't wisely monitor their time and activities.

3. *Don't be naive.* If you are going to be a guest on talk shows or be interviewed for articles or news programs, you're likely to be working with reporters and moderators who disagree with you. Some may be downright hostile. That's the nature of the media environment. Be sure you're mentally prepared (again, by doing your homework beforehand) and psychologically prepared as well.

Don't Expect Fair Treatment

When my friend Sy Rodgers (an extraordinary advocate for balanced ministry to homosexuals) was a guest on a prominent talk show, the host approached him just before the show began and greeted him with these words: "I think you are offering false hope when you say homosexuals can change, and I'm going to nail you when we get out there."

When Dr. Joseph Nicolosi (a psychologist offering help to homosexuals desiring change) spoke to a school-board meeting in San Francisco, he was drowned out by shouts and catcalls; the school board officials did nothing to intervene.[4] And when a conservative activist addressed a Northern California church, gay activists surrounded the building, blocking entrances and vandalizing property. Yet the local media was virtually silent; had conservatives been staging such a disruption, there is no question it would have been front-page news.[5]

"The establishment media," notes commentator Cal Thomas, "have developed a relationship with the political objectives of gay-rights activism that has shamefully compromised their ability to report objectively and fairly on this issue."[6] A polling of the media in the early 1990s confirmed Thomas's observation: 80 percent of the newsmen questioned said they did not believe homosexuality was wrong, 90 percent favored abortion rights, and only 20 percent attended church or synagogue. A fair interview, under these conditions, is not a foregone conclusion.

Yet we can hardly expect the world to celebrate the Christian view. Jesus gave us fair warning: "If ye were of the world, the world would love his own: but because ye are not of the world, but I have chosen you out of the world, therefore the world hateth you" (John 15:19 KJV).

When you openly criticize any form of gay ideology, including the pro-gay theology, you are going against the tide. The disapproval of the world cannot be avoided; indeed it's often a confirmation that you're on the right track.* In fact, when I consider the moral and philosophical views of the people throwing their support behind the gay-rights and gay Christian movement, I am amazed that gay Christians (who should know enough of the Bible to know better) are glad to get their support. If Phil Donahue, Joan Rivers, Cher, and Elizabeth Taylor supported my moral views, I would be gravely concerned.

All media and public work is not, of course, hostile or imbalanced. I have found much of it to be challenging, fruitful, and sometimes downright fun. But it's best to go into it prepared for anything. So take Jesus' advice—be wise as a serpent yet innocent as a dove (Matthew 10:16).

Since others have been publicly speaking on this issue for years, we might as well learn from their mistakes and their triumphs. In my opinion, the following are the most crucial mistakes to avoid, and the best ideas to implement, when confronting the pro-gay theology in the public arena.

---

* When Ronald Reagan was castigated by the American Civil Liberties Union for proclaiming 1983 the "Year of the Bible," he said he wore their criticism like a badge of honor!

What Doesn't Work

1. Do not attack the character of homosexuals. Some Christians seem bent on proving that homosexuals are neurotic, sex-obsessed, or hateful. (During the Anita Bryant campaign, for instance, one well-known pastor remarked, "Those so-called gay folks would just as soon kill you as look at you!")

This backfires for two reasons. First, it speaks poorly of the person doing the attacking and gains sympathy for the gay viewpoint. "The Church is discredited," a pro-gay author once noted, "occasionally by an inexcusable error of fact, but far more often by some exaggeration or tendentious assertion."[7] Attacking the character of an opponent betrays a weak argument while making the opponent look all the better. "Abuse a man unjustly," Edgar Watson Howe observed, "and you will make friends for him."

Second, this tactic skirts the issue. If homosexuality is wrong, it's wrong whether practiced by a scoundrel or a wonderful person. Attacking the character of homosexuals raises an obvious question: Would same-sex contact be all right if the people involved in it were nice people? If that were the case, then homosexuality would certainly be legitimate. I know many lesbians and gay men who are responsible, likeable, hardworking people; I know far too many heterosexuals who are outright despicable.

Keep the issues straight. The character of the person is not in question. The person's behavior is.

2. Do not relay loathsome, explicit "facts" about homosexual sex. Some Christian speakers feel a need to not only condemn homosexual behavior, but to describe its more sensational aspects in the most lurid of terms. Instead of just saying sex between men or women is unnatural, they reach for the wildest sexual practices committed by some (definitely not all) in the homosexual community, hold those practices up as the "gay norm" and, like a camera zooming in on a bloody corpse, linger over the crude details. This serves no good purpose. In fact, it needlessly alienates us from gays who hear these remarks.

I remember, in 1978, sitting in a gay bar where someone had brought in some literature put out by Christians on homosexuality. The pamphlets and flyers elaborately detailing all the sexual things we allegedly did to each other were being passed from barstool to barstool. By the fresh eruption of laughter, you could tell another man was reading them. We found these Christian materials hilarious! They were largely untrue and were obviously designed to excite revulsion toward homosexuals by accusing us of practices most of us had never heard of, much less indulged in.

This also backfires for both reasons listed previously: It discredits the speaker, and it skirts the larger issue. Homosexuality is wrong, whether an act is committed 5000 times a year during sadomasochistic rituals or once in a 50-year monogamous relationship. It's wrong in and of itself.

3. Do not portray gay extremists as examples of all homosexuals. People see through such tactics. Extremists can be found in any group, Christian and non-Christian alike. To point out the extreme factions of the gay-rights movement and hold them up as the norm is just as cheap and manipulative as picking out the "pro-lifers" who shoot abortionists and saying they are representative of the whole pro-life movement. Let's avoid such games.

4. Do not use cliches. Cliches are grating. They weaken the argument of the person using them, and they make their user sound as though she or he is relying on bumper-sticker sayings rather than sound reasoning. Here are a few of my least favorites:

- "Gay lifestyle." There is no such thing. Homosexuals live their lives in many ways. Some are militant; many but not all are promiscuous; some are moderate, some conservative. To categorize one lifestyle as the norm for all of them is inaccurate and will cast doubt on other statements you make.

- "We love the sinner but hate the sin." That's true, but let's find another way to say it. This one is almost certain to get a laugh if you use it in public, just because it has been so overused. (Also, I suspect, because it's simplistic.)

• "If you are gay, that's your choice." It is not. No one chooses to be homosexual. People do choose, however, to act on their homosexual desires. Make the distinction and keep it clear.

• "God made Adam and Eve, not Adam and Steve." I mentioned this one earlier in the book, but I would avoid using it in public. It sounds sarcastic, like mockery of homosexuals. Sarcasm never wins an argument.

What Does Work

1. Stick to verifiable facts rather than anecdotes or rhetoric. "The Bible says…"; "Studies have shown"; "Surveys have proven…"; all these are verifiable and tough to argue against. For example, rather than just saying, "I know homosexuals can change because I did," I prefer saying, "Treatment programs for people like me who wanted to change have certainly been successful," and then I name the programs or studies so the audience can check for themselves (see chapter 6).

2. Admit error. I have found it helpful to admit the past mistakes of some Christians, rather than blindly defend everything we've done in the past. We've made mistakes, and if we refuse to admit them, we can hardly expect gays or society to take us seriously. For instance, theologian Richard Mouw told *Christianity Today,*

> We have treated homosexuals horribly in the past. And if homosexuals today are angry with the church, we first need to repent of our past sins and then try to seek the credibility in this society to begin speaking.[8]

3. Stay flexible when discussing theories, yet adamant when discussing the Bible. What the Bible says about homosexuality is absolute, but theories that often come up—such as those on the origins of homosexuality, whether or not homosexuality is changeable, and how the average homosexual lives—are all subject to question. When discussing the Bible we can be adamant; when discussing our theories, more caution is needed.

We can't be certain, for example, what makes people homosexual (theory), yet we can be certain that homosexuality is wrong (Scripture). So, although I strongly feel that family dynamics have a lot to do with the development of homosexuality in most cases, I'm open to other theories as well, and I say as much when speaking on the subject. Likewise, I'm not at all convinced that homosexuality is inborn; when speaking on the subject, I give the same reasons against this view that I list in chapter 6. The studies are inconclusive at best. But I'm open to future evidence. However, that won't change my position on homosexuality one bit. If it is biblically condemned, then how it begins is secondary.

Stay flexible enough to admit that any theory may be wrong, and stick to the facts of Scripture. A discussion of the pro-gay theology should return, again and again, to what the Bible says. That is the bottom line—don't let yourself get sidetracked!

4. Remember that confrontation need not always *seem* successful in order to have *been* successful. We may walk away from a debate, interview, or discussion feeling as though all our points fell flat. Or our denomination may swing toward the pro-gay theology despite our best efforts. Or a gay friend may ignore all our arguments, no matter how carefully thought out and presented, and still join the gay Christian movement. All of this can leave us feeling as though we have failed.

It's best to remember, when confronting the gay Christian movement, the parable of the sower:

> When he sowed, some seeds fell by the way side, and the fowls came and devoured them up: Some fell upon stony places, where they had not much earth...And some

fell among thorns; and the thorns sprung up, and choked
them: But other fell into good ground, and brought forth
fruit (Matthew 13:4-5,7-8 kjv).

The sower's job was to sow; the type of ground the seeds fell on was
not his responsibility. If we looked at his work statistically, we might
say he was a failure. Most of his seeds did not take root; most of the
ground the seeds fell on was hard, or scorched, or thorny. But there
were results as well—there always are some results, even if they may
seem minimal.

We are not called to persuade, but to present. As stewards of truth,
our job is to present the truth clearly, lovingly, and responsibly. When
standing before the judgment seat of Christ, we will not be asked how
many homosexuals we were able to persuade out of the gay Christian
movement. But surely we'll be asked how faithfully we stewarded the
truth we've been given, and how lovingly yet boldly we presented it.

When asked that question, may it please God that we may answer
with confidence and then hear Him say, "Well done, good and faithful
servant."

15

A SATISFIED MIND

*"When we want to be something other than
the thing God wants us to be, we must be wanting
what, in fact, will not make us happy."*

C.S. LEWIS

I began this book by recounting the day I visited the nearby Metropolitan Community Church. I listened, I watched, and then I stepped into the aisle and went forward to receive communion with my gay Christian comrades. It had taken less than 60 minutes for me to convince myself that God and gay were compatible. It would be another six years before I reconsidered the gay gospel, and what kind of life I'd made for myself by accepting it.

At first, back in 1978, it had been exhilarating. After all, up to that point two of the most potent forces in my life—my spirituality and my sexuality—had been at war. I'd tried to kill one in the interest of the other, with miserable results. Now they were coexisting peacefully...or so I thought, and would continue to think for years. So initially, my

237

decision to step into the aisle of the gay church was followed by relief and excitement: relief because the battle between gay and God was resolved, and excitement at the prospect of a new church, new identity, new everything.

And in no area of life was that newness more keenly felt than in the new friends I was making. I'd lost my old Christian friends when I joined the gay community, but I had been unable to develop close ties with the gay men I met at the bars because I'd had so little in common with them.

Not so with these men and women. We had both our faith and our sexuality in common, and our shared experiences as Christians who'd wrestled with the homosexual issue bound us tightly together. Soon I began meeting former Baptists, Pentecostals, evangelicals, and believers from every conceivable denomination who, like me, had kept a painful secret from their home churches until they decided, also like me, to stop keeping "the secret."

These newfound friends who called themselves "gay Christians" weren't shallow, uncommitted game-players. They were sincere, both in their faith and, in many ways, their way of life. I met some truly reprehensible people too, as one meets anywhere. But by and large, my fellow congregants at the gay church had a genuine faith in Jesus, a faith that showed itself in their conversations and lifestyle.

No one who's familiar with me or anything I've written on this subject could ever assume I think homosexuality is anything less than unnatural and immoral. My recognition, then, of my newfound friends' sincerity doesn't imply an endorsement of their homosexuality. But I've come to believe, as I hope I've shown earlier in this book, that people can be sincere, yet sincerely wrong. Their sincerity doesn't make their wrong right, nor does their wrongness prove they are insincere. To be both is not only possible; it's painfully common.

All of which made it easier for me to tell myself that I'd made the right decision. If the members of the Metropolitan Community Church had been a bunch of openly salacious orgy enthusiasts, I'd have quickly spotted their error. But the warmth and, yes, even the integrity I sensed in them only strengthened the grip of the error that was taking over my own life.

Over the years, I've been asked repeatedly how, as a born-again Christian from a Christ-centered church, I could have been so deceived as to believe and promote the "gay gospel." I can't speak for others who've been in the same position, but in my case, the recipe was pretty simple. I had a long-standing problem—sexual attractions toward the same gender—that I had neither created nor chosen. But I did make a series of wrong choices that set me up for deception.

The first wrong choice lay in keeping my sexual struggles a secret, refusing to bring them into the light of accountability, counsel, and prayer support, where they belonged. That alone would have spared me years of error and moral tragedy. I followed that decision with an even worse one...by finally indulging the desires I'd pushed down for so long. That led to a general hardening of my heart toward God and an increasingly darkened mind.

And that, inevitably, led me to say "yes" to the seduction of pro-gay theology and to the cementing of a deception that would last too long and cost me far too much. But the deception wasn't something that mugged me while I was innocently walking down the street. I set myself up for it, willfully and quite stupidly. Rebellion is, after all, no accident, and the rebel is no victim.

Within a year, I'd accepted a post as the church's pianist and had entered a two-year training program for acceptance onto their ministerial staff. (In fact, I planned to become a licensed minister with the Universal Fellowship of Metropolitan Community Churches, a plan I pursued but then backed out of shortly before I left the gay community.) And over the next four years, I regularly taught Bible studies, preached sermons, and, in time, began counseling men and women who visited the church wondering what to do with their sexuality. I did my best to persuade them that the answer to their conflict lay in accepting the claims of the gay gospel. My memories of that erroneous counsel will always provoke an ache in my heart.

During this time, along with getting new friends and church responsibilities, I also attempted a series of relationships with men. None of them lasted more than six months. Intimacy had never been my strong suit, a fact borne out by the multitude of short-term affairs I'd had with men and women since my junior-high-school days. As a self-identified gay Christian, I tried forming partnerships with other men in the church—sometimes ministers; sometimes laity; always disastrous.

And while I believe most sexual relationships among men are, by their nature, incapable of longevity and monogamy, I'd have to say the problem was more *me* than my sexuality. I simply had no patience with the give and take necessary for long-term commitment, so I'd leave at the first sign of trouble. In retrospect, I'm grateful that none of these partnerships lasted, as that may have impeded me from ever facing the wrongness of homosexuality itself. But I'll also admit to deep remorse for the way I so casually jumped into relationship after relationship.

Still, I tried. I also tried, with a bit more success, to quash whatever pangs of conscience I still had over the question I'd considered back in 1978, when I first joined the gay church: *What about the Bible?*

I'd adopted the pro-gay theology by then and could hold my own when defending it. But articulating an argument is one thing; being personally convinced of it is another. And at times I wondered, very uncomfortably, *Was I really convinced that pro-gay theology was true? Or was I just doing a darned good job* pretending *to be convinced?*

Occasionally a Christian friend from my old days would write, call, or even confront me face-to-face. Word had gotten out, of course, that Joe Dallas had gone gay, and many of my former acquaintances had to have been shocked and appalled. Some tried to get through to me, and to this day I'm sure they have no idea how much impact they had, nor what doubt they stirred in me.

Not that I would admit it at the time—I made it a point to keep my bravado intact as I explained to them why I believed what I believed, and how wrong they were to challenge me. But afterward when I was alone, away from the need to put the best face possible on my "gay Christian" persona, I'd be plunged into piercing doubts. Sometimes I'd talk myself out of them by parroting the revisionist lines. Other times, when logic and pro-gay theology weren't getting along in my mind, I'd silence the argument with a six-pack, hoping to put the matter behind me in the morning.

Only so many mornings can pass, though, before your doubts won't be gagged any longer—so by the early part of 1984, mine spoke up.

By then, at age 29, I'd decided to pursue a career in counseling instead of the ministry. I had dropped out of the gay church entirely. (More from burnout, I suspect, than rejection of pro-gay theology.) I was single, and I had a good job and an active social life of dating, partying, and generally having a pretty good time.

But then there were the brief interludes when it stopped being good, and those times were becoming more frequent. At the oddest hours—midday at work, for example, or early in the morning—I'd feel a cold, lonely pain in my gut that was hard to identify. It wasn't a longing for a lover or friend, as I had plenty of company but no desire to try yet another "relationship." No, this was a longing for something ill-defined and always just out of reach. And this uneasy, depressing yearning festered and persisted, sometimes to the point of drawing tears.

Whatever it was, it was becoming downright scary, especially because I saw nothing in my life warranting it. I was in excellent physical shape, having taken up bodybuilding with a vengeance. I was reasonably popular and sought out for companionship. My finances were in order, as was, indeed, every other part of my life. I'd taken enough coursework to become a therapist shortly and was looking forward to getting an internship somewhere. Good friends, great health, career goals, and financial security...*So what's not to be happy about?* I'd ask myself whenever "it" reared its head. But during the holiday season of 1983 and early 1984, while my undiagnosed emotional pain got worse and worse, its source was elusive.

Until what started as an uneventful evening became a turning point. I'd gone straight to the gym after work as usual, then trained, showered, grabbed a quick dinner, and headed home. It was nearing eight o'clock by then and, being an early riser, that's when I preferred being indoors on weeknights. Parties were for weekends; work and studying took precedence Monday through Thursday.

But tonight's for relaxing, I remember telling myself, as there was no upcoming test to prep for and no papers to write. So I grabbed a Bud Lite, plopped myself onto the couch, shucked my wingtips off, and clicked the remote. When the screen lit up, my mouth dropped, then broadened into a grin.

There, on the Christian station I'd happened to tune into, was an old friend from my early ministerial days. He'd been one of the most well-known and widely respected Christian musicians of the 1970s, and, in fact, he continues to have a thriving music ministry even now. But that night it was himself, not his music, he was discussing on this talk show. Not just himself—but his *problems* as well, problems I'd never known him to have.

He openly described, to my astonishment, his alcoholism. It had dogged him for years, disrupting his ministry and marriage, nearly costing him both. Now he'd been sober for some time, and he was en-couraging viewers to admit whatever secrets they struggled with, bring them into the light, and deal with them openly the way he'd finally had to admit and deal with his. It was possible, he said, for a Christian to have an ongoing sin in his life that he feels terrified to let anyone know about. But whatever difficulties might come as a result of finally admitting the problem paled, he said, when compared to the nightmare you could make of your life by not dealing with it.

Click.

I'd turned the TV off without realizing it and was staring into space, stunned not so much by my old friend's testimony, but by the thought it was bringing up in me.

The nightmare you could make of your life…the nightmare you have made of your life…

"Wait a minute!" I shouted at no one in particular. "My life's no nightmare." Then I reeled off, one by one, the reasons I was a success by any standard. All of them were valid; none were arguable. *So there—case closed. Have another beer.*

And yet—no. The case had been reopened, I knew, skipping the beer and sitting back down.

My old friend had a secret problem, I reflected, just as I'd had six years earlier. But unlike me, he'd dealt with his by calling it what it was, rather than by redefining it. And he'd done so openly, in the church, without running away. I, on the other hand, had dealt with my problem by deciding to indulge it, then trying to make peace with it by redefining it, then running away from anyone who challenged that redefinition. And if I'd really been sure I was right, why did I run from anyone (or any thought, for that matter) that challenged me?

After another 30 minutes of silent reflection, I found it boiled down to this: A life not lived with a clear conscience and satisfied mind becomes its own nightmare, the very nightmare my old friend was warning against. And that, in a nutshell, was the "it" that had haunted me for months. I simply wasn't sure anymore—nor, perhaps, had I ever been sure—that I was right about God or my way of life. And those two things, I admitted bleakly, were things a man had better be sure of.

But what, I wondered, *is making me so unsure of both?*

The answer flew at my face like a basketball held underwater for too long: *The Big Question, that's what.* The hard one; the one I'd crammed into the back file for too long. Time to pull it out, with the lights turned on and no wishful thinking. My old musician friend had done it; couldn't I?

I looked around my apartment's living room—piano, bookcase, entertainment center, plants, mirrors, and stereo—with a strange certainty I was about to raise issues that would forever change everything. So I quietly said goodbye to my surroundings, knowing that what I was about to ask myself would drive a stake through the heart of my life as I knew it.

The stake was a question, and the question was simple: *When I embraced the "gay and Christian" identity, was that a decision based on the belief this was God's will for my life…or on the hope that this was what God might allow?*

Plain question; enormous implications. I knew I could content myself with the grace of God while shunning His will, though it's a stupid,
dangerous thing to do. But there was, I remembered, such a thing as
"cheap grace"—a willingness to be forgiven but not obedient. Scripture,
church history, and modern experience are rife with examples. There were
believers, and there were disciples. And wasn't one of the church's greatest
tragedies the number of people who chose to be one instead of both?

My house of cards was caving in, blown down by the first honest
look I'd had at myself since I'd erected it.

All this time I'd contented myself with some facts I knew to be
true, using them to obscure other equally important ones. God loved
me, no question. I had been born again, grounded in the Word, and
established in a life that did, in many ways, testify to my faith. I made
no bones about my belief in Christ when I was on the job, often referring to myself as a churchgoing Christian. I read the Bible, sometimes
daily, sometimes not, but regularly nonetheless. I had a prayer life and
was certain I sensed God's presence, especially during worship or private
devotions. These were facts, and they spoke loudly.

So loudly they had helped me ignore the quieter, inconvenient ones;
the ones that emerged now, dusting themselves off so I could give them
a fresh look.

Fact: God's love and His approval are far from the same. The prodigal
rebel is as loved by God as the obedient disciple, but only one walks in
the light of His approval.

Fact: Anyone can pray, read the Word, and call himself a Christian.
Satan himself quoted Scripture to Christ, atheists pray under stress…and
Christians can be carnal, deceived, wrong. The habit of reading the
Bible, no matter how fervently, doesn't guarantee one's life is in line
with it. It's the *doers,* not the hearers, who live in God's favor. Maybe I'd
never lost my salvation; maybe God's Spirit still dwelled in me; maybe
at times He even blessed or provided for me. So what? Salvation alone
can't be enough. To call Him Savior at all times but Lord at some times
is the lot of the lukewarm or the deluded.

Fact: God never held my sexual orientation against me. But where did I get the idea He created it? I'd always known man's sin nature expressed itself differently from person to person. Sometimes it shows itself in common ways; other times, it manifests itself through uncommon, even unnatural desires. Regardless of what created those desires, like all believers I was expected to ask myself not whether my feelings seemed natural to me, but what He expected me to do with them. Instead, I'd decided for myself what was right, usurping the Creator's privilege and making it my own.

And there it was in plain, ugly view. Exhibit A, the most damning evidence against me. I'd removed myself from God's authority, then made a god of Joe Dallas. And like all fools trying to play god, I'd been wrong.

Wrong when I'd stepped into the aisle, taking communion as a gay Christian. Wrong when I'd encouraged others to do the same. Wrong when I'd spoken to college campuses as a "proud, gay Christian," eagerly taking on the students who thought homosexuality was sick, shooting down arguments from well-intentioned but poorly informed Christians.

And wrong—God help me, so wrong!—when entering into relationship after relationship, trying time and again to form partnerships, which would inevitably fail.

I have no idea how much time had passed that evening while I went through this internal struggle. It was dark and quiet; the silence seemed to make it easier, in the end, to say what had to be said, boldly and finally.

"I've been wrong for years, and there's nothing I can do to atone— nothing I can do at all but face it and weep."

So I did, sobbing bitterly into the early morning hours, then praying the only appropriate words—*God be merciful to me a sinner!*—before finally slipping into the deepest, fullest sleep I'd enjoyed in years.

I began packing the next morning.

More than 20 years have passed between then and the time of this writing. They have been years of new relationships, unique situations, and undeserved privileges unthinkable that dark winter night I repented. I've enjoyed a 19-year marriage to an extraordinary woman who still reduces me to the awkwardness of a love-struck kid; I've fathered two sons who own my heart; I've had the honor of authoring five books and the joy of full-time ministry. I am a prodigal returned, forgiven, and restored, and perhaps best of all, I've got a satisfied mind.

But it's a troubled one too. How could it not be? The state of both the church and the nation should trouble us, and our concern needs to be translated into constructive, redemptive action.

Acting and Speaking with Grace and Truth

In Ephesians 2:10, Paul referred to the church as God's "workmanship," the Greek word for which is *poema,* from which we get our word *poem.* I love this concept, sobering as it is. God's the poet; we're the poem—His earthly work of art, His visible representatives. That puts both tremendous honor and responsibility on us because, as His workmanship, we've been commissioned to represent Him accurately. John said as much himself when he reminded his readers,

> He who says he abides in Him ought himself also to walk just as He walked (1 John 2:6).

And when describing how He walked, John mentions two of Jesus' most noticeable qualities:

> We beheld His glory, the glory as of the only begotten of the Father, full of grace and truth (John 1:14).

To represent Him properly, then, is to exhibit grace and truth. And on no issue are we more challenged to express both grace and truth than on this one.

Jesus showed immeasurable grace when dealing with sinners, both sexual and otherwise. When interacting with an adulterous woman, tax collectors, or prostitutes, He consistently showed respect, a propensity to dialogue and socialize with them, and even a readiness to defend them from mistreatment, always with an eye toward their earthly safety and their eternal well-being.

The Influence of Grace

There's our standard for grace when dealing with homosexuals:

- respect in our speech and actions
- a willingness to dialogue, relate, and find common ground when possible
- a readiness to defend them against verbal or physical mistreatment
- and all of the above done with an eye toward their fair treatment in this life and, more important, their salvation

To fall short in this area is to relinquish our influence and credibility. And let's sadly but clearly admit we're guilty. Too often, the Christian expressing his views on homosexuality has done so with a contempt, in both tone and words, seldom expressed when he describes other sins. "We're all sinners," he seems to say, "but gays are a special class of the worst sort." Or, as my friend Mike Haley of Focus on the Family often says, some speak of homosexuality as the sin Jesus "had to hang on the cross a little longer for."

Imagine a doctor seeing a patient with a rare disease. After examining the person, he curls his lip with distain and says, "I've seen lots of sick people, but you're the sickest. Your problem's rare and disgusting; I can barely stand treating you for it. I don't know how you got this way, though I can only guess it's your own fault. Anyway, you have a repulsive disease. Here's a prescription for it—now go take it and please don't soil my office with your presence again."

The doctor is correct in telling the patient he has a problem and in offering him a remedy. But that's about all he's correct about. His attitude is deplorable; his words brutal. He's guilty of exercising atrocious bedside manners, so could we really blame the patient if he reacts negatively?

When there's a lack of grace among us for gays, I believe we contribute to the growth and strength of the gay movement. Of course, individuals will answer to God if they embrace error, but what about us? To what extent have we helped them along the way?

Perhaps they can best tell us themselves:

> We grow because hundreds of thousands of gay and lesbian Christians who are despised and rejected by the Catholic and Protestant churches of their childhood have no where else to go.[1]
> —Mel White

> If the church had really done their missionary work, I don't think that MCC [Metropolitan Community Church] would have ever existed.[2]
> —Troy Perry

Jesus wept openly over Jerusalem, knowing all it could have been, yet foreseeing its doom. Paul's heart's desire was to see the Jews (who at times opposed him violently) saved. But today, who weeps for homosexuals? Whose heart cries out to see them brought to the truth? A lack of impassioned, Christlike tears may be a measure of our compromised grace.

The Influence of Truth

But a compromise of truth is no less atrocious. Jesus refused to soft-pedal truth for the sake of grace when referencing sexual immorality. So when extending grace to an adulteress, He also called her behavior a sin (John 8:1-11). His Sermon on the Mount, an epic model of grace, also includes one of the most stringent standards for sexual purity in Scripture: "Whoever looks upon a woman to lust after her has committed adultery in his heart" (Matthew 5:28). He categorized adultery, fornication, and lewdness alongside blasphemy and murder (Mark 7:21), and when rebuke was called for, whether against His adversaries or against His disciples, He never withheld it. (See Matthew chapter 23 or Matthew 16:23, for example.) To walk as He walked, then, is to be as unsparing of the truth as we are of grace.

Imagine another doctor—this one beset with a need to be liked and a greater concern for getting lots of patients than for providing adequate care. Upon discovering his patient's life-threatening illness, he fears the reaction he'll get when he tells the patient and his family about it. He's heard stories of people hating their doctors for telling them bad news—and how he hates being hated! He's even heard of those who never visit the doctor again after getting a frightening diagnosis, and how will he keep his practice open if that happens? So he calls the illness something else: something nicer; less offensive. The patient's happy, nobody's offended, and the doctor's practice keeps growing.

Until, of course, his patients start dying because he refused to tell them the truth while they could have done something about it. In his quest to be popular, he's set himself up for some enormous malpractice claims.

In his defense, he might protest, "I wanted my patients to be comfortable when they came to see me!"

"Fine," we'd respond, "so long as you didn't make them comfortable at the expense of telling them the truth about their condition."

"But," he'd object, "I can't keep my practice open by telling people things that upset them."

"If popularity and a large clientele mean more to you than sound medical practices," we'd answer, "then drop medicine and go into politics. A doctor's calling is to treat illness, not to make friends."

A growing segment of the church seems likewise guilty of malpractice. In our desire to be "seeker-friendly" and sensitive, we're in danger of shunning truth and all the inconvenience and discomfort it evokes—because we hate confrontation, need to be liked, and prefer large churches to truthful ones. And while our desire to be nonoffensive seems noble to some, I can't help but wonder where I'd be if the only Christian messages I'd heard were the "nice" ones.

Believe me, few people recognize their need for salvation through being told how likeable they are. Nor are people born again by being made comfortable in their sin. Perhaps one of the greatest errors infecting modern Christian thought is the assumption that if people like us, then we've reached them. However, Titus Brandsma, a Christian martyr who died at Dachau in 1942, had a more biblical perspective on the matter:

Those who want to win the world for Jesus Christ must
have the courage to come into conflict with it.[3]

To those for whom sensitivity takes precedence over truth, we'd
respond as we did to our codependent medical friend: Comfort is
fine, so long as you don't make people comfortable at the expense of
telling them the truth about their condition. And if popularity and a
large congregation mean more to you than sound doctrine, then drop
the ministry and go into politics. A preacher's calling is to give the full
counsel of God, not to make friends.

Blessing Comes from Being Inconvenienced

Now imagine a third and last medical scenario. Suppose a renegade
new movement sought to redefine a deadly illness as something less
destructive than it really was. Suppose the movement was supported by
a new breed of doctors, who developed a sophisticated set of arguments
to support this strange idea. And suppose a doctor's patients started
coming to him wanting to know who was right: the Traditionalists or
the Revisionists?

We'd forgive the doctor if, at first, he found it hard to argue the
obvious. He'd need time to study and consider the new arguments,
understand them, and then develop a response. But eventually we'd
expect him to have done his homework and prepared an answer, and
to go on speaking and defending the truth.

A new religious movement is seeking, with much success, to redefine
homosexual sin as something else. The movement is supported by both
heterosexual and homosexual advocates who misread the Bible, but do
so using a sophisticated set of arguments. Being ill-equipped to respond
was, at first, forgivable. After all, who among us thought we'd be called
on to defend the obvious? But today, the deadline for excuses has come
and gone. To be relevant is to be equipped to address the issues of the
time, and like it or not, this issue is too relentless to die a quiet death,
either now or anytime soon.

Ultimately, then, the church's ability to withstand the gay Christian
movement will be determined by our willingness to be inconvenienced.

It will be inconvenient to study pro-gay theology and learn how to refute it. It will certainly be inconvenient to train up Christian spokesmen to stand for truth on our campuses and in our television studios and sanctuaries. It will be inconvenient and controversial to establish ministries in our churches to repentant homosexuals. And getting involved with them, through one-on-one discipleship and relating, will no doubt be a major inconvenience as well.

Yet nothing less will stem the tide of pro-gay theology. And if we should refuse to be inconvenienced and let the tide sweep over us, for whom but ourselves do we think the bell is going to toll?

I was fortunate. Loving friends took me in when I repented. Strong brothers welcomed me into their fellowship. I was forgiven, accepted, and restored. I could only wish the same for every woman or man who, by God's grace, is also brought beyond delusion. And perhaps, with an awakening among Christians to our need for each other no matter what our background or former sins, more prodigals will find a celebration waiting for them when they too return to their Father's house.

It is not a pipe dream. Episcopal seminarian William Frey envisioned it some time ago and, as he relates it, it sounds like nothing more than basic Christianity:

> One of the most attractive features of the early Christian communities was their radical sexual ethic and their deep commitment to family values. These things drew many people to them who were disillusioned by the promiscuous excesses of what proved to be a declining culture. Wouldn't it be wonderful for our church to find such countercultural courage today?[4]

Wonderful indeed.

Wonderful, admirable, and—most important—*entirely possible.*

Resources

For more information on Joe Dallas's seminars and educational materials, or to reach Joe for your conference or church engagement, please contact him as follows:

Joe Dallas
c/o Genesis Counseling
17632 Irvine Blvd., Suite 220
Tustin, CA 92780
714-508-6953
www.joedallas.com

NOTES

Chapter 1: Where We Are Now

1. From Jeff Levi's speech to the National Press Club during the 1987 Washington Rally; cited in William Dannemeyer, *Shadow in the Land* (San Francisco: Ignatius Press, 1989), p. 86.

2. Quoted are, respectively: Mel White, *Stranger at the Gate* (New York: Simon and Schuster, 1994), p. 311; Troy Perry, *The Lord Is My Shepherd and He Knows I'm Gay* (Los Angeles: Nash Publishing, 1972), p. 3; Malcom Boyd, *Gay Priest* (New York: St. Martin's Press, 1986), p. 2.

3. "Episcopalians approve gay bishop," CNN.com.us, August 6, 2003.

4. "Q&A with Chuck Smith Jr.," *Dallas Morning News*, December 10, 2005.

5. "HERC Sneaks into THE WEST WING," *Ain't It Cool News*, www.aintitcool.com/display.cgi?id=7220.

6. "A Personal Mission Statement from Cynthia Clawson" cited by *The Record: A Newsletter of Evangelicals Concerned*, Fall 2005, *www.ecinc.org*.

7. Ken Medema's endorsement of the pro-gay viewpoint is documented in the video "Bitter Sisters/Suffering Sons" (1994) produced by His Way Ministries, P.O. Box 4005, Ottowa, Kansas 66067.

8. Cited in *The Record: A Newsletter of Evangelicals Concerned*, Winter 2006, www.ecinc.org.

9. "Brian McLaren on the Homosexual Question: Finding a Pastoral Response," Leadership Journal.net, blog.christianitytoday.com/mt-tb.cgi/43.

10. "Ordination Dilemma for LA Bishop," *Los Angeles Times*, 13 January 1996.

11. *National and International Religion Report*, 1 November 1993; cited in *The Exodus Standard*, December 1993, p. 11.

12. "Church and Society," *Time*, 24 June 1991, p. 49; "Goings on Behind Bedroom Doors," *U.S. News and World Report*, 10 June 1991, p. 63.

13. "Clinton's Church Hosts Gay Activist Event," *Lambda Report*, January 1996, p. 1.

14. Interview with Ken Korver, pastor of Emmanuel Reformed Church of Paramount, California, 2 February 1996; "New Head of Disciples of Christ Would Permit Gays in Ministry," *Los Angeles Times*, 31 July 1993; "4 Churches Expelled for Outreach to Gays," *Los Angeles Times*, 13 January 1996.

15. "Rethinking the Origins of Sins," *Orange County Register*, 15 May 1993.

16. Victor Paul Furnish, *The Moral Teaching of Paul* (Nashville: Abingdon Press, 1979).

17. Ron Rhodes, *The Culting of America* (Eugene, OR: Harvest House Publishers, 1994), p. 27.

18. "Non-Traditional Churches Welcoming Gays to Flock," *Los Angeles Times*, 21 June 1991; *Penpoint Journal*, June 1991, p. 1.

19. Rhodes, p. 35.

Chapter 2: Why Bother Arguing?

1. Paul Campos, "What is it with conservative Christians and homosexuality?" *Orange County Register*, 26 March, 2006, p. 6.

2. George Grant and Mark Horne, *Legislating Immorality* (Chicago: Moody Press, 1993), pp. 165-170.

3. Paul Varnell, "Learning from Catholics' Change," *Out NOW!* 27 June 1995, p. 15.

4. Hank Hanegraaff, *Christianity in Crisis* (Eugene, OR: Harvest House Publishers, 1993), p. 291.

5. "Non-Traditional Churches Welcoming Gays to Flock," *Los Angeles Times,* 21 June 1991.

6. The Metropolitan Community Church is not unique in this respect. Statements and beliefs doubly alarming were expressed at the 1993 ReImaging Conference in Wichita, Kansas, which was attended by women representing mainline churches from across the country. See "Earthquake in the Mainline," *Christianity Today,* 14 November 1994.

7. Mel White, *Stranger at the Gate* (New York: Simon and Schuster, 1994), pp. 132-133.

8. Troy Perry, *Don't Be Afraid Anymore* (New York: St. Martin's Press, 1990), p. 20.

9. Troy Perry, in *Dallas Voice,* 19 July 1989; cited in William Dannemeyer, *Shadow in the Land* (San Francisco: Ignatius Press, 1989), p. 101.

10. "Shaun Proulx talks to Rev. Troy Perry," www.gayguidetoronto.com/1_shaun/troy_perry.html.

11. Grant and Horne, p. 172.

12. Sylvia Pennington, *Ex Gays? There Are None!* (no city: Lambda Christian Fellowship, 1989), p. 161.

13. "Goings on Behind Bedroom Doors," *U.S. News and World Report,* 10 June 1991, p. 63.

14. Perry, *Don't Be Afraid Anymore,* p. 340, emphasis added.

15. As cited in F. LaGard Smith, *Sodom's Second Coming* (Eugene, OR: Harvest House Publishers, 1993), p. 130.

16. "Fallout Escalates Over Goddess Sophia," *Christianity Today,* 4 April 1994, p. 74; cited in Greg Laurie, *The Great Compromise* (Wheaton, IL: Grason, 1994), p. 11.

17. "Earthquake in the Mainline," p. 40.

18. "Earthquake in the Mainline," p. 40.

19. Kristi Hamrick.

20. Ronald Bayer, *Homosexuality and American Psychiatry: The Politics of Diagnosis* (New York: Basic Books, 1981), p. 172.

21. Bayer, p. 119.

22. Kenneth Lewes, *The Psychoanalytic Theory of Male Homosexuality* (New York: Simon and Schuster, 1988), p. 222.

23. Lewes, p. 222.

24. See Bayer, chapter 3, for a fascinating, detailed account of this.

25. "Pedophilia Not Always a Disorder?" *NARTH Bulletin,* April 1995, p. 1.

26. "Pedophilia Steps into the Daylight," *Citizen* magazine, 16 November 1992, p. 6.

27. "Pedophilia Steps into the Daylight."

28. "Pedophilia Steps into the Daylight."

29. "Interview: John Money," *Paidika: The Journal of Pedophilia* (The Netherlands), 2:7, p. 5.

30. "Progress in Empirical Research on Children's Sexuality," *SIECUS Report,* 12:2, p. 2.

31. "Pedophilia Steps into the Daylight," p. 7.

32. "Pedophilia Steps into the Daylight."

33. Judith Reisman, *Kinsey, Sex and Fraud* (Lafayette: Huntington, 1990), p. 131.

34. "Cradle to Grave Intimacy," *Time,* September 1981, p. 69.

35. "Interview: John Money," p. 9.

36. "Stonewall Celebrates 25 Years of 'Gay Rights,'" *The Lambda Report*, July 1994, p. 10.

37. Gregory King of the gay-oriented Human Rights Campaign Fund, for example, doesn't even consider NAMBLA to be a gay organization, whereas lesbian author Camille Paglia states, "It [pedophilia] has been at the center of gay male sex for thousands of years" ("Stonewall Celebrates").

38. Cited in Dinesh D'Souza, *Illiberal Education: The Politics of Race and Sex on Campus* (New York: Free Press, 1991), p. 12.

39. "Gay Rights/Special Rights" video. Dobson also cites gay advocates allowing for bisexual or homosexual trios. See Dobson, p. 117.

40. Eric Buehrer, *The Public Orphanage* (Dallas: Word, 1995), p. 14; Buehrer, p. 15; Dobson, pp. 167-168.

41. Dennis Praeger, "Why Judaism Rejected Homosexuality," *Mission and Ministry: The Quarterly Magazine of Trinity Episcopal School for Ministry*, Summer 1995, emphasis added

42. Praeger.

Chapter 3: How the "Gay Christian" Movement Began

1. Dennis Praeger in *Broward Jewish World*, 16 October 1990; cited in George Grant and Mark Horne, *Legislating Immorality* (Chicago: Moody Press, 1993), pp. 24-25.

2. See John Boswell, *Christianity, Social Tolerance, and Homosexuality* (Chicago: University of Chicago Press, 1980), pp. 61-87; Grant and Horne, pp. 21-38; and Wainwright Churchill, *Homosexual Behavior Among Males* (New York: Hawthorne Books, 1967), pp. 121-141.

3. Ronald Bayer, *Homosexuality and American Psychiatry* (New York: Basic Books, 1981), p. 15.

4. Dennis Praeger, "Why Judaism Rejected Homosexuality," *Mission and Ministry: The Quarterly Magazine of Trinity Episcopal School for Ministry*, Summer 1995, p. 13.

5. Kinsey in 1948, of course, and others. See Kenneth Lewes, *The Psychoanalytic Theory of Male Homosexuality* (New York: Simon and Schuster, 1988), pp. 48-122; and Bayer, pp. 68-69.

6. Bayer lists some organizations pre-existing Mattachine, but cites Mattachine as the most important and, in retrospect, the most easily identifiable starting point.

7. Neil Miller, *Out of the Past: Gay and Lesbian History from 1869 to the Present* (New York: Vintage Books, 1995), pp. 333-344; Bayer, p. 71.

8. Glenn Wood and John Dietrich, *The AIDS Epidemic: Balancing Compassion and Justice* (Portland, OR: Multnomah, 1990), p. 75.

9. Wood and Dietrich, p. 75; and Churchill, p. 293.

10. Bayer, p. 76.

11. Bayer, pp. 83-88.

12. Churchill, pp. 200, 293.

13. Bayer, p. 92.

14. Bayer, p. 92.

15. Bayer, p. 93.

16. Quote from the *Dallas Voice*, 19 July 1989, p. 24; cited in William Dannemeyer, *Shadow in the Land* (San Francisco: Ignatius Press, 1989), p. 101.

17. Troy Perry, *Don't Be Afraid Anymore* (New York: St. Martin's Press, 1990), p. 7.

18. Perry, *Don't Be Afraid Anymore*, p. 34.

19. Leigh Rutledge, *The Gay Decades* (New York: Penguin Books, 1992), pp. 19-20. See also Martin Duberman's *Stonewall* (New York: Dutton, 1993) for a full treatment of the event.

20. Rutledge, p. 2.

21. Roger Biery, *Understanding Homosexuality: The Pride and the Prejudice* (Austin: Edward William Publishing Co., 1990), pp. 194-197. See also Rutledge, p. 7, for one of too many examples of this, in which a group of English youths beat a gay man to death with clubs as he was walking down the street in Wimbledon Common. "When you're hitting a queer," a proud young "fag basher" commented afterward, "there's nothing to be scared of 'cause you know they won't go to the law."

22. Rutledge, pp. 16,98-99; Baird and Baird, *Homosexuality: Debating the Issues* (Amherst, NJ: Prometheus Books, 1995), p. 23.

23. This is not to suggest a favorable comparison between the civil-rights movement and the gay-rights movement. I see the two as being fundamentally different. But the militant gay-power movement linked itself, both in its title and tactics, to the civil-rights and black-power movements—sometimes with, and sometimes without, their approval (see Rutledge, p. 23).

24. Erica Goode, "Intimate Friendships," *U.S. News and World Report,* 5 July 1993, p. 50, emphasis added.

25. Goode.

26. See Baird and Baird; Ronald Bayer, *Homosexuality and American Psychiatry: The Politics of Diagnosis* (New York: Basic Books, 1981); Duberman; and Neil Miller, *Out of the Past: Gay and Lesbian History from 1869 to the Present* (New York: Vintage Books, 1995).

27. Some Christian bookstores order pro-gay books without knowing it. Many times I've found these materials in stores run by conservative Christians who wouldn't consider having the gay view promoted on their shelves. But the titles of the books *(Is the Homosexual My Neighbor?; Christianity, Social Tolerance, and Homosexuality; Can Homophobia Be Cured?)* are often innocent or compassionate-sounding. When I've pointed the books out to the owners, they've always removed them, surprised to find they'd been peddling the gay ideology without realizing it.

28. Perry, *Don't Be Afraid Anymore,* pp. 208, 211, 183-185, 185-187.

29. Perry, *Don't Be Afraid Anymore,* p. 171.

30. William Dannemeyer, *Shadow in the Land* (San Francisco: Ignatius Press, 1989), p. 104; Mel White, *Stranger at the Gate* (New York: Simon and Schuster, 1994), p. 268; Perry, *Don't Be Afraid Anymore,* p. 283.

31. Rutledge, pp. 4, 47.

32. Rutledge, p. 100. It is disturbing to note that nearly 20 years later (February 1996) a heresy trial was in progress within the Episcopal church over the ordination of a gay deacon. Compare that to the events seven years later when no less than an openly gay bishop was confirmed by the same church.

33. Isamu Yamamoto, *The Crisis of Homosexuality* (Wheaton: Victor Books, 1990), pp. 79-80.

34. Bayer, p. 204.

35. Bayer, pp. 156-159.

36. Bayer, pp. 156-157.

37. Bayer, p. 157; Yamamoto, p. 49.

38. Anita Bryant, *The Anita Bryant Story* (Old Tappan, NJ: Fleming Revell, 1977).

39. Bryant, p. 79; Biery, p. 201; Perry, *Don't Be Afraid Anymore,* p. 140; Bryant, p. 35.

40. Perry, *Don't Be Afraid Anymore,* p. 145.

41. Bayer, p. 155.

42. Perry, pp. 146-171; White, p. 270; Rutledge, p. 140; and see Perry, *Don't Be Afraid Anymore*, p. 279, White, pp. 291-296, and Rutledge, pp. 146, 186, 197.

Chapter 4: The "Gay Christian" Movement Comes of Age

1. • Derrick Bailey, *Homosexuality and the Western Tradition* (Hambden, CT: Shoe String Books, Inc., 1975).

• Wainwright Churchill, *Homosexual Behavior Among Males* (New York: Hawthorne Books, 1967).

• Tom Horner, *Jonathan Loved David* (Philadelphia: Westminster Press, 1978).

• Clinton Jones, *Homosexuality and Counseling* (Philadelphia: Fortress Press, 1974).

• John McNeil, *The Church and the Homosexual* (Kansas City: Sheed, Andrews and McMeel, 1976).

• Troy Perry, *The Lord Is My Shepherd and He Knows I'm Gay* (Los Angeles: Nash Publishing, 1972).

• Norman Pittenger, *Time for Consent* (London: SCM Press, 1970).

• Richard Woods, *Another Kind of Love* (Chicago: Thomas Moore Press, 1977).

2. Evangelicals Concerned, a national group of pro-gay Bible studies and fellowships founded by New York psychotherapist Ralph Blair, is probably the most theologically conservative of all the gay Christian groups and is the most articulate in defending the pro-gay theology.

3. See Paul Morrison, *Shadow of Sodom* (Wheaton, IL: Tyndale House, 1978), p. 15, for one of many examples about education; Anita Bryant, *The Anita Bryant Story* (Old Tappan, NJ: Fleming Revell, 1977), p. 35.

4. Troy Perry, *Don't Be Afraid Anymore* (New York: St. Martin's Press, 1990), p. 41.

5. An example: "Paul [the apostle] did not like homosexuals, but Paul did not take to women's rights...Not once did Jesus say, 'Come unto me all ye heterosexuals'—No! Jesus said, 'Come unto me all ye that labor and are heavy laden, and I will give you rest.' And that includes homosexuals, too. God doesn't condemn me for a sex drive that He has created in me" (see Perry, *The Lord Is My Shepherd*, pp. 150-151).

6. Horner, p. 98.

7. F. LaGard Smith, *Sodom's Second Coming* (Eugene, OR: Harvest House Publishers, 1993), p. 120.

8. If academic credentials alone prove that what a person says is credible, then what are we to make of Angela Davis or Timothy Leary?

9. Leigh Rutledge, *The Gay Decades* (New York: Penguin Books, 1992), p. 170.

10. John Boswell, *Christianity, Social Tolerance, and Homosexuality* (Chicago: University of Chicago Press, 1980), p. xv.

11. Elodie Ballantine Emig, "1 Corinthians 6:9—Part III," *Where Grace Abounds Newsletter*, P.O. Box 18871, Denver, CO 80218-0871.

12. Boswell, p. 117.

13. "The Murder of Matthew Shepherd," www.geocities.com/corkymcg/crime/proj005.html?20067.

14. "The Murder of Matthew Shepherd."

15. For a detailed account of relevant court rulings and other cultural landmarks regarding homosexuality, see *The Homosexual Agenda* by Alan Sears and Craig Osteen, Broadman and Holman, 2003. For detailed arguments regarding same-sex marriage from a distinctly Christian perspective,

see *Outrage: How Gay Activists and Liberal Judges Are Trashing Democracy to Redefine Marriage* by Peter Sprigg, Regnery Publishing, 2004. For a series of well-articulated secular arguments for traditional marriage, also see *The Meaning of Marriage* by Robert P. George and Jean Bethke Elshtain, Spence Publishing, 2006.

16. "The Murder of Matthew Shepherd."

17. "NBC defends Couric's 'anti-Christian' comments," www.freerepublic.com/focus/f-news/1299316/posts.

18. "NBC defends."

19. "Students Assemble to Protest Network," The Hoya.com, www.thehoya.com/news/120304/news17.cfm.

20. "A Promise Kept: Equality Riders go to Wheaton," www.soulforce.org/article/790; "Leaders urge caution as campuses brace for Soulforce," BaptistPressNews.com, bpnews.net/printerfriendly .asp?ID+22798.

21. "Supreme Court Decision on Scouting," supct.law.cornell.edu/supct/html/99-699.ZS.html; "The American Gay-rights Movement: A Timeline," www.infoplease.com/ipa/A0761909.html.

22. For a detailed account of relevant court rulings and other cultural landmarks regarding homosexuality, see *The Homosexual Agenda* by Alan Sears and Craig Osteen, Broadman and Holman, 2003. For detailed arguments regarding same-sex marriage from a distinctly Christian perspective, see *Outrage: How Gay Activists and Liberal Judges Are Trashing Democracy to Redefine Marriage* by Peter Sprigg, Regnery Publishing, 2004. For a series of well-articulated secular arguments for traditional marriage, also see *The Meaning of Marriage* by Robert P. George and Jean Bethke Elshtain, Spence Publishing, 2006.

23. "Episcopal Bishops give consent to consecration of Canon Gene Robinson," Anglican Communion News Services, www.anglicancommunion.org/acns/articles/35/25/acns3538.html.

Chapter 5: Pro-Gay Theology

1. See Hank Hanegraaff, *Christianity in Crisis* (Eugene, OR: Harvest House Publishers, 1993), p. 317, for the roles these creeds play in the essentials of Christianity.

2. Troy Perry, *Don't Be Afraid Anymore* (New York: St. Martin's Press, 1990), p. 342.

3. Perry, p. 339.

4. Randy Frame, "Seeking a Right to the Rite," *Christianity Today,* 4 March 1996, p. 66.

5. Perry, p. 39.

6. Mel White, *Stranger at the Gate* (New York: Simon and Schuster, 1994), pp. 295, 300, 309, 315.

7. Robin Scroggs, *The New Testament and Homosexuality* (Philadelphia: Fortress Press, 1983), p. 127.

8. Paul Morrison, *Shadow of Sodom* (Wheaton, IL: Tyndale House, 1978), p. 89.

9. Perry, p. 39; White, pp. 36-39, 156.

10. Sylvia Pennington, *Ex-Gays? There Are None!* (no city: Lambda Christian Fellowship, 1989), p. 388.

Chapter 6: Pro-Gay Arguments on the Nature of Homosexuality

1. Thomas Schmidt, *Straight and Narrow? Compassion and Clarity in the Homosexuality Debate* (Downers Grove, IL: InterVarsity Press, 1995), pp. 172-173.

2. Paul Gebhard, *The Kinsey Data* (Philadelphia: Saunders Press, 1979), p. 23; Alan Bell and Martin Weinberg, *Homosexualities: A Study of Diversities Among Men and Women* (New York:

Simon and Schuster, 1978); Mel White, quoted in Randy Frame, "Seeking a Right to the Rite," *Christianity Today,* 4 March 1996, p. 66.

3. Joseph Shapiro, "Straight Talk About Gays," *U.S. News and World Report,* 15 July 1993, p. 48.

4. "Rethinking the Origins of Sin," *Los Angeles Times,* 15 May 1993.

5. Simon LeVay, "A Difference in Hypothalamic Structure Between Heterosexual and Homosexual Men," *Science,* 30 August 1991, pp. 1034-1037.

6. John Ankerberg, "The Myth that Homosexuality Is Due to Biological or Genetic Causes," research paper, PO Box 8977, Chattanooga, TN 37411.

7. "Is This Child Gay?" *Newsweek,* 9 September 1991, p. 52.

8. "Is This Child Gay?"

9. *Los Angeles Times,* 16 September 1992, p. 1; cited in *NARTH Newsletter,* December 1992, p. 1.

10. "Sexual Disorientation: Faulty Research in the Homosexual Debate," *Family* (a publication of the Family Research Council), June 1992, p. 4.

11. "Is This Child Gay?" p. 52.

12. Nakamura, as quoted in *Los Angeles Times,* 30 August 1991; Fausto-Sterling, as quoted in *Time,* 9 September 1991, p. 61.

13. Quoted in *Newsweek,* 9 September 1991, p. 52; "Gay Genes Revisited," *Scientific American,* November 1995, p. 26.

14. Michael Bailey and Richard Pillard, "A Genetic Study of Male Sexual Orientation," *Archives of General Psychiatry,* 1991, no. 48, pp. 1089-1096.

15. David Gelman, "Born or Bred?" *Newsweek,* 24 February 1992, p. 46.

16. Gelman.

17. Gelman.

18. King and McDonald, "Homosexuals Who Are Twins," *The British Journal of Psychiatry,* March 1992, p. 409.

19. Frank Siexas, former director of the National Council on Alcoholism; quoted in William Dannemeyer, *Shadow in the Land* (San Francisco: Ignatius Press, 1989), p. 55; Joe Dallas, "Born Gay?" *Christianity Today,* 22 June 1992, p. 22, and *Chronicle of Higher Education,* 5 February 1992, p. A7; "Rethinking the Origins of Sin"; Robert Wright, "Our Cheating Hearts," *Time,* 15 August 1994, pp. 44-52.

20. Richard Isay, interviewed on "Gays and the Church," *ABC World News Tonight,* 28 February 1996; Richard Isay, *Being Homosexual* (New York: Farrar, Straus, Giroux, 1989), p. 112.

21. Mel White, *Stranger at the Gate* (New York: Simon and Schuster, 1994), p. 5.

22. Troy Perry, *Don't Be Afraid Anymore* (New York: St. Martin's Press, 1990), p. 64.

23. Letha Scanzoni and Virginia Mollenkott, *Is the Homosexual My Neighbor?* (New York: Harper and Row, 1978), p. 107; Sylvia Pennington, *Ex-Gays? There Are None!* (no city: Lambda Christian Fellowship, 1978), p. 108.

24. Schmidt, p. 155.

25. Bell and Weinberg.

26. Ruben Fine, *Psychoanalytic Theory, Male and Female Homosexuality: Psychological Approaches* (New York: Hemisphere, 1987), pp. 84, 86; Irving Bieber, *Homosexuality: A Psychoanalytic Study* (New York: Basic Books, 1962), pp. 318-319.

27. Masters and Johnson, *Homosexuality in Perspective* (Boston: Little Brown and Company, 1979),

p. 402; Glenn Wood and John Dietrich, *The AIDS Epidemic: Balancing Compassion and Justice* (Portland, OR: Multnomah, 1990), p. 238; June Reinisch, *The Kinsey Institute New Report on Sex* (New York: St. Martin's Press, 1990), pp. 138, 143.

28. Stanton Jones, "The Loving Opposition," *Christianity Today,* 19 July 1993, cited in Baird and Baird, *Homosexuality: Debating the Issues* (Amherst, NJ: Prometheus Books, 1995), p. 252.

29. Ronald Bayer, *Homosexuality and American Psychiatry: The Politics of Diagnosis* (New York: Basic Books, 1981), pp. 39-40.

30. Bayer, pp. 99-126.

31. Bayer, p. 142.

32. Bayer, p. 148.

33. Bayer, pp. 159-162.

34. Scanzoni and Mollenkott, pp. 111-112; Roger Biery, *Understanding Homosexuality: The Pride and the Prejudice* (Austin: Edward William Publishing Co., 1990), p. 185.

35. Bayer, p. 34.

36. Bayer, p. 128.

37. Bayer, p. 167.

38. Alfred Kinsey, *Sexual Behavior in the Human Male* (Philadelphia: Saunders Press, 1948), p. 625, 638.

39. Reinisch, p. 138.

40. Judith Reisman, *Kinsey, Sex and Fraud* (Lafayette: Huntington, 1990), p. 9.

41. Lesbian activist with ACTUP, interviewed in "Gay Rights/Special Rights" video.

42. Stanton Jones, "The Loving Opposition," *Christianity Today,* 19 July 1993, reprinted in Baird and Baird, *Homosexuality: Debating the Issues* (Amherst: Prometheus Books, 1995), p. 253.

Chapter 7: Pro-Gay Arguments from Social Issues

Epigraph: Marshall Kirk and Hunter Madsen, *After the Ball: How America Will Conquer Its Fear and Hatred of Gays in the '90s* (New York: Doubleday, 1989).

1. Isay, *Being Homosexual* (New York: Farrar, Straus, Giroux, 1989), p. 145; Joseph Nicolosi, *Reparative Therapy of Male Homosexuality* (Northvale: Jason Aaronson, 1991), p. 138.

2. Mel White, *Stranger at the Gate* (New York: Simon and Schuster, 1994), p. 307.

3. Andrew Sullivan, *Virtually Normal: An Argument About Homosexuality* (New York: Alfred Knopf, 1995), p. 212.

4. Roger Biery, *Understanding Homosexuality* (Austin, TX: Edward William Publishing Co., 1990), p. 201.

5. White, p. 236.

6. John Boswell, *Christianity, Social Tolerance, and Homosexuality* (Chicago: University of Chicago Press, 1980), p. vii.

7. "Homosexuals Can Change," *Christianity Today,* 16 February 1981, p. 37.

Chapter 8: Religious Pro-Gay Arguments

1. Mel White, *Stranger at the Gate* (New York: Simon and Schuster, 1994), p. 214.

2. George Barna, *What Americans Believe* (Ventura: Regal Books, 1991), p. 36; cited in Ron Rhodes, *The Culting of America* (Eugene, OR: Harvest House Publishers, 1994), p. 23.

3. In Stephen Lang, "Is Ignorance Bliss?" *Moody,* January/February 1996, p. 13.

4. Charles Colson, *The Body,* as excerpted in *Christianity Today,* 23 November 1992, p. 29.

5. Elliot Miller, *A Crash Course on the New Age Movement* (Grand Rapids, MI: Baker Book House, 1993), p. 16.

6. Cornelius Plantinga, "Natural Born Sinners," *Christianity Today,* 14 November 1994, p. 25.

7. Lang, p. 13.

8. White, p. 268.

9. Sylvia Pennington, *Ex-Gays? There Are None!* (no city: Lambda Christian Fellowship, 1989), p. 138.

10. "Gays and the Church," *ABC World News Tonight,* 28 February 1996.

11. Roger Biery, *Understanding Homosexuality: The Pride and the Prejudice* (Austin: Edward William Publishing Co., 1990), p. 176.

Chapter 9: The Nature and Use of the Bible

1. Stanton Jones, "The Loving Opposition," *Christianity Today,* 19 July 1993, pp. 18-25.

2. Letha Scanzoni and Virginia Mollenkott, *Is the Homosexual My Neighbor?* (New York: Harper and Row, 1978), p. 71; Roger Biery, *Understanding Homosexuality: The Pride and the Prejudice* (Austin: Edward William Publishing Co., 1990), p. 146; Mel White, *Stranger at the Gate* (New York: Simon and Schuster, 1994), p. 305.

3. "Straight Talk About Gays," *U.S. News and World Report,* 10 June 1991, p. 63.

4. "Gays and the Church," *ABC World News Tonight,* 28 February 1996.

5. Joseph Gudel, "That Which Is Unnatural," *Christian Research Journal,* Winter 1993, p. 12.

6. Troy Perry, *Don't Be Afraid Anymore* (New York: St. Martin's Press, 1990), p. 339; Scanzoni and Mollenkott, p. 1.

7. Biery, p. 143; John Boswell, *Christianity, Social Tolerance, and Homosexuality* (Chicago: University of Chicago Press, 1980), p. 335.

8. Elodie Ballantine Emig, "1 Corinthians 6:9—Part III," *Where Grace Abounds Newsletter,* P.O. Box 18871, Denver, CO 80218-0871.

9. Troy Perry, *The Lord Is My Shepherd and He Knows I'm Gay* (Los Angeles: Nash Publishing, 1972), pp. 150-151.

10. Perry, *Don't Be Afraid Anymore,* p. 39.

11. White, p. 305; Scanzoni and Mollenkott, p. xi.

12. Perry, *Don't Be Afraid Anymore,* p. 140; White, p. 311.

Chapter 10: Genesis and Homosexuality

1. Thomas Schmidt, *Straight and Narrow?* (Downers Grove, IL: InterVarsity, 1995), p. 41.

2. Stanton Jones, "The Loving Opposition," *Christianity Today,* 19 July 1993, p. 22.

3. John Boswell, *Christianity, Social Tolerance, and Homosexuality* (Chicago: University of Chicago Press, 1980), pp. 93-94; Derrick Bailey, *Homosexuality and the Western Christian Tradition* (Hambden, CT: Shoe String Books, 1975).

4. Letha Scanzoni and Virginia Mollenkott, *Is the Homosexual My Neighbor?* (New York: Harper and Row, 1978), pp. 57-58.

5. Scanzoni and Mollenkott.

6. Schmidt, pp. 88-89.

7. Bruce Metzger, "What Does the Bible Have to Say About Homosexuality?" *Presbyterians for Renewal* magazine, May 1993, p. 7.

Chapter 11: Moses and Homosexuality

1. Transcript from *The West Wing*, episode: "The Midterms," aired 18 October 2000.
2. John Boswell, *Christianity, Social Tolerance, and Homosexuality* (Chicago: University of Chicago Press, 1980), p. 100; Troy Perry, *Don't Be Afraid Anymore* (New York: St. Martin's Press, 1990), p. 341.

Chapter 12: Jesus and Homosexuality

1. Troy Perry, *Don't Be Afraid Anymore* (New York: St. Martin's Press, 1990), p. 341.
2. Tom Horner, *Jonathan Loved David* (Philadelphia: Westminster Press, 1978), pp. 82-125.

Chapter 13: Paul and Homosexuality

1. John Boswell, *Christianity, Social Tolerance, and Homosexuality* (Chicago: University of Chicago Press, 1980), p. 109.
2. Letha Scanzoni and Virginia Mollenkott, *Is the Homosexual My Neighbor?* (New York: Harper and Row, 1978), pp. 65-66, emphasis added.
3. Bennett Sims, "Sex and Homosexuality," *Christianity Today,* 24 February, 1978, p. 25.
4. Troy Perry, *Don't Be Afraid Anymore* (New York: St. Martin's Press, 1990), p. 342.
5. Thomas Schmidt, *Straight and Narrow?* (Downers Grove, IL: InterVarsity, 1995), pp. 78-79.
6. Timothy Dailey *The Bible, Church and Homosexuality* (Washington, DC: Family Research Council, 2004), p. 11.
7. Boswell, pp. 341, 344.
8. Boswell p. 342.
9. Dailey, p. 11.
10. Boswell, pp. 109, 340.

Chapter 14: A Time to Speak

1. Cal Thomas, "Religious Wing Has Too Much Faith in Caesar," *Los Angeles Times,* 21 March 1995.
2. "Gays and the Church," *ABC World News Tonight,* 28 February 1996.
3. "The Homosexual Movement," cited in Baird and Baird, *Homosexuality: Debating the Issues* (Amherst, NJ: Prometheus Books, 1995), p. 34.
4. "Bitter Sisters/Suffering Sons" (video), His Way Ministries, 1994.
5. A survey conducted by the Media Research Center in 1993 found 150 stories on "pro-life intimidation" of abortion clinics; no reporting was found on this extreme demonstration at Hamilton Square in San Francisco.
6. Cal Thomas, "Gay Scientists Can Count on Compliant Media," *NARTH Newsletter,* December 1995, p. 17.
7. Roger Biery, *Understanding Homosexuality: The Pride and the Prejudice* (Austin: Edward William Publishing Co., 1990), p. 174.
8. Richard Mouw, as interviewed in *Christianity Today,* 14 August 1995, p. 25.

Chapter 15: A Satisfied Mind

1. Mel White, *Stranger at the Gate* (New York: Simon and Schuster, 1994), p. 317.
2. Troy Perry, quoted in Paul Morrison, *Shadow of Sodom* (Wheaton, IL: Tyndale House, 1978), p. 29.
3. As cited in Alan Sears and Craig Osten, *The Homosexual Agenda* (Nashville, TN: Broadman and Holman, 2003) p. 205.
4. *Time,* 24 June 1991.

About Joe Dallas

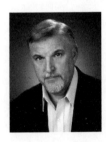

Joe Dallas, past president of Exodus International, lectures extensively at churches and seminars and directs a biblical counseling practice in Tustin, California. His articles have been featured in *Christianity Today*, *Christian Research Journal*, and the *Journal of the Christian Association of Psychological Studies*.

For more information on Joe Dallas's seminars and educational materials, or to reach Joe for your conference or church engagement, please contact:

Joe Dallas
c/o Genesis Counseling
17632 Irvine Blvd., Suite 220
Tustin, CA 92780
714-508-6953
www.joedallas.com

Joe Dallas's other books on homosexuality include...

Desires in Conflict: Hope for Men Who Struggle with Sexual Identity

For more than a decade, *Desires in Conflict* has been the definitive "must-read" for those who wonder, *Can a homosexual change?* This new edition with updated information offers more compelling reasons why the answer is "Yes!"

When Homosexuality Hits Home: What to Do When a Loved One Says They're Gay

The heart-wrenching declaration that a loved one is a homosexual is increasingly being heard in Christian households across America. How can this be? What went wrong? Is there a cure?

In this straightforward book, Joe Dallas offers practical counsel, step by step, on how to deal with the many conflicts and emotions parents, grandparents, brothers and sisters or any family member will experience when learning of a loved one's homosexuality.

Drawing from his own experience and from his many years of helping families work through this perplexing and unexpected situation, Joe offers scriptural and compassionate advice to both struggling gays and those who love them.

If The Gay Gospel? has helped you understand this issue more clearly, here are some other excellent books you might enjoy...

God's Grace and the Homosexual Next Door: Reaching the Heart of the Gay Men and Women in Your World
Alan Chambers and the Leadership Team at Exodus International

Author Alan Chambers—a former homosexual himself—and four of his colleagues at Exodus International offer practical and biblical insights on how both individuals and churches can become a haven for homosexuals seeking freedom from same–sex attraction.

> "One of the great movements in our time is that of the ex-homosexuals and ex-lesbians. These are broken people who have admitted their brokenness and found true happiness—not the so-called 'gay' lifestyle—but by living for Jesus Christ. One such man is Alan Chambers, currently president of the largest umbrella organization of ex-homosexuals, Exodus International. Alan Chambers' book provides believers with Christian and loving (but uncompromising) answers to this controversial issue."
>
> —D. James Kennedy, Ph.D., Senior Minister, Coral Ridge Presbyterian Church

101 Frequently Asked Questions About Homosexuality
Mike Haley

Almost daily we hear news reports that confirm the acceptance of homosexuality in our culture. Homosexuals are adopting children, appearing as characters on television programs, taking vacations catering to an exclusively gay clientele, and even seeking the right to "marry" their partners. But is this acceptance healthy for society?

Few topics can raise questions so quickly. And for many readers, those questions hit close to home as they learn of the homosexuality of a loved one or close friend.

Here are the answers to the most often asked questions about homosexuality, fielded by an expert on the subject...and a former homosexual himself.

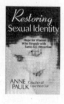

Restoring Sexual Identity: Hope for Women Who Struggle with Same-Sex Attraction
Anne Paulk

Restoring Sexual Identity offers answers to the most commonly asked questions from both homosexuals desiring change and friends and relatives of women struggling with same-sex attraction.

Is lesbianism an inherited predisposition or is it developed in childhood? Does becoming a Christian eliminate all desire for members of the same sex? What support is available for women who struggle with lesbianism? Can a woman be a lesbian and a Christian at the same time? How does childhood sexual abuse relate to the development of lesbianism? These and other important questions are answered as the author draws from her own experience and that of many other former lesbians who participated in an extensive survey on same-sex attraction.